.U. Ross

INVOLUNTARY
JOURNEY TO
SIBERIA

Andrei Amalrik

INVOLUNTARY JOURNEY TO SIBERIA

Translated from the Russian

by

Manya Harari and Max Hayward

READERS UNION

Newton Abbot 1971

© 1970 by Harcourt Brace Jovanovich, Inc.
and Harvin Press Ltd

The English translation has been somewhat abridged from
from the Russian original published under the title
Nezhelannoye puteshestvie v Sibir
by Harcourt Brace Jovanovich, Inc.

First published in Great Britain by Collins and Harvill Press

This edition was produced in 1971 for sale to its members
only by the proprietors, Readers Union Limited, PO Box 6,
Newton Abbot, Devon, TQ12 2DW. Full details of
membership will gladly be sent on request

Printed in the UK for Readers Union by
Redwood Press Limited at Trowbridge

Contents

Foreword

ANDREI AMALRIK is among the growing number of Soviet
intellectuals who in recent years have suffered imprisonment, deportation to a remote part of the country, or con-
finement in a lunatic asylum for protesting against actions
of their government which they find morally inadmissible,
for putting to a practical test the rights they theoretically
enjoy under the Soviet Constitution, or for refusing to
accept unwritten conventions that intolerably restrict their
creative activity and private life. Pavel Litvinov, the grandson of a former Soviet Foreign Minister, and Larissa Daniel
(the wife of the writer imprisoned in 1966) have been exiled
to Siberia for demonstrating on Red Square against the inva-
sion of Czechoslovakia; two of Amalrik's associates, Alexander Ginzburg and Yuri Galanskov, were sentenced to forced
labour in 1968 for circulating, among other things, documents about the trial of Sinyavsky and Daniel. These are
only two of dozens of cases, many tried behind closed doors
in cities other than Moscow – which means that the outside
world hears only the vaguest rumours of them.

What happens to people who have been sentenced to
forced labour has been described in the remarkable book
My Testimony by Anatoly Marchenko who spent six years
(1960-66) in the notorious labour camps of the Potma district. Amalrik's book is the first circumstantial account to
reach the West of what it means to be 'exiled' – the punishment that Litvinov, Larissa Daniel, and others are now
undergoing. Amalrik was arrested in 1965 on a charge of
'parasitism' that is, failing to have regular employment –
though the real reason, as he plainly saw during the proceedings against him, was the fact that he was a non-con-
formist in his literary and artistic tastes, showed an active

interest in *avant-garde* painters such as Anatoly Zverev and Dmitri Plavinsky (who are forbidden to hold exhibitions in the Soviet Union), and occasionally met foreigners (including an American diplomat) who shared this interest. In several ways his case was analogous to that of the poet Joseph Brodsky who in the previous year (1964) was sentenced to five years' exile nominally for 'parasitism' (but in reality for his poetry: probably the most talented being written in Russia today). Brodsky was allowed to return to Leningrad the following year after world-wide protests and intensive efforts on his behalf by some of his compatriots, notably the late Frieda Vigdorov, a journalist and Deputy of a Moscow district Soviet mentioned in Amalrik's book, who made a record of Brodsky's trial, thus contributing greatly to his release.

The decree on 'parasitism' passed under Khrushchev in 1961* was originally intended to help clear the big cities, mainly Moscow and Leningrad, of vagrants, alcoholics, and workers guilty of absenteeism by deporting them to underpopulated and inhospitable areas to which it is not easy to attract free labour. It was soon found a convenient way of dealing with 'awkward' intellectuals as well. In a sense it was a resumption on a minor scale of Stalin's policy of supplying labour to Siberia and the Far North by the mass deportation of 'undesirables'. There was an even earlier precedent, as Amalrik mentions, in Peter the Great's decree under which vagrants were rounded up for work in his factories in the Urals. Then, as now, it was not effective in economic terms.

Like Brodsky, Amalrik was released before his term came to an end – not as a result of any outcry on his behalf but through patient efforts on the part of friends (including Alexander Ginzburg) and his lawyer to get his sentence reversed as a miscarriage of justice. The story of his dealings with the Soviet authorities over the period of his detention, trial, and exile throws much light on some salient features

---

* It was, however, in operation before its formal enactment, in 1960. It was abolished in May 1970.

of a totalitarian structure in decline: the present Soviet system since – and because of – the death of its creator offers the first such spectacle in history (the Nazi system was smashed by outside forces before it was fully fledged). Two aspects of this decline are very evident from Amalrik's testimony: First, the tendency for the post-Stalin bureaucracy, even the police, to take some account of the law, such as it is, in dealing with people who have fallen foul of it. They may still honour it more in the breach, but at least they wish to appear to be observing it. There is a marked contrast with the flagrant arbitrariness of Stalin's times. As one of the officials in his case actually put it to Amalrik: 'The Committee [i.e. the K G B, as the secret police is now called] isn't what it was. In the old days you would have disappeared for twenty years ...' Secondly, the striking development of interdepartmental rivalry in the bureaucracy. Amalrik cites much evidence that, in dealing with his case, the ordinary police and the secret police were working at cross-purposes, and even fighting each other – the ordinary police being inclined, on the whole, to take a more rational, common-sense view of its functions. Amalrik shows that someone like himself, who is prepared to insist on his rights, can to a certain extent exploit these bureaucratic rivalries – unthinkable in Stalin's time, when the hierarchy of power was strictly pyramidal, with a vertical subordination going right up to Stalin at the apex, and no nonsense about overlapping horizontal jurisdictions (this was the essence of 'pure' totalitarianism, never achieved by Hitler). The emergence of 'bureaucratic pluralism' may be the one most important feature of post-totalitarian decline: important in the sense that it points a possible way to gradual political change.

After losing his fight against the K G B's move to have him expelled from Moscow as a 'parasite', Amalrik was sent to work on a collective farm (*kolkhoz*) near Tomsk in Siberia. About half his book is thus taken up by a description of life and work among the most underprivileged section of the Soviet population and gives a valuable picture of a world

which to most educated Russian city dwellers seems as
remote as any foreign country. The gulf between the intel-
ligentsia and the ordinary people (i.e. the peasants) has
always been great in Russia. Partly because of their
ignorance of it, the nineteenth-century intellectuals tended
to idealize 'the people' and look to them with varying
degrees of mysticism, as a source of light, and even salva-
tion. The experience of Soviet intellectuals, through
enforced contact with 'ordinary people' as prisoners in concentration camps, and latterly as 'parasites', sharing their
life in kolkhozes, has been, on the whole, sobering and dis-
illusioning. In *The First Circle* Solzhenitsyn has described
his own disenchantment with his earlier 'populist' ideas and
his realization that peasants, being no better and no worse
than other people, must be judged each on his merits, as an
individual. Amalrik was even more disillusioned by his
experience, and though one may find his judgments somewhat too harsh, there is no doubt about the general validity
of his observations. He shows that the Russian peasant has
in Soviet times become a curious social hybrid. As a result
of forcible collectivization in the early thirties he has lost his
peasant instincts and his proprietary attachment to the soil,
but at the same time he has not developed the outlook and
habits of a worker. The result is a kind of rootlessness which
may be paralleled in other countries only by migratory
agricultural workers. But the Soviet peasants (who account
for a little under half of the total population) do not have
the mobility of agricultural workers elsewhere – they
cannot leave their collective farms without permission
and they are not allowed to carry the identity cards without
which no Soviet citizen can travel inside the country. They
are the victims of a literally arrested economic development,
consigned to a limbo between industry and agriculture.

In his essay *Will the USSR Survive until 1984?* (written
after this book and recently published in the West),
Amalrik reaches sombre conclusions about the chance of
change in the Soviet system as a result of internal social
pressures and shifts. From his book it is easy to see the origin
of this pessimism: the inertia, ignorance, apathy and lack

of solidarity of the peasants he observed in the kolkhoz near Tomsk made him feel that the ordinary people in the Soviet Union are incapable as individuals or *en masse* of any initiative, and that they are readily manipulated by the authorities to whom, despite their passive discontent, they are entirely submissive. Not all Russians would share this view, but it is undoubtedly widespread in Moscow intellectual circles. It has led, in Amalrik's case, to grave doubts as to whether Russian society has the inner resources to change spontaneously, rather than in response only to directives 'from above'. The corruption of traditional values, the destruction of natural ties (such as the peasant's feeling for the soil) – so Amalrik seems to be saying in his essay – have gone too far to make any self-regenerative process conceivable.

There are certainly arguments against this view. Perhaps the best is the example of Amalrik himself. It is clear from what he says of himself that, like others who have chosen the same path of defiance, he has no particular 'ideology', but only an almost blind belief in the need to assert one's rights, in so far as they have been officially defined. He has concluded, like many of his contemporaries, that it is rarely effective to resist the encroachments of a bureaucratic police state in the name of an idea, or on the basis of moral indignation. It does make sense, on the other hand – and not merely as a last despairing, existentialist gesture – to study the rules and regulations, and quote them at one's persecutors. Amalrik may represent a tiny minority, but in an era of apparent social stagnation and political impasse, perhaps only minorities have any prospect of growth. If more and more people insist, as Amalrik does, on their rights as defined in Soviet law, there is a chance of evolution without the external conflict (a Soviet-Chinese war) that he postulates in his essay as the only possible agent of change.

Russia was always notoriously deficient in a sense of law, but the trend in the nineteenth century was towards a gradual increase of respect for law (even in the lower reaches of society) and the establishment of legal institutions. There are signs – of which Amalrik's book provides evidence – that this trend, after decades of arbitrary rule, is slowly reasserting itself. The example of Yugoslavia, which has moved farthest in the evolution away from 'pure' totalitarianism, shows that progress towards a kind of *Rechtsstaat* (state based on the rule of law) is possible without radical change in the political structure. The evidence of Russian history in the nineteenth and early twentieth century (and now in the post-Stalin period) would suggest that a general feeling of the need for law, springing from a desire for stability in which all are ultimately interested, is the only 'natural' antibody that a society is likely to develop against the wasting disease of bureaucratic arbitrariness. As Amalrik says in his book : 'Those in high office ought surely to reflect that without a proper rule of law they themselves may one day share the fate of Sinyavsky and Daniel. As long as we live in a State that violates its own laws, nobody, from the rulers of the country down to unregistered attic-dwellers, will have any sense of responsibility for their actions, or feel assured of their personal safety.'

Judging by the continuing arrest of protesters in the Soviet Union, there is admittedly not much sign that the holders of high office have reflected very profoundly on these lines, but there is nevertheless a great difference from Stalin's time : they hesitate to resort to indiscriminate terror, and the growth of 'bureaucratic pluralism', among other factors, does appear to impose considerable restraints; people are not arrested without some technical reason, and the desire to give an appearance of due legal process is, if anything, stronger than under Khrushchev. One cannot help feeling, therefore, that there is considerable wisdom in the advocacy by some Soviet intellectuals of a legalistic pragmatism which *may* be favoured by a logical trend in the history of their society. For some of the most sceptical, this is indeed almost an article of faith. The gifted mathematician and poet, Alexander Esenin-Volpin, in a statement on the trial of Sinyavsky and Daniel, expressed it like this: 'I do not believe in anything, or try not to; in all my reflections I try to proceed from nihilism, from extreme philosophical scepticism – not applying it, however, to juridical and logical norms.' It remains to be seen whether this faith is well grounded in reality, that is, whether 'juridical norms' can become the main cohesive force in a society that for too long was held together only by terror.

MAX HAYWARD

Author's Preface

What happened to me is not anything surprising or exceptional in my country. But that is just why it is interesting.

I have tried to write as simply as possible, without omitting the boring details of which the life of a prisoner or exile mostly consists – otherwise I could not have conveyed the atmosphere in which I lived. I very much wanted to write objectively; if I have not altogether succeeded in this and if here and there a note of irritation slips through, I am very sorry about it. I wanted the reader, while seeing everything through my eyes, nevertheless to judge what he sees for himself. To me, what happened seems at times absurd to the point of being monstrous, and at others, completely natural.

I will be satisfied if my book, even in a minor way, will help to disprove the notion that any positive result can be achieved by force.

N.B. All footnotes are the translators'.

CHAPTER I

'Newsweek' Interview

ONE morning, late in January 1965, I was awakened by a telephone call, and an unknown woman's voice told me that a catalogue of Zverev's* exhibition had been reserved for me. This is how I learned that the exhibition, which had been so much talked about and seemed so improbable, was being held after all. Here, briefly, is the story that led up to it.

At the time of his first visit to Moscow, the French conductor, Markevich, had seen a private collection of pictures by such painters as Kandinsky, Chagall and Tatlin, and among them those of the young Moscow artist Anatoly Zverev. Eventually, he met Zverev himself – a man of medium height, unshaven, long unwashed, wearing hand-me-down clothes and shoes with holes in them, a man with a small face, hunted eyes and nervous gestures. Markevich already knew that Zverev was one of the most interesting Russian painters of the present time, but perhaps his decision to arrange an exhibition of his works abroad was chiefly influenced by his interest in Zverev the man. Indeed, it seemed to me that Markevich and Zverev were very much alike and it occurred to me that if Zverev had been somewhat more self-assured, the similarity between them would have been even more striking.

I got to know Igor Markevich at the time of his last visit to the Soviet Union in the autumn of 1964, when he told me that the exhibition was definitely to be held and that he had made all the arrangements with the owner of a picture gallery in Paris. All the same, I found it hard to believe, just because he talked about it so much and so openly, whereas we in Moscow were used to wrapping up even the smallest

*Zverev is a Russian painter who is regarded by the Soviet authorities as too 'modernist' to be exhibited at home, but was allowed to hold an exhibition in Paris.

initiative in the domain of 'modernist' art in the strictest
mystery. Now I realized that I had been wrong.

The exhibition opened on the 3rd of February 1965. I
don't know what impression it created in Paris, but for
Russian artists, the first exhibition abroad of the works of an
avant-garde painter of the post-war generation was, it seemed
to us, a great event. It also had another interesting aspect:
for the Soviet officials in charge of art it was a test case.
Zverev was not regarded as an artist in the Soviet Union; his
exhibition was a private undertaking by Markevich, who
had not negotiated it officially with the Soviet Ministry of
Culture. Still, once it had opened, the authorities were
obliged to react in one way or another, all the more because
other exhibitions might be held abroad of the works of
Russian artists who were far removed from the academic
style of Socialist realism.

In Moscow the last to hear of the exhibition was Zverev
himself. I couldn't find him for a long time. He had no apartment of his own and he wandered about Moscow, sometimes
renting a room or spending the night wherever he happened
to be. He dropped in to see me nearly every day but just
then I hadn't seen him for a week. My father, the painter
Plavinsky, and I were already celebrating the opening of the
exhibition when Zverev turned up unexpectedly, wearing
an enormously long, red coat that he had borrowed from
a friend. Our news didn't seem to excite him particularly –
his only comment was that we were ahead of time: it was
still only the 2nd of February, the day before the opening.
Since none of us went regularly to work, we were always
getting the date wrong!

Meanwhile, the most ridiculous rumours were spreading
around Moscow – for instance that Picasso had visited the
exhibition and bought all the pictures, or that Markevich
had flown to Moscow and taken Zverev back to Paris with
him for two days. It was said that Zverev had disliked Paris
and immediately asked to return to Moscow. It was also
said that the paintings in the exhibition had really been
painted by Zverev's wife – Zverev had only signed them –
and that I had sold them for huge sums to Markevich, who
knew nothing about art.

Finally, the Ministry of Culture began to take an interest in Zverev. The head of one of the departments of the Ministry, which was in charge of the export of paintings, tried to get in touch with Zverev through the collector Kostaki. Kostaki gave Zverev the telephone number of the Ministry officials and Zverev rang them up towards the middle of February. According to him, they were delighted by his telephone call and asked him to go round at once and take some of his pictures. This he refused to do, saying that he was going into hospital to have an operation in a few days time; but he promised to call during his convalescence.

Zverev had been about to have an operation during the whole of the past year; he really needed one – it was a question of removing the metal pins which held his broken arm together – but it was put off again and again. He only spoke of it now to avoid going to the Ministry. He thought that the authorities, trying to cash in on the exhibition in Paris and make some foreign currency out of it, would pick out the more conformist of his paintings for the gallery that had recently been opened in Moscow. He was afraid that in this way they would gradually take him in hand, depriving him of the possibility of painting as he wished and of selling his pictures to whomever he liked. The prospect of profitable sales through the gallery was not enough to counterbalance these fears.

I doubt however that the situation was as simple as this. It was more likely that the officials in the Ministry had split into two factions: those who wished somehow to 'legalize' Zverev now he had become well known, and those who proposed simply to ignore him as a madman. What with the invariable bureaucratic delays, there was in any case little chance of his being forced to exhibit in the gallery – until they had taken a closer look at him. But if the authorities were in no hurry to sell Zverev's paintings themselves, this did not mean that they would in future countenance the private sale of Russian 'modernist' art abroad. Although they avoided showing their disapproval of the Paris exhibition (Soviet diplomats even attended its opening) it was quite possible that they would take measures to ensure that no more such exhibitions were held without authorization from the Government, and to close all the real or imagined channels by which Russian *avant-garde* works of art reached the West.

In Moscow the attitude towards the exhibition was highly ambiguous. We were eager to know what the reaction to it was abroad. The most contradictory rumours reached us. We formed the impression that the French had treated it with some reserve but that the English and Americans liked it. This was confirmed by the few newspaper cuttings I saw. Zverev cursed the French, especially Louis Aragon, who was said to have attacked the exhibition in *Lettres Françaises*.

I thought it might be very interesting at this point for Zverev to give an interview to some foreign journalists in Moscow. Zverev was not against it but thought it would be dangerous to discuss his exhibition or even art in general and said he would talk mainly about how he loved tortoises. Nevertheless, we decided to go ahead and arrange the interview; the only question was who the interviewer should be.

I decided to consult an American diplomat I knew. It so happened that on the day before we were to meet him, another Soviet artist had invited Zverev and me to meet an American journalist whose name I had forgotten – I only remembered that his wife was called Christina and that he was interested in Russian painting. This was quite sufficient for us. That evening the journalist was not at home – the artist arranged over the telephone with Christina that he would ring again in a couple of days and said (though without giving our names) that he would like to bring two friends of his to see them. When I told my friend the American diplomat about this and asked him if he knew the journalist, he said it was Robert Korengold, a correspondent of *Newsweek*, and that it was all right for me to talk to him about the interview.

We were going to telephone Korengold the following evening, but early that morning the diplomat called me and said he would like to come and see me with the friend whom he had mentioned the day before. I realized that he meant Korengold. We agreed that they should come the next day at noon. Zverev was supposed to phone me that day and I meant to tell him what had happened.

It turned out that on the day we had tried to see Korengold he had received a telegram from his paper telling him to interview Zverev, as the next issue of *Newsweek* was to deal with the exhibition. He was to do this as soon as possible or it would be too late. In other words, at the very time when we had been trying to arrange the interview through his wife, Korengold himself was vainly hunting for Zverev all over the town. He had at first tried to reach him through some dubious Russian friends, young artists and writers about whom I shall have some more to say later. They found Zverev, but by then Korengold had arranged to meet him and me through the diplomat.

Zverev didn't ring me up when he had said he would, but I still hoped that he would either call or drop in. Next morning, however, Plavinsky came and told me that Zverev had unexpectedly gone to the hospital for his operation. I tried to get in touch with Korengold, but there was no answer from his house and at his office I was told he was out and no one knew when he would come back. As I came out of the telephone booth I noticed a young man leaning against it with a bored expression. By now it was nearly eleven thirty so I went home.

I lived in a communal flat, in a huge building put up before the Revolution by the 'Russia' Insurance Company for its employees. The flat had been planned for one family, but four were now living in it. It was divided in two by a passageway: immediately to the right of the entrance was the room occupied by my father and me; we had partitioned it into two cubicles. Farther along the same side of the passageway were the bathroom, kitchen and a small pantry, so that we had no one living next to us. A door from the kitchen led to the back stairs, which the architect of the insurance company had considerately put up for cooks and other members of the domestic staff. On the left of the entrance, opposite us, lived an old woman with her grandson and his wife. The next room was occupied by a woman clerk from the police with her husband and daughter, and the last one, opposite the kitchen, by the house manager and his wife. There was a telephone in the passage.

Our guests arrived at twelve sharp. Korengold was a balding, shortish gentleman, obviously Jewish. I apologized for having unintentionally misled him and explained that Zverev had unexpectedly gone to the hospital. He was not particularly upset as he had evidently been told that I could speak for Zverev.

While Korengold was looking at the pictures on my walls, I heard the woman police clerk making a telephone call in the passageway. The only reason I noticed this was that she spoke almost in a whisper, instead of the usual loud tones that greatly disturbed me when I was trying to work. Plavinsky, who had been with me since morning, noticed this as well.

I don't remember exactly what we talked about with Korengold. I think I asked him what impression the exhibition had made on American visitors and told him about Zverev's telephone call to the Ministry. Korengold asked me whether Zverev was likely to get into any sort of trouble because of the exhibition. I said apparently not. Then he told me about the telegram from his paper, of which I already knew, and asked me what he could do about the interview. The latest he could send his article was the next morning, so could I speak for Zverev? Lying on my desk was Zverev's autobiography and Korengold suggested getting the answers to his questions out of it. But I had a different idea. Let Korengold write his questions down, I said, and I would go straight to the hospital and bring him the answers and a photograph of Zverev by the evening. I also offered to take photos of several of Zverev's paintings in case his paper wished to reproduce any of them. He gladly agreed. Everything seemed to be settled; the diplomat and I were arguing about which collection to take the reproductions from, and Korengold was writing his questions, when there was a ring at the door.

There was one bell for all the tenants; if the caller was for us he rang five times. I asked my father to tell whoever it was that I was out. I heard our neighbour opening the door; my father went into the passage but immediately reappeared looking upset. 'It's for you, Andrei,' he said, as, pushing him aside, four men came into the room, three in civilian clothes and one in a policeman's uniform. My guests looked frightened. I knew the man in uniform: he was the district superintendent Captain Kiselev; two of the civilians were young men with blank faces which had not yet assumed the characteristic expression of experienced police agents; the third was older, with a splendid fur hat and a highly professional face – I guessed that he was the most important man in the group.

Although I was to some extent prepared for this incident, it still gave me a most unpleasant feeling. I knew that I had been watched for a fairly long time, evidently on the simple assumption that, since I knew foreigners on the one hand and was friendly with 'modernist' artists on the other, I must surely work as an intermediary between them. I don't of course know what evidence they had collected against me, but I was not important enough for the surveillance to be carried out in such a sophisticated way that I would know nothing about it.

As early as the spring of 1963 agents of the Moscow CID – the Criminal Investigation Department – had supposedly made inquiries about my activities as an art collector in the office of the magazine *Sport Abroad*, where I was working at the time. It is unlikely that they heard anything of interest there. A little later, our neighbour in the building – an elderly housewife who afterwards went to work as a clerk for the police – was detailed to keep an eye on me. Since I never spoke with her, her only duty was to report on my visitors and telephone calls. As far as I could make out, she had no direct contact with the people interested in me, and made her reports only to the superintendent at the local police station. Much more hope was placed in another neighbour who was recruited at the beginning of 1964. This was a man of my own age whom I had known all my life – as children we had even played soldiers together. His assignment was to cultivate me and get to know my friends. To help him do this, he was provided with tickets to all the art exhibitions. Members of the *druzhiny** were also asked to

---

* *Druzhiny*: Volunteer auxiliary police units which were formed in the early years of Khrushchev's rule to fight hooliganism and other petty crime. They swiftly acquired a reputation for lawlessness themselves. Its members are known as *druzhinniki*.

keep a watch on me, and in the spring of 1964 the local
police superintendent himself, Captain Kiselev, began to
come and see me occasionally to find out whether I was
working or not. All this surveillance was evidently co-
ordinated by Goncharenko, the KGB* operative for the
Frunze district† of Moscow, about whom I shall have more
to say later.

Despite all this, I continued to meet my foreign friends
since, in my view, there was nothing criminal about it.
Moreover, I saw no great harm in my semi-literate neighbour reporting, after the event, that some foreigner had been
to see me. In any case, these foreigners were themselves probably under surveillance. It might be asked, nevertheless, why
I decided to go ahead with this 'interview', even though I
knew that the authorities must have known about it beforehand. Why didn't I go out on the street at the last moment,
wait for Korengold's car to appear, and then signal him to
go away again? The reason was that I did not regard it as
a breach of Soviet law to see foreigners, and moreover, if
the police wanted to check on whether Korengold had come
to get some pictures from me, they would stop him as he
left and find that he had nothing with him. In any case, I
had decided to risk it in Russian fashion: I'd never had
trouble before, so why should I have trouble now? But
things had turned out differently, and I would now have to do
a little explaining to the man in the fur hat:

'Giving an interview, are you?' he said, still standing in
the doorway.

'What do you mean, an interview?' I asked with surprise.
Korengold had hidden away his list of questions in his
pocket. The man in the fur hat (which he never took off)
then tried a different tack:

'It's time you came to your senses, Andrei Alexeyevich,'
he said, with a hint of friendliness in his voice. 'We have
had statements from your neighbours that you don't work
anywhere, and are always having suspicious gatherings in
your room.'

---

* KGB: Committee on State Security – i.e. Soviet Secret Police.
† District in central Moscow.

'I don't have any permanent work,' I replied, 'because my father is an invalid and has to be looked after.'

'Well, you should help your father then,' he said.

'I do help him,' I said, trying to be punctilious in my answers and not allow myself to be put out. 'As for gatherings in my room – it's not true. I have far fewer visitors than the neighbours – and then only a few friends.'

'Are these your friends too?' he asked, pointing at Plavinsky, Korengold and the diplomat.

'Yes,' I said.

'Let me see your papers,' he then ordered in an official tone of voice.

'You show me your authorization first,' I replied.

'Certainly,' with a faint air of disdain for the ritual I had initiated, he showed me – without, however, letting it out of his hands – a document identifying him as a lieutenant in the Moscow C I D. 'You can write down my name,' he added.

But I did not bother to write down his name, or even to remember it, since it would have been meaningless. From the very start I realized I was dealing with a member of the Moscow branch of the K G B.

'And these young people here are *druzhinniki*,' he continued, pointing at his two companions in civilian clothes – this evidently more for the benefit of the Americans than for mine. And indeed, the two young men bowed politely, not to me but to the Americans.

'So you don't work anywhere,' the Lieutenant repeated, examining my identity papers. I explained I did not work anywhere *permanently* but that I did temporary jobs.

'And where do *you* work,' he asked, turning to Plavinsky.

'I've been working in television,' Plavinsky replied; the use of the ambiguous tense was insidious, but the Lieutenant did not pursue the matter.

'And you, where do you work?' he at last asked the Americans sternly, as though expecting them to say they didn't work anywhere. But both of them, unlike Plavinsky and me, turned out to have employment: one with the American Embassy, and the other with *Newsweek*.

'So that's who your friends are,' said the K G B man portentously, returning the Americans' papers. 'Have you been in contact with them long?'

'What do you mean; in contact?' I replied. 'I know them, but I am not "in contact" with them.'

'Why did they come to see you then?'

'To look at pictures.'

'Yes, we came to look at pictures,' both Korengold and the diplomat chimed in. They were both very frightened, and were evidently afraid they might have to leave here not for their flats in Kutuzovsky Prospekt,* but for the Lubianka;† though it was not clear what they had done wrong. It is scarcely a crime to look at a collection of pictures, or even to conduct an interview.

All the walls of my tiny apartment were covered with pictures, and there were many others lying on top of the cupboard and on the floor.

'Are these the pictures you sell to foreigners?' the Lieutenant asked politely.

'I don't sell pictures,' I replied.

'Well, couldn't they look at pictures somewhere else?' The tone was now not at all polite.

'They evidently wanted to see my collection,' – here I decided to brag a little and added: 'Only one or two people in Moscow collect modern art, and I am well known among them.'

My boast did not go down well with the two *druzhinniki*. One of them muttered something to the effect that these were not pictures but 'trash'. The other observed ironically that I was thus apparently not the only one to go in 'for this kind of thing'.

After this the Lieutenant told the two Americans they could go home. Watched by one of the *druzhinniki*, I went out into the corridor to see them off. As they said goodbye to me with a bewildered look on their faces I felt extremely embarrassed, since I thought that Korengold, if not the diplomat, might well suspect me of being an *agent provocateur* who had fixed up this whole episode on purpose.

* *Kutuzovsky Prospekt*: residential area where many members of Moscow's foreign colony reside.

† *Lubianka*: headquarters of the secret police.

'And now let's go,' the Lieutenant said to Plavinsky and me when the Americans had gone.

'Have you got a warrant?' I asked.

At first they didn't even understand and thought I was asking whether they had a car (as it turned out, they had: for some reason it was a disguised taxi), and when they realized what I meant, the Lieutenant was quite taken aback:

'What do we need a warrant for?' he said, 'we're just inviting you round for a chat.'

'I won't go without a warrant,' I insisted.

'Yes you will.'

'Take me by force, if you like,' I said, 'otherwise I won't go.'

'Get ready and come along,' Captain Kiselev snapped all at once. Until this moment he had been a silent extra on the scene, but he was now very displeased by my stubbornness: 'You're not a real Soviet man, disobeying the authorities like that.'

'I'm willing to obey the Soviet authorities, but not you,' I answered. The Captain was perplexed by this Jesuitical answer.

'Come along, or things will be worse for you ... come on now, we just want to have a talk with you,' the Lieutenant went on pleading and threatening for a long time, but I had made up my mind not to go. This was not because I thought it was the most sensible thing to do (perhaps, on the contrary, it was the least sensible thing), but simply because I wanted to be awkward, because I was unwilling to give in.

Seeing that I was determined not to go, the Lieutenant changed his tone. 'Very well,' he said, 'sit down. Here's a piece of paper: write out the names of the people who were here, the date and purpose of their visit, and certify that they were found here by us.'

'I won't do that either,' I said. 'All I am willing to do is to write down that on such and such a date, for purposes unknown to me, I was visited by a police captain, a lieutenant of the CID and two *druzhinniki*.'

'That's no good to us,' the Lieutenant said angrily. He now turned his attention to Plavinsky and, finding that he had no papers with him, demanded that I confirm that this really was Dmitri Petrovich Plavinsky. I gave my word that this was so. 'If he isn't, you'll answer for it!' the Lieutenant said and went into the next room to ask my father to confirm Plavinsky's identity as well. After this he let Plavinsky go, and again began to argue with me and threaten me. Perhaps he thought that without a witness I would be more compliant. But I wouldn't give in. 'Very well,' he said grimly, 'we shall be meeting again,' and he left, followed by the others. I also thought we should meet again, but I was wrong: I have never seen him since. In the doorway both *druzhinniki* – if that's what they were – unaccountably asked me to excuse them for 'troubling' me. I excused them.

CHAPTER 2

I Leave Home

IT WAS quite obvious that the departure of my unexpected guests was not the end of it but only the beginning. It was even possible that they would return in half an hour, this time with a warrant for my arrest. It was true, or so it seemed to me, that there was no evidence against me on which to base a criminal charge, but I was vulnerable in another way: for almost a year I had not had any permanent job and therefore fell under the provision of the so-called 'decree concerning the intensified struggle against persons leading a parasitic, anti-social way of life'. This decree, passed in 1960 after a shrill newspaper campaign against 'parasites', laid down that anyone who had not had a proper job for more than a month could be exiled for two to five years to one of the traditional Russian places of exile – the North of European Russia, Siberia or the Far East – 'and forced to do physical work'. This punitive measure was evidently meant to kill several birds with one stone: liquidate unemployment, provide a labour force for the remote areas, and cleanse the large cities of their 'anti-social elements'. It was also a useful way of dealing with 'awkward' intellectuals, such as the Leningrad poet and translator Joseph Brodsky, who was exiled to the North in 1964. It is true that the decree should not have applied to me because I was living with my paralysed father, an 'invalid of the first category' (which included only those who needed constant care), but this might easily be overlooked. Therefore I decided for the present to leave home and avoid all contacts with the police until I managed to get a job.

I took a notebook, some money, my art notes, and the catalogue of Zverev's exhibition; I collected the manuscripts of my plays – the writing of which I regarded as my real job, though alas, it was not one that would have commended

me to the police – said goodbye to my father, telling him
that a friend of mine would visit him every day, and left the
house by the back stairs: I was afraid they might be waiting
for me at the front door.

My plan was to get a job as secretary or research assistant
to some professor of history. This would be more or less a
sinecure and I had thought of it from time to time, realizing
that sooner or later I would have to get a permanent post. No
one could offer me anything definite that day; I was asked to
ring back 'tomorrow'. I realized that there was little hope
in this direction, but in case nothing should come of it I had
an alternative plan, of which I shall speak later. All that
day was spent in telephone calls and visits; in the evening
I visited my friends and told them about my troubles.

As I have already said, it was unpleasant to think that
the Americans would perhaps imagine I had purposely invited them to my flat as a provocation, on orders from someone else. Apart from that, even if the diplomat (who had
known me for some considerable time) did not suspect me of
being an *agent provocateur*, he might think that, once in
the power of the security police, I would allow myself to be
used in some way against him, or say something to his dis-
advantage on the basis of which he could be declared *per-
sona non grata*. It was even possible that he or his superiors
at the Embassy might try to get in first and somehow attempt
to discredit me in the eyes of the KGB. I therefore asked
a woman friend of mine to go at once to the diplomat's
house to tell him that I had not been arrested and to reassure
him generally. Besides this, I felt in honour bound to provide *Newsweek* with the material of the interview with
Zverev, and I therefore asked her to tell the diplomat that
if Korengold agreed, tomorrow morning he would be handed
a photograph of Zverev in his hospital dressing gown together with the answers to his questions.

I carefully explained to her how to find the diplomat's
flat and even drew a plan – if she lingered too long in front
of the building to see whether it was the right number
and the right entrance, the policeman on duty outside would
come up and question her about where she was going and
why. To be on the safe side I told her what she was to

say in such an event; but in fact she got safely to the door of the diplomat's flat. She could hear women's voices inside; evidently there was a party going on. When she rang, the voices quietened for a moment, but then became even louder. No one came to the door. She rang once more. The noise inside the flat grew louder, and the door stayed closed. She rang several times again but with no result, though she had the impression that someone was standing on the other side of the door. Then she resolved upon extreme measures and hammered on the door with her fists.

The door opened and the diplomat came out on to the landing to talk to her. He was very excited and kept interrupting my friend, saying again and again: 'This is a new provocation ...' 'It is a new provocation ...' Then he asked her, 'Where are Andrei and Dima Plavinsky? Are they in prison?'

'Don't worry, neither has been arrested,' said my friend, but he clearly did not believe her. So far as I could make out, the conversation was rather confused. The diplomat kept saying that he was merely interested in modern Russian art and started to explain which artists he liked best, adding that he had not spared money to buy their paintings; then he started to say again that it was all a 'provocation', until my friend finally asked him why, in that case, he was talking about it to her in such a loud voice on the landing and – after all, she could have brought other people with her and left them on the landing below where they might be making a tape-recording of the conversation. In the end it seemed that the diplomat did believe that she had been sent by me, but all the same they got nowhere, even after he had gone back into the flat several times to consult his wife. When my friend mentioned the interview for the magazine he pretended to know nothing about it. Realizing that she had failed in her mission, my friend said that it would evidently be better for me to see him myself and asked how this could be arranged.

'Do you know any foreigners in Moscow at whose home we could meet?' asked the diplomat. 'My embassy has strictly forbidden me to visit Russians.'

My friend said she would ask me and left. She took the

underground home. On the way two young men went up to her and said: 'Would you come with us, Miss?' As she told me, she felt her blood curdle, but fortunately the intentions of the young men were more frivolous than she had at first supposed.

After some hesitation I decided to call on the diplomat myself. I went early next morning; I had no time to waste, and besides, I had to catch the diplomat before he went off to the Embassy. I got out of the bus almost opposite his house and looked carefully to see if there were a car with a Soviet registration plate waiting anywhere near, but I noticed nothing suspicious and went in together with two negroes. It was not yet 8 a.m., but I had underestimated the industriousness of American officials: the diplomat had already gone to the Embassy, and it was left for me to explain matters to his frightened wife, who looked at me as though I were a ghost. To make matters worse, she didn't understand a word of Russian. Eventually, after I had taken a piece of paper and drawn a car leaving the Embassy, she rang her husband who arrived a few minutes later – luckily the Embassy was very near.

We could now talk in less hectic circumstances. As I left, I asked him why, the night before, he had been so frightened that he had not even been willing to open the door. He said that he had simply not heard the doorbell as there was a lot of noise in the flat. We agreed that I should come to see him again a few days later. I went several times, but I was not able to say goodbye to him before he left the country. We did not always see eye to eye during the two years I knew him in Moscow, and I don't know if I'll ever see him again, so I should like to say here that, unlike many foreigners in Moscow who buy pictures by Russian painters, he won me over by his genuine love and understanding of art. His attractive red-haired wife could have become a good painter herself if she had not, like many women, chosen instead to look after her house and family.

After leaving him I went to see Dima Plavinsky, but he was out. His wife told me that Dima was so frightened that he had spent the whole of yesterday wandering about the streets. Fearing an ambush, he had not come home until the early hours and had then gone straight out again. At six o'clock he was to meet his wife in Smolensk Square, and I asked her to tell him that I was staying with my friends and would be glad if he could come and see me. I saw him that evening; the next morning he left for Central Asia.

That day I was also able to clear up some of the circumstances that had led up to my ill-fated meeting with Korengold. As I have already said, the day I telephoned his wife – the 22nd of February – Korengold had received a telegram from his magazine asking him to interview Zverev. On the morning of the 23rd the diplomat had called on me and I had asked him which journalist I should see. At the same time, Korengold had asked a friend of his, Eddie Steinberg, a young Soviet painter, to find Zverev for him and added that, if necessary, he would get permission for the interview from the Ministry of Culture. I don't know if he did in fact obtain this. At any rate, that same evening Korengold ran into the diplomat who told him about me. Next morning he rang me up and we arranged to meet on the 26th as I reckoned that Zverev would get in touch with me on the 25th. Later, on the 24th or 25th, Korengold called on Steinberg to find out whether he had discovered where Zverev was. Meanwhile a lot of people who for one reason or another had become involved in the search for Zverev had gathered in Steinberg's flat – Bohemians of various kinds, young men who claimed to be writers, an ageing poet and even a trolleybus driver. The driver was to play no further part in the story and I mention him merely as a curiosity. None of this motley crew had found out where Zverev was. Then, in front of them all, Korengold said to a friend of mine who was there and who had once invited me to his house with Zverev, that on the morning of the 26th he was to see Zverev at the house of a good friend, the meeting having been arranged by 'a tall man with glasses whose wife is a painter'. He meant the diplomat. But this attempt at a misleading description was naïve. An informer who was at the party went off at once to report Korengold's words to the KGB, who already knew about the interview and decided to sabotage it. It was easy to establish who the tall man in spectacles was, and it was known that I was a friend

of his as well as a close friend of Zverev's. Even before Korengold gave away the time of my meeting with Zverev, the
KGB must have known that the interview would be
arranged by me, as the informer had spent the past few days
making every possible effort to get into my house. Once the
date was known, my neighbour was instructed to remain
at home all day and to ring up the moment any foreigners
came to see me. In addition, arrangements were evidently
made to have the house watched. What happened as a
result I have already described.

Soon after Korengold left Steinberg's flat, all these dubious
people saw Zverev (I think he happened to drop in on Steinberg on his own initiative) and told him that an American
journalist was looking for him and wanted to interview him.
Zverev listened with considerable interest, said nothing and
drove straight from Steinberg's to the hospital where he was
operated on at once. I don't know if he went in order to
avoid meeting the journalist or simply because he visited the
hospital nearly every day. The reason he was operated on
that day was either that it really was due to be done then
or, perhaps, because instructions had come that the operation should take place on that particular date. I had met the
informer several months earlier at the apartment of a young
woman who was interested in art; I did not, of course,
realize what part he was to play in my life. He was a very
dapper young man of about twenty-three, the son of an important government official from one of the wine-growing
areas of the country; his name was Volodya Anikanov. He
was a writer of short stories, and that evening he expatiated
on the theme that art must be the vehicle for bringing
noble ideals to the masses.

The day after my flight from home it became clear that
my attempts to get a job as secretary or assistant to some
historian had failed. Evidently the historians were too
cautious. I then resolved upon a risky step. I had heard that
a proof-reader was needed for the newspaper *Soviet Policeman*. I had worked with a member of its staff on another
paper and hoped that, not knowing of my recent troubles,
he would pull strings for me. I thought it unlikely that the
paper would undertake detailed inquiries in the case of a

man who applied for so insignificant a job as proof-reader, a temporary job at that. All my papers were in order, I had never been in prison, none of my relatives lived abroad, and I was not Jewish – if I had been, it would (unofficially) have barred me from working in any such place. The idea of protecting myself from the police by getting a job on a police newspaper struck me as amusing; besides, the office was near my home and I could always drop in at lunchtime to see my father. I thought I would be fairly safe so long as I held the job, and it would not be altogether easy to dismiss me without good grounds.

I telephoned my acquaintance, got a pass from the Ministry of Public Order (formerly the M V D*) and went to the newspaper office. The stout elderly lady in charge of proof-correcting welcomed me warmly, even joyfully; she asked me about my previous jobs, told me that I could start the very next day, that I was just the person she was looking for and took me to see the editor. The editor was a resolute-looking man who wore the uniform of a colonel of the Internal Security forces.

'If you like him, he's all right by me,' he said amiably to the stout lady. 'I'll ring up Garanov right away.'

Without asking me anything further, he called Major Garanov, the head of the Personnel Department of the Central Police Administration.

'It's a temporary job,' the lady in charge of proof-correcting told me while the Colonel was waiting to speak to Garanov. Turning to him, she added: 'After that I think we'll keep him in the service.'

'We'll see about that,' the Colonel said non-committally, but giving me an encouraging wink, as though to say: 'Cheer up, if you do well, we'll certainly keep you in the service.'

By this time he had been put through to Garanov.

'Garanov? Klyachkin speaking,' the Colonel began breezily. 'I'm sending you a young fellow. Take care of his application so that he can start as proof-reader for us to-morrow.'

Garanov must have objected that according to the regulations a month's investigation was needed before a new per-

*M V D: Ministry of the Interior.

son could be appointed. Lowering his voice, the Colonel said: 'We don't need a month ... it's only for a proof-reader, and a temporary one at that....'

After this the Colonel sent me to Garanov. The Ministry was housed in a hideous five storey building without a lift, put up at the end of the forties when the fashion for Stalinist pseudo-Classicism was at its height.

From one end to the other of each floor ran huge wide corridors which, unlike those in other Soviet institutions, were deserted: no officials smoking and chattering, no haunted-looking visitors waiting for appointments; only occasionally did a solitary figure in military uniform rush by and immediately disappear behind a firmly closed door. To tell the truth, I felt a little frightened, but I decided not to retreat.

To judge by Garanov's office, in which two other people had desks as well, the rooms which gave on to the enormous corridor were very small. Garanov, a colourless individual who was either bald or else slicked his hair down so that it had become invisible, greeted me without any expression of pleasure. The conversation, too, was colourless. He asked me where I had worked before and how I knew that the *Soviet Policeman* needed a proof-reader. At this point we were interrupted by the arrival of a captain who was exceptionally thin and had sloping feminine shoulders. He was making an appeal, which seemed strange to me, on behalf of some young man. He kept repeating that 'the boy feels he is a poet, he has suddenly started showing his poetic gifts' – and that it was necessary 'to help the boy by giving him a job in the M V D'. None of this, however, seemed to strike the Major as odd, and the only thing that worried him was whether the poetic gift, so suddenly revealed, had been officially approved. To this the Captain replied that a collection of his poems was already at the printers. The Major then appeared to agree and the Captain went away looking pleased. What the connection was between poetry and a Security job I failed to understand.

The mention of poetry gave a new direction to the Major's thoughts.

'Do you read books?' he asked me. I was a little taken

aback but realized that what interested the Major was the level of my education.

'Yes, I do,' I said nervously fearing that Garanov would ask me just what books I read. But he had no more questions and merely told me to sign a form, write out my biographical details and bring my papers in the following day.

While I was in the Major's office I overheard another strange conversation. The two officials at the other desks were talking about a man – I can't remember his name, let's call him 'Ivan Ivanovich' – who had made some mistakes which had resulted in innocent people being victimized. The question now was whether to correct the mistake and release the people who had been sentenced unjustly, or 'to spare' Ivan Ivanovich – an elderly man who was very touchy and whose feelings would be hurt if his mistake was rectified. Whom they decided to spare in the end – the people who were in prison through no fault of their own or the touchy Ivan Ivanovich – I don't know.

I dropped in at home to see how my father was feeling. He said he was all right and that Kiselev had been in and left a note for me. The note was an order to appear the next day at 5 p.m. at Police Station No. 5, where I was to ask for Interrogator Vasilyev. I heard our neighbour, who had seen me, talking on the telephone, and I hastily left home again.

I think it was that day that I decided to visit Zverev in the hospital. There was a notice requiring everyone to wear sterilized gowns and the cloakroom attendant refused to accept my coat. No one, however, prevented me from going in as long as I kept my coat on.

Zverev had already heard what had happened. Dima Plavinsky, thinking that after he had left I must have been handcuffed and taken away to prison, had said as much to Zverev's half-crazed mistress, and she had told not only Zverev but half of Moscow, embellishing the tale with such exaggerations that all who met me during my remaining days of freedom stared as though they had seen a ghost. Zverev's operation was a very minor one and it had been entrusted to some interns. The interns took too long over it, the anaesthetic wore off, and Zverev, waking up in pain, heard someone say: 'That's the famous Zverev.' Morbidly suspicious as he was, he decided that they were about to finish him off and started to yell at the top of his voice. They managed to calm him down, took out the pins, and let him go.

Next morning, while the local police were looking for me, I walked into the office of the head of the Personnel Department of the Central Police Administration. Garanov greeted me with even less enthusiasm than he had shown the day before. He took a long time reading my *curriculum vitae* and turning the pages of my work-book.* At last he sighed and asked: 'Why do you keep changing your job? How long are you going to be temporary?'

I mumbled something to the effect that it was difficult for me to find a good job as I had no university degree. The fact that I had been thrown out of the university was not, of course, to my advantage.

'Naturally,' said Garanov. 'One has to study. Me, I worked in the Security Service and went to evening classes. It wasn't easy in those days, you know, the Security Service worked so hard that you never had a moment's leisure – not like today.'

I had a fairly good idea of how it had been in the Security Service in those days.

'So now,' added Garanov, 'it's time for you to settle down. Call me the day after tomorrow, in the morning.'

I wasn't keen on meeting Vasilyev or anyone else from Police Station No. 5 until the question of my job was settled. Nevertheless at 5 p.m. I rang up and asked for Vasilyev.

'Will you please come here at once,' Vasilyev said.

'I'm sorry, I'm not feeling very well, could we put it off for a couple of days?' I asked with as much self-assurance as I could muster.

'All right,' said Vasilyev after a short pause. 'Come at five o'clock on the 5th of March.'

Clearly, my time was running out, as was proved to me by

---

* Under pre-war regulations introduced by Stalin to tighten up 'labour discipline', all Soviet workers must possess 'work-books' which contain a full record of their previous jobs, reasons for dismissal, etc. They must be presented whenever a new job is applied for.

an incident which took place that evening. The friends with whom I was staying went out and I volunteered to stay at home and baby-sit. At about nine o'clock there was a ring at the door. I opened it a crack, and from the manner in which a nondescript-looking man in a black overcoat silently pushed his way in, I realized that things were not too good.

'What can I do for you?' I asked politely.

Without a word the man in black showed me a small red book.

'Don't worry,' he said after having enjoyed the effect of his gesture. 'All I want is some information about your neighbours.' He pointed to the right. 'What kind of people are they? But,' he put his finger warningly to his lips, 'not a word to anyone.'

'You will have to ask the people who live in the apartment,' I replied. 'They are out at present, I'm only the baby-sitter. I don't know anything about the neighbours except that one of them works for the police.'

'For the police!' The agent was taken aback and, mumbling once again that I was not to say a word to anyone, quickly withdrew.

Evidently, he had either stupidly got the instructions wrong and come to question my friends about the policeman who lived next to them instead of vice versa, or else he was merely using the familiar pretext of seeking information about the neighbours in order to find out whether I was there.

Later that evening, when we were all sitting in the small kitchen, I told my friends about this incident. Their neighbour on their left was a caretaker, the one on the right was a policeman; it was perfectly clear that no one would have come to question my friends about either of them. The kitchen was the place we usually went to when we wanted to speak freely. Not until some time later did we discover that, in the flat above, which was occupied by a member of the house committee, police agents had fixed up a tape-recorder and recorded all our conversations through the ventilator. I was reminded of a conversation I'd had with Markevich in his room at the Ukraina Hotel. Markevich was annoyed because Zverev had refused to come to see him at his hotel.

'Zverev is a frightened man,' I said. 'There are likely to be a lot of KGB agents snooping around the hotel, and in addition many of the rooms are bugged, which makes sensitive people nervous.'

It must not be imagined that I said all this in a conspiratorial whisper, Markevich was hard of hearing so I had to shout at the top of my voice.

'Nonsense,' said Markevich calmly. 'I have been staying here for a long time and I know that everything keeps breaking down in the hotel – either the lights go out or the water doesn't run from the tap. I'm sure the microphones have broken down long ago.'

I think Markevich was underestimating the achievements of Soviet technology. For many people in Moscow microphones are a real plague: they think that somebody is listening in to them all the time. I remember one curious incident. A friend of mine had a party at his apartment one evening and among the guests was a foreigner. The conversation was perfectly innocent but all the same he turned the radio on loud for fear of people listening. Towards midnight there was a ring at the door and two policemen came in. Everyone was terrified. As it happened, they need not have been: new buildings, like the one in which my friend lived, had very thin partitions; the tenants who had the flat overhead had been kept awake by the loud music and had telephoned the police. Stories about bugging are very amusing in retrospect, but it was an unpleasant shock to me when I discovered that all our conversations had been overheard.

Realizing that the police knew where I was, I decided to go back home. Captain Kiselev arrived a quarter of an hour after my return. He asked me where I had vanished to, but his tone was informal and without insisting on an answer he handed me another summons from Interrogator Vasilyev for the date we had arranged by telephone. i.e. the 5th of March.

'Will you be there?' Kiselev asked.

'I'll see.'

'Be sure you are,' Kiselev said in a friendly voice, 'there's nowhere for you to hide anyway.'

Sometime earlier, my father had asked a friend of his to find out from the police what had happened to me. The police said they didn't know – I might already have been arrested. Evidently the police thought the K G B might have taken over my case without letting them know.

On the morning of the 5th of March I phoned Garanov; he said in a voice which was now positively funereal that, unfortunately they couldn't hire me at the moment, but that he would ring me, 'if they needed me later'. It was clear that this would not happen. This meant that on the eve of my meeting with Vasilyev I was deprived of my trump card. But I must say that on the whole I was almost pleased that nothing had come of my attempt to work for the police.

I had to decide what to do next. Of course I didn't have to obey the summons, but I wasn't sure that would be best for me. If Vasilyev still meant only to warn me or to give me more time to find a job my disobeying the summons might make things worse. But all this was mere speculation. I hoped in any case to learn from Vasilyev just what they wanted from me, and what I had to fear or hope.

CHAPTER 3

The Wheels Begin to Turn

I HAD expected that either Vasilyev would turn out to be a KGB officer pretending to be a policeman or that someone from the KGB would be present at the interview. But nothing of the sort occurred. In the squalid office of the CID in the 5th Police Station I found Vasilyev and three young men who were typical police agents; they sat at their desks and took hardly any part in our conversation. One of them was questioning an old man, who, as far as I could make out, was a stableman at the race-course.

I was struck by Vasilyev's manner. He seemed to be choking with rage, but he spoke very clearly and distinctly as though doing his best to hide it. I don't know if this was his usual way of talking or whether I really had enraged him by something I had done. He began by asking me how I had dared to refuse to accompany the two policemen. If he had been there, he would have brought me along even if it had meant putting me in a strait-jacket, and I would have got two weeks in prison for my refusal to obey representatives of authority. He mentioned the decrees of 1961 about resisting the representatives of authority. In fact, these decrees are so worded that if you interpret them widely enough they can be taken as an invitation to policemen or *druzhinniki* to break into people's homes and haul them off without more ado. However, not having such a low opinion of Soviet law, I started arguing with Vasilyev. At this, he lost his temper altogether and began to shout. I said I would refuse to talk to him if he adopted this tone. He quietened down and spoke more politely, though still seething with rage and pronouncing every word so clearly that he seemed to feel it carefully with his tongue before allowing it to come out.

At first he kept asking where I had been during the past

few days. As I have already said, the police and presumably Vasilyev himself knew this perfectly well; evidently, he was only trying to catch me out. In any case, wherever I might have lived during those days, it was not a crime, so I gave the most absurd answers, not bothering to make them convincing and trying to make Vasilyev realize that he was getting nowhere. Suddenly one of the agents at the neighbouring desk butted in and said, 'None of your bloody lies, you ...' But Vasilyev quickly gave him a warning sign and said something like 'Don't talk like that,' indicating that he shouldn't swear, and that I was the sort who had to be handled with a certain delicacy. Then, he took out a sheet of paper and said:

'All right, if you don't want to say where you were, you needn't. Here's a piece of paper for you, make out a complete list of your friends.'

'I won't do that,' I said.

'Why on earth not?' asked Vasilyev.

'Why should I get my friends into trouble?' I asked ingenuously. 'In making inquiries about me you'll start dragging them to the police station and at the best cause them nothing but unpleasantness.'

'Why are you trying to make out that the police station is a frightening kind of place?' Vasilyev asked. 'When, on the contrary, we defend the rights of the Soviet citizen.'

'Good for you,' I replied, whereupon the conversation took a new turn.

'All right,' he said, 'if you don't want to write you needn't,' his rage expressing itself in the long pauses between the words. Then for some reason he put the blank sheet of paper in his safe, and, evidently following a prearranged plan, began to question me about where I worked and how I earned my living. I said that my father was seriously ill, and so was my aunt who was all alone since she had been widowed three months ago; for this reason I couldn't do regular work but managed with temporary jobs such as proof-correcting, modelling and technical translation which I did at home.

'How much do you earn?' asked Vasilyev.

'About thirty roubles a month. My father has a pension of

sixty roubles, so we manage quite well.'

Vasilyev argued that no one could live on thirty roubles a month and claimed that he, Vasilyev, couldn't manage on his salary of a hundred and fifteen. I told him that I had no television set.

'I only have an old one,' he shouted. 'I can't even afford a meal at the cafeteria.'

'No, you can live on thirty roubles a month,' the stable-man from the race-course suddenly broke in. 'As long as you live at home.' He had been trying for some time to butt into the conversation between Vasilyev and me. He had probably meant to support Vasilyev in order to impress his own interrogator, but in a practical matter like this he couldn't help but take my side.

'You shut up,' his interrogator said severely, 'and don't interrupt other people's conversation.'

The old man shut up while Vasilyev continued to argue that it was impossible to live on thirty roubles a month and that I must therefore have some other source of income. I didn't think at the time of accusing him of anti-Soviet propaganda, inasmuch as thirty roubles a month is the official minimum wage in towns, so that whether we like it or not, we must all know how to manage on thirty roubles. Instead of using this 'ideological' argument, I offered to work out my expenses to the last penny. Losing his temper altogether, Vasilyev commented that I was 'too clever by half'.

'That's not surprising,' I said modestly. 'I had ten years of high school.'

'I'm not talking about school – that's a different sort of cleverness,' Vasilyev said darkly and told me to write down in detail where and at what jobs I had worked and what I was doing now, stressing the fact that I spent a rouble a day.

'One rouble a day on the average,' I corrected him, 'occasionally two and sometimes nothing.'

I wrote down the details of what I spent. Vasilyev hid the answer in the safe and without saying another word, left the room. I was astonished at his having asked me nothing about either foreigners or paintings. I took this to be on the whole alarming. Evidently the KGB had given up the idea of 'talking me round' and decided to act through the police who were to question me along narrowly defined lines.

Vasilyev was replaced by his deputy, Captain Kiselev. He put on an official expression and asked me again where and at what jobs I had worked; he carefully wrote down my replies and asked me to sign his report of the conversation. He then asked me to sign another paper, which said that I had been informed of the text of the decree passed by the Presidium of the Supreme Soviet of the RSFSR* on the 4th of May 1961 'concerning the struggle against persons who avoid doing socially useful work and lead an anti-social, parasitical way of life', and gave me until the 20th of March to find a job, after which I would be held criminally responsible for not having one. I signed the paper to confirm that I had taken cognizance of it, but said that in view of my father's illness I would not get a permanent job.

'If you won't, you'll be sent to Siberia,' said Kiselev – though unlike Vasilyev, he behaved in a friendly manner towards me. There followed an argument about my work-book, a repetition of the one which had taken place between me and Vasilyev. I didn't want to give up my work-book, in which all my previous jobs were entered, but Kiselev and some other police captain, who came in, talked me round and I took it to them on the following day. I thought that I would only land myself in further trouble by refusing, but it might have been better not to take it all the same. They carefully copied out all there was in it for their files and returned it to me. In this way the case against me as 'an anti-social parasite' was formally initiated.

The police had given me so little time to find a job that I could not have got one for which I was qualified even if I had wanted to. The only thing I could have got was a job as a handyman, loader, stoker, or some other kind of unskilled worker, in other words, a job of no interest to me which in view of my weak heart would have been bad for my health and which would have left me no free time. I did at first try to find this sort of job, purely out of fear of the police, but I soon changed my mind and firmly decided not to get a job at all. Of course at first sight it would seem that it would have been more prudent of me to find myself

* The Russian Republic of the Soviet Union.

work. But even prudence must have its limits. One must insist on one's rights to an independent existence. Why should I go and work as a handyman or a night watchman when I believe that my proper work is to write plays and poems, or to do research on history and art? Loyalty to the State must not turn into slavish obedience, I told myself; one must stand up for one's dignity and not give way to fear. As disagreeable memories of my encounter with the police gradually faded and no one bothered me for a while, my resolution grew firmer and firmer.

There was, as I've already said, another reason why it was difficult for me to take a permanent job, and I thought the police ought to take it into account. Since my mother had died in January 1961 I had lived alone with my father who was seriously ill, half paralysed, scarcely able to speak and had had several strokes and heart attacks. At times he had to lie motionless, so that I was obliged to feed him with a spoon, though it is true that he was quite often able to warm up his dinner, move about the apartment and some-times even come out with my help and sit on a bench on the boulevard. I don't mean that I spent all my time look-ing after my father and that I never left the house, but it was perfectly obvious that without my care he could not survive. His condition was not, needless to say, improved by all these visits from the police.

Apart from this, ever since the beginning of the year I had also to look after my aunt – my mother's sister. Her husband had died in December 1964, and she lived alone. She, too, was ill: a haemorrhage of the brain had left her almost blind and she could not leave the house by herself. Her husband's relatives helped her to some extent, but I went to see her nearly every day, taking her food and medi-cines. In these circumstances it was very difficult for me to take on a full-time job.

And there was still another thing that decided me against getting a job. I thought that the accusation of being a 'parasite' was only a pretext for this police harassment and that if I managed to get a job, it would not save me but would merely force my persecutors to find some other pre-text and perhaps to accuse me of some crime or other. This would have been much worse. As will be seen, I was not altogether wrong in my assumption.

Although the date by which I had to find myself a job had passed, no one had bothered me as yet. True, at the beginning of April, Captain Kiselev came to see my father a couple of times and asked him whether I had found work. When my father said no, Kiselev sighed and shook his head, saying: 'What are his plans then? What is he hoping for?' Then he tried questioning my father about the foreigners who came to see me. Another time he said to my father that here I was, not working, not helping him either, and probably looking after him very badly, so wouldn't my father care to write a report about me to the police? My father told him that these visits tired him and asked him not to come again.

It was obvious that this lull was only temporary, that the bureaucratic machine was grinding away: notes were being written, orders given, information gathered and gigantic wheels were turning which sooner or later would crush me. Perhaps I would have started to look for work again if it had not been for a depressing event: in the middle of April my aunt had another stroke and died after a few days.

My aunt, Zoya Grigoryevna Teodorovich, née Shableyev, was the last of the old Shableyev family. The name comes from the word *shabla*, an old form of *sabla*, i.e. 'sabre'. My grandfather, Grigory Shableyev, the only son of an official in the Russian administration of Poland, had at the end of the last century married a gypsy, the daughter of a horse-thief. He had three children: Evgeni, born in 1895, Zoya in 1900 and my mother, Claudia, in 1903. After which my grandparents had divorced. In my grandfather's family the marriage was regarded as disgraceful; my mother and my uncle were brought up almost from birth by my grandfather's married sister, while my aunt remained with my grandfather and was regarded as a sort of Cinderella by the rest of the family, until the Revolution wiped out all such absurd distinctions. My grandfather was killed during the Civil War in Siberia and my grandmother died in Orenburg where she had been evacuated during the war in 1942. My uncle was shot as 'an enemy of the people' in 1937, my mother died of cancer of the brain in 1961; my aunt, the last of the Shableyevs, survived her for only three years.

My aunt had had a good voice, and in her youth her singing teacher had told her that her path would be 'strewn with flowers'. In the thirties she was an opera singer in Tbilisi, then in Saratov, until the Saratov opera lost its subsidy from the State and she was transferred to musical comedy. After the war she sang in Moscow and I remember her in the role of Silva, wearing an enormous ostrich feather in her hat. That feather – I can still see it as I once found it in her trunk together with her black sequined dress and fan – is one of my most vivid childhood memories; recently I heard by chance that the feather went to a distant relation of my aunt's and that her grandchildren still use it for play-acting. My aunt had to give up the theatre in 1951, when her husband was arrested. The warrant for his arrest stated that he was 'socially dangerous as the son of an "enemy of the people"' (his father had been a Commissar in Lenin's government after the October Revolution), and he was charged with 'slandering socialist realism' and sentenced to five years – not very much for those times. To earn her living my aunt made artificial flowers for hats and dresses in the Soviet style of the early fifties. In this way her teacher's prophecy was strangely fulfilled.

My aunt's death left me very depressed, and I decided to leave Moscow for a while. I arranged for our neighbour's charwoman to look after my father for three days and went to Tallin, in Estonia, where I wandered by myself in the narrow streets of the old city.

Soon after my return Captain Kiselev dropped in and he said I must go through a medical test to show whether I was fit for physical work. He took me to the district clinic where I was given a general examination and seen by an oculist and a lung specialist; analyses were made of my blood and urine and I was X-rayed and had a cardiogram taken. We wandered side by side from room to room, like two inseparable friends working on the same job, and Captain Kiselev gradually accumulated a whole armful of medical forms. All this took several days. I asked Kiselev what would happen after the test.

'You'll get another warning,' he said, 'then, if you still haven't found a job, we'll send you up for trial.'

While we were waiting for the results of the cardiogram, we went into the psychiatric office; this was my first meeting with psychiatrists. I was questioned by two women and one man.

'Why aren't you working?' they asked me. By then I was sick to death of medical procedures and of stupid questions.

'I've got too much to do,' I answered.

'Oh, what is it that you do?' they asked politely.

'I go to see my friends.'

'But aren't your friends working most of the day?' the psychiatrists objected cautiously.

'No,' I said, 'my friends are like me.'

After this the psychiatrists looked at one another and told me I was free to go. As I gathered from what followed, they reported that I was completely sane.

A couple of days later, on my way home, I ran into Kiselev.

'You need treatment,' he said in a sympathetic tone of voice. 'I have just received your cardiogram, your heart is no good at all, Siberia is quite out of the question.'

I felt completely relieved though not at all surprised. My heart had been weak from birth, which was why I had been exempted from military service and had recently been feeling not at all well.

When all the medical certificates had been collected, Kiselev and I drove to the Department of Forensic Medicine on the outskirts of Moscow. This was on the 30th of April. Kiselev took a long time finding something out and finally said we would have to wait. The waiting also took a very long time. We sat with several women covered with bruises who had come to be examined after being beaten by their husbands. At last we were called out and I appeared before a medical 'commission' which consisted of one thin, nondescript man who was as snub-nosed as a baby mouse and wore overalls as grey as his face.

'Do you drink vodka?' he asked in a sugary voice after listening absentmindedly to my heart.

'Hardly at all.'

'Ah, hardly!' he quickly wrote something on a scrap of paper which he handed to Kiselev. I expected that I would also be seen by the neuro-pathologist whose office was next door, but the examination was over.

'Well, what's the verdict?' I asked as we went out.

'Limited capacity for work, no lifting of heavy objects,' replied Kiselev. 'Now we'll go to the police station to talk things over with the chief.'

I didn't argue; from what Kiselev had said I expected that I would be given a 'fatherly' lecture and the whole thing would be over. However, when we got to the police station, instead of the 'chief' I saw Vasilyev once again. A bad sign, I thought.

'Well, how's life?' he asked urbanely.

'The same as usual,' I replied.

'The same, but not quite,' he said mysteriously and again asked me to write an account of where and when I had worked and studied, why I wasn't working now, and how I managed to live. While I was writing this down, he suddenly asked me what category of disability I belonged to. I said I hadn't been assigned to any.

'You soon will be,' Vasilyev promised. 'But as you haven't got a permanent job I don't know on what basis they will calculate your benefits.'

He took my statement, told me I was free to go, and said goodbye in a friendly manner. I went away, forgetting my identity papers in his office.

I left the police station in a happy mood, hoping that everything would now end well, though not completely sure it would. It may seem unnatural that a man should rejoice in having a weak heart, but this is explained by the unnatural circumstances in which we live. If I were registered as disabled, it would give me a certain freedom as well as a small disability pension which would be anything but superfluous considering the minute sums I earned.

It was the beginning of May. There seemed no prospect of my getting the pension soon, and no sign either that the police had lost their interest in me. As I expected, all my neighbours were questioned, and Vasilyev said he would also have to question my father. This might be considered a mere formality connected with winding up my case and fixing the amount of my pension. I telephoned Vasilyev myself and asked him to come soon, as my father had been invited to the country and was to leave Moscow for two weeks in a day or two.

He had been invited by an old woman friend of his, with whom he had occasionally stayed before; I knew that one of her relatives was indirectly involved in the investigation of my case, but I attached no importance to this fact. At about the same time I was offered a job as librarian not far from my home. This suited me, and I arranged to call on the personnel department as soon as I had seen my father off to the country.

Vasilyev called two days before my father was to leave; he came with a young man in civilian clothes whom I had never seen before or since. During the interrogation I sat in another room and came in only at the very end. As far as I remember, Vasilyev asked my father whether I looked after him, what means we were living on, whether I was working and if not why not, and whether my father got help from the neighbours. My father answered with great difficulty and very slowly, but clearly and sensibly. He said that I looked after him all the time, bought his food and cooked it, washed him and did whatever else was necessary; that we were living on his pension and my occasional earnings, and that I had given up trying to keep a permanent job in order to care for him. At this point Vasilyev suggested that another reason for my not working permanently was, presumably, that I had a weak heart, and my father confirmed this. As for the neighbours, he said that with the exception of one woman, so far from helping him, they actually tried to make life as difficult as possible for him.

Vasilyev read out his notes and my father, using his left hand, scrawled his initials at the bottom of the page. Before leaving, Vasilyev asked me what I was doing about getting a job. I said that I might soon have one.

'They may put you down as disabled,' he said, 'but I advise you to get a job as soon as you can all the same.' He did not, however, give me back my papers, although he knew I couldn't get a job without them. I replied that I had tried to get a job on the *Soviet Policeman,* but that they must have made inquiries with the local police, i.e. presumably from Vasilyev himself, and on getting the answer had refused to take me on.

'No, you are wrong there,' said Vasilyev. 'The Ministry has its own means of checking up – they wouldn't ask the police. Our business is to help people get jobs.'

In the doorway he met our neighbour and she said how-do-you-do to him as to an old friend. This confirmed my belief that the neighbours had already been questioned.

CHAPTER 4

The Prosecutor; Arrest; Meeting
with the Judge

ON the morning of the 14th of May I saw my father off to the country. As soon as I was back Zverev came and told me that his exhibition was opening that day in Geneva – it was the same exhibition that had earlier been held in Paris. In the interval between the two exhibitions he had at last found time to go to the Ministry of Culture where, as far as I could make out, they talked to him in much the same way as they had talked to me at the police station. He was received by Druzhkov, head of the Department of Conservation and Restoration of Ancient Monuments, who for some reason was also responsible for the export of works of art. In Druzhkov's office (which according to Zverev was very small – there is a shortage of space for bureaucrats in Moscow) there were two other young men with athletic figures and official expressions on their faces. As he suffers from persecution mania, Zverev decided that after his conversation with Druzhkov they would beat him up in order to teach him not to arrange any more exhibitions in Paris.

'Why are the Western papers making such a fuss, saying that you are living on bread and water in Moscow? Are you really so badly off?' Druzhkov asked him severely.

Zverev, who drank beer as well as water, glanced at the two young athletes and said that these were bourgeois lies. The conversation continued in the same spirit for about twenty minutes, after which Druzhkov told Zverev to come another time and bring some of his paintings. Zverev left the room under the disapproving eyes of Druzhkov's assistants; happy to have emerged unscathed, he never visited the Ministry again.

To celebrate the Geneva exhibition, Zverev and I went to

a café. However, neither of us had enough money for anything more than a glass of soda-water each.

When I came home the neighbours told me that some officer had been to see me. Then the 'officer' arrived in person and turned out to be none other than Captain Kiselev.

'Things are bad,' he said, 'I have to take you to see the Prosecutor.'

'And what will the Prosecutor do?'

'The Prosecutor wants to talk to you, then he may either stop the case or give the order for your arrest,' Kiselev explained.

The Prosecutor's office for the Frunze district was on the first floor in the right wing of a large old house not far from Trubnoy Square. The Prosecutor, Fetisov, had summoned me for four o'clock, but he was not yet there when we arrived. We waited in a large dark passage, sitting on a wooden bench of a kind found only in police or railway stations. A policeman sitting next to us was telling another about the trouble he'd had arresting a prostitute: she went from one client to another, and it wasn't easy to track her down. Then a young woman came in and for some reason asked whether this was the clinic. The Prosecutor arrived shortly before five. He was a tall man of over fifty in a black shiny suit and looked very much like the film actor Samoylov who usually plays the role of a Party bigwig. As soon as he arrived we were summoned to his room; without looking at us, he told us to sit in two large black leather armchairs near his desk. A portrait of Lenin hung on the wall behind him. Sitting at his desk, he spent about three minutes looking at my file, which Kiselev had handed him. The file was fairly thick.

'Well, it certainly looks like a case of social parasitism and there might be an element of *fartsovka*,'* said the Prosecutor to no one in particular. He gave me a hard look and asked, 'Well, so you're tired of living in Moscow?'

'No, not at all,' I replied truthfully.

'Let him wait,' the Prosecutor nodded at me.

'Go outside and wait a bit,' said Kiselev; I went out into

---

* *Fartsovka*: Moscow slang for illegal business deals with foreigners: Amalrik was suspected of selling pictures to foreigners.

the passage. Kiselev spent about twenty minutes with the Prosecutor alone.

'Let's go over to the 5th Station,' he said as he came out of the Prosecutor's office. 'The Prosecutor will take advice and ring us up there.'

He left me in the guardroom of the 5th Station and immediately disappeared. After waiting for about ten minutes I got up to leave.

'Stay where you are, you are under detention,' said the duty officer, and the policeman at the door barred my way. I realized that Kiselev had lied to me so that I should not try to escape on the way from the Prosecutor's office to the police station – though it might well be that the Prosecutor was really taking advice before signing the order for my arrest.

A man may be caught quite by chance in the wheels of the huge bureaucratic machine. He may think that only a fold of his jacket has got caught, and that everything is all right except for a certain discomfort under the armpits; but all the time, it is not just his jacket getting tighter and tighter, it is the slow movement of the machinery, gradually pulling him in and mangling him. As I walked with Kiselev across Trubnoy Square, feeling the warmth of the spring sun and thinking that at the police station I would write a statement for the umpteenth time and continue to go about for a while in a rather tight jacket, I did not realize that the wheels which had been slowly turning for two years had just completed their final revolution.

Needless to say, all such literary similies occurred to me only much later. I had other things to think about at the time. I spent about an hour in the guardroom which was divided in two by a wooden counter. The duty officers of the 5th and 11th Police Districts sat at the back of the room, behind a counter; the rest of the space was intended for visitors and for policemen coming on and going off duty. One door opened on to the street and a lieutenant was posted in front of it; another led to the back of the building, and a third, which was locked, into a narrow corridor between two rows of so-called P D C's (Preliminary Detention Cells). Still another door directly behind the counter led to a large cell which I gathered was reserved chiefly for drunks and other people detained for only a short time. This door had a small panel of plexiglass. Through it we could see some boys who were banging on the door and shouting that they had come to give evidence and refused to be locked up. The duty officer lazily exchanged insults with them, but soon they were led out and taken somewhere else. When they had left, the senior lieutenant on duty asked me to hand over my watch, money, papers, belt, shoelaces and spectacles; I realized that I was to be put into the cell. I was unwilling to give up my glasses and the senior lieutenant did not insist, but he said that if some drunk smashed them for me it would be my own fault.

The cell was about sixteen yards square and had a small barred window high up in the wall opposite the door; most of the space was taken up by benches rather as in a small auditorium; a narrow passage was left between the benches and the wall where the door was. I did not sit on a bench: people had walked on them and they were covered with mud; moreover, the prisoners were not often allowed out to the toilets, so they had urinated in the corner against the walls or, if they were drunk, straight on to the benches which were wet and stank to high heaven. When I was brought in, there was a man lying on a bench with his legs tucked up; he was dishevelled, his face was covered with bruises and scratches and he wore filthy workman's clothes. I walked up and down the narrow passage between the benches and the wall. For some reason I vividly recalled that in the spring of the previous year I had been in the country near Smolensk just when the floods were beginning and I had walked several miles barefoot over the flooded fields; at this recollection I sensed my lack of freedom more sharply than I was ever to do again.

I now saw that the talk about 'disability benefits' and about a 'second warning' was only a trick to make sure that I *wouldn't* get a job and thereby make it more difficult to deport me from Moscow. It is also possible, though not very likely, that someone really did have the idea of registering me as disabled and thereby closing my case, but that this plan was not approved at a higher level. I did not yet regard my case as lost: my trial was still to come and I hoped then to answer all the arguments of the police, naïvely failing to realize that the trial was just as much a formality as the policeman's report or the questioning of my father, and that the outcome of my case had been decided at the very moment at which it was begun. Even so, by walking feverishly up and down the room and brooding on how best to defend myself, I was acting in the best possible way, for it helped me to bear the loneliness and enforced idleness of prison and to keep up my spirits.

While I was walking up and down, my cellmate woke up, looked around him with bleary eyes and said: 'No, this is not the diplomatic corps.' I was quite astonished – nothing about him suggested that he belonged to diplomatic circles, and neither did he look like an informer who had been put into my cell to find out about my foreign contacts. He continued to mumble drunkenly, something almost incomprehensible about the American Embassy and then dropped off to sleep again. In the end the explanation proved to be very simple. He worked as a mechanic for the department of the Soviet Foreign Office responsible for servicing the houses of diplomats; having received his pay he had got blind drunk and was unceremoniously delivered to the police station. Soon another drunk was brought in. He was an innocuous-looking old man in a shabby hat and with a large black eye. He kept whimpering and complaining: 'Me, a patriot, a devoted son of my fatherland, to be sent to jail!' In the intervals, he knocked on the door and begged for 'just one little cigarette'. The senior lieutenant gave him a cigarette and he fell silent, except for an occasional muffled sob. Several more people were brought in, and then a young policeman came and told me to follow him.

I had been summoned by the Judge – not just an ordinary one, but, as the policeman told me with awe, the 'Chief Judge'. The court was not far from the police station and we went to it on foot; I walked in front, holding up my trousers, while the young policeman followed me. He had a proud and eager expression on his face – evidently because his charge was going to be tried not by just any sort of

judge, but by the 'Chief Judge'. Captain Kiselev was waiting for us at the door, a thick file in his hands. I reproached
him with having tricked me at the Prosecutor's, but he did
not reply; when I expressed astonishment at things moving
so fast – I had only just been arrested and now I was about
to be tried – he said: 'Nothing of the sort. The Judge only
wants to have a talk with you.'

We climbed to the first floor, crossed a small courtroom
and walked into the office of Yakovlev, the Chief Judge of
the Frunze district. He had a turned-up, shiny nose and a
bald patch from his forehead to the back of his head, with
curly and abundant hair on either side of it; he struck me
at once as extremely unprepossessing, and I felt that if he
were going to hear my case, I could expect the worst. A
short young man with a shaven head and very black eyes
sat on a sofa in his room. When we went in the Judge was
talking to him and telling him to go somewhere to find out
about a job and also to buy himself some drug at the chemist
– presumably he was an alcoholic.

As he left the Judge turned to Kiselev and asked him:
'Do you know who that is? That's Pushkin, the greatest
pickpocket in Moscow.' (I assumed that he was nicknamed
Pushkin because he looked a little like the poet.)

'He wrote to me from the camp,' the Judge continued,
still addressing Kiselev, but glancing sideways at me so
that I realized he was speaking for my benefit. 'He said that
he had lied to me in court when he told me he had done
seven years at school, but that he would complete his
schooling in camp. And in fact he did. We corresponded
for a while and I petitioned the Supreme Court of the
R S F S R to release him before he had served his term – that's
always a tricky business,' he added. The Supreme Court had
either released him, or annulled his sentence and pardoned
him – I no longer remember – but in any case, Pushkin the
pickpocket had returned to Moscow, and now Judge Yakovlev was getting him a job and having him treated for
alcoholism. After telling his story the Judge looked at me
triumphantly as if to say: 'What do you think of that?' Only
then did he take the file that Kiselev had brought him.

As I expected, the first thing he asked was why I was not

working. I repeated briefly what I had already told the police. Looking through my work-book, he asked me what I could do and it became clear to him that I could do very little. Then he asked about my health and, learning that I had a bad heart, looked at my draft board report which pronounced me 'unfit in peacetime, though fit for non-combatant service in war'.

'Well yes, in wartime people like that are used as drivers,' said Yakovlev, pursing his lips and obviously expressing his contempt at my unfitness for active service.

'You can't do without drivers either,' Kiselev said in my defence.

Yakovlev grudgingly assented and went on to another subject.

'Who were those foreigners who were always going to see you?'

I said that I collected paintings by young artists and that foreigners came to see them. I added that there was considerable interest in modern Russian painting abroad and that one Russian painter, Zverev, had had an exhibition arranged for him by art collectors in Paris. I said this more out of devilment than for any particular reason, and immediately realized that it was a mistake.

'And what has happened to Zverev now?' asked the Judge.

'Nothing, as far as I know,' I replied.

'It would be interesting to see what sort of pictures he paints,' said the Judge. He then asked Kiselev whether my house had been searched – apparently it never occurred to him that there might be any other way of getting to see my paintings. Kiselev replied that it had.

'Do you know of any artist,' Yakovlev asked me solemnly, 'who is unrecognized at home but famous abroad?'

'Yes,' I said, 'there is for instance the American artist Rauschenberg who first got recognition in France.'

'I'm not asking you about Americans,' the Judge objected crossly. 'I mean any Russian artist, say even a modernist?'

'Plenty,' I said. 'Kandinsky, Chagall, Soutine, Archipenko, Malevich – in fact nearly all the most important Russian artists in this country.'

'And who do you think these artists were painting for?

Who, do you think painting is for in general.'

'That's a complicated question,' I said.

'Have you ever been to the Tretyakov Gallery?'

'Occasionally,' I said modestly.

'Do you know who painted the picture "Life Is Everywhere"?'

'Yaroshenko,' I said. 'It was painted in the nineteenth century and shows prisoners in a railway carriage looking through the windows at pigeons.'

'There was someone who painted for the people,' said Yakovlev. 'The lowliest Russian peasant considered that picture as his own. Painters should paint for the ordinary people, not for connoisseurs, foreign or even Russian. They can never be real artists otherwise.'

I did not feel much like getting into an argument about art but, using his own criterion, I agreed that the artist should paint for someone.

'I suppose they should paint for people who are interested in art – after all people are not a homogeneous mass all interested in one and the same thing. Some people like music, others painting, still others like sport or science, and there are some people who are not interested in anything.'

I might have added that if artists must paint for 'the people' then illiterate bureaucrats should not stand between them and their public, laying down the law on what is suitable and what isn't.

Yakovlev listened and shook his head sadly. Our conversation on art finished on this note.

I told him there were rumours going around in Moscow that the decree concerning 'parasites' was going to be abolished; I asked him whether this was true. (These rumours had been circulating for the past month, and I had already mentioned them to Kiselev, who had said : 'They'd be right to abolish it. It makes no sense – the only people we deport under it are drunkards.')

'No, it's not true,' Yakovlev replied, 'though there is a group of writers in Moscow, as well as a few assessors,* who are trying to get it abolished.'

---

* In the Soviet legal system judges are assisted during trials by assessors who play a part similar to that of a jury.

'What do you yourself think of the decree?' I asked him.

'It's a good decree,' he replied. 'It's just what you people deserve.'

He then explained that having been born in the Soviet Union we were endowed from birth not only with a great number of privileges but also with certain duties, including the one to work.

'If you don't want to work in Moscow you can go to Siberia to help look after the red foxes. It's true that they stink,' he added with a sadistic leer on his face. 'But the country needs them for their fur.'

Yakovlev then explained to me my rights and obligations. The trial had to take place no later than five days after my detention, and I was allowed to engage a defence counsel, to summon witnesses and examine the evidence against me.

'You'd better read your file if you haven't already done so,' he said, as though this had been open to me earlier. 'Then, if you like, you can make a written application to me asking for a defence counsel and witnesses.'

As Kiselev and I went out into the empty courtroom, he handed me the file. It consisted, I remember, of the report of the District Inspector, i.e. Kiselev, extracts from my work-book, the evidence of the two *druzhinniki* who had been to see me in February, references from my last employers, and other evidence collected by Vasilyev from my father and neighbours; I think the warrant for my arrest was there as well.

The evidence of one of the *druzhinniki* was very short, that of the other very long. They stated that they had gone to my apartment on the 25th of February together with the District Inspector of the 5th Police Station, and, as one of the two wrote, 'another colleague' (not mentioned by the other *druzhinnik* at all). At my apartment they had found 'two foreign citizens and a man who called himself Plavinsky'. They went on to speak of the pictures hanging on my walls – pictures that were evidently especially intended for sale to foreigners since they were painted in gloomy colours and 'gave a distorted idea of Soviet life'. They were particularly indignant at a picture which showed 'a Soviet rouble sinking into the sea together with a row of broken-down hovels'. I realized that what they had in mind was Oscar Rabin's 'One Rouble'. Indirectly influenced by American Pop art, Rabin had painted a careful reproduction of a huge rouble piece against a background of a Moscow suburb; there was no sea in the picture. Both the *druzhinniki* had concluded that I was a potential traitor to our country and ought to be deported to Siberia as soon as possible, if only as a 'parasite'. In the reference supplied at the request of the police by the newspaper *Water Transport* where I had worked a year earlier it was said that I had worked badly, sometimes failed to turn up and even left my trade union.* I'll come back to this point later.

The basic 'proof' of my guilt consisted in the evidence of my neighbours: the chairman of the house committee who lived in our apartment, the woman police clerk and her husband, and the young man who lived next door with his wife and grandmother. At least two of them had been watching me at the request of the police and the K G B for over a year, but you can imagine how much all this evidence was worth.

The chairman of the house committee wrote briefly that though I was 'in the prime of life' I lived as a 'parasite' and that it would be better for me to work. The woman clerk stated that I had no job, was often away for long periods and had left my father to his own devices – fortunately, his neighbours helped to look after him. The young man and his wife also said that I neither worked nor looked after my father. It was true that the evidence was to some extent conflicting; some of the witnesses wrote that I could not be doing any work since I spent all day at home, others that I neglected my father because I was out from morning to night. The most interesting was the evidence supplied by the young man's grandmother, the oldest tenant in our flat. It was known that, at the end of the thirties, enraged by her husband's infidelities, she had informed against him, alleging that he indulged in anti-Soviet talk; her husband was duly shot. Now she had discovered a new object

* Soviet trade unions are under the control of the State and the Communist Party; membership in them is a formality that involves the obligatory payment of dues.

for her zeal. Her evidence, painstakingly recorded by Vasilyev, read like a thriller, complete with passwords, a secret safe, suspicious visitors, foreigners with spying equipment, a mysterious woman with long hair and an escape down the back stairs. All this was deduced from such 'evidence' as the following: my father had once been heating some glue in the kitchen, and when she asked him what it was for he had replied: 'It's not your business.' She concluded, therefore, that he was heating it in order to stick wallpaper over a secret safe. On another occasion, when some people came to see me I had told them 'My father's seriously ill', and this had obviously been a password. The 'fact' that I neither worked nor looked after my father was thrown in merely for good measure. The neighbours also stated that I was often visited by foreigners who brought and carried away abstract paintings. I was amused at the idea of their being able to tell that the paintings were abstract; whenever my friends or I brought or carried away paintings, we always carefully wrapped them up.

The most unsavoury and mendacious part of the neighbours' evidence were the references to my father. To begin with, except for one woman who, as it happened, gave no evidence, none of them had ever helped him. On the contrary, he was persecuted by them, especially by the witness I. Kagan (the woman police clerk and informer), who got so annoyed at his shuffling his feet as he walked along the passage that he hardly dared to go out of his room. Whenever I tried to stand up for him, the neighbours threatened to report us to the police. Statements that my father was able to look after himself were also untrue. He was so depressed at not being able to work, read books that interested him or even talk, that the doctors had advised him to occupy his mind by doing as much of the housework as he could. For this reason he occasionally warmed up his dinner and sometimes even swept the floor. But, as the neighbours knew perfectly well, he could not have lasted out a day without someone's help. Finally, the 'long periods' during which I had allegedly left him alone amounted in fact to two: in the whole of our life together I had left him once after the visit from the *druzhinniki* (having first arranged for a friend to come and see him every day) and another time after the death of my aunt when I went to Tallin for three days and hired a charwoman to look after him while I was away.

In order to refute all this false evidence, I wrote a formal application for the court's permission to call a witness who came often to our apartment and knew how we lived. Not that I had much hope of her evidence influencing the course of the trial, but I wished in this way at least to let my friends know what had happened to me, otherwise, they would never hear whether I had been tried or not. I also asked the court to appoint a defence counsel for me. Yakov-lev took my statements and said that the trial would probably be held on the following Monday or Tuesday, and that counsel would probably come to see me either the next day (Saturday) or on Monday.

Kiselev, who was impatiently awaited by some friend of his outside, but who could not leave until the Judge had talked to me and I had read my file, was now at last able to take me back to the police station. On the way, perhaps to justify himself, he told me that, if I had not been charged with 'parasitism' a criminal case would have been started against me. This was the only time anyone spoke to me so frankly; everyone else, both before and after the trial, kept telling me that I was my own worst enemy; if I had got myself a job just for appearance's sake nothing would have happened to me.

CHAPTER 5

Mogiltsev Street

I WAS put back into the same cell, where by now there were quite a lot of drunks, some sleeping on the floor or on the benches, while others walked on top of them waving their arms and swearing aimlessly. It was after 10 p.m. and I had had nothing to eat since morning so I knocked on the plexiglass panel in the door and asked the lieutenant who opened it whether I would be fed.

'Why didn't you tell me earlier?' asked the lieutenant. 'You've got money, I'd have gone round to the shop to buy you something. Now it's closed, and as from tomorrow you'll be on prison food.'

There was nothing to do but hold out till the morning, though I wondered how on earth I was going to sleep. At midnight, however, the door opened and I was called out.

I was led out into a courtyard and heard that I was to be taken to Mogiltsev Street, but I didn't know what that meant. Two policemen got on to a motorcycle, made me sit in the sidecar, and off we went. It turned out that I was only being transferred from the 5th District to the 60th, which was housed in one of the quiet side streets near the Arbat. The duty officer unlocked the door at the back of the guardroom, and I found myself in a sort of miniature prison. It consisted of three cells with doors giving on to a passage. The door on the right led to the lavatory. At the far end, under a dim light, stood a small cupboard, a table, a chair and a pail of hot water. There was a policeman on duty in the corridor and the only way to get into it was by unlocking the door from the guardroom side; it could not be unlocked from the inside. In this corridor I was met by a good-natured jailer who frisked me once more, in his own words 'as a formality'; he took away my glasses and put me into the first cell, which, though clean struck me as very gloomy. It was completely empty and had a high ceiling that made it look larger than it was. Afterwards, when I measured it, it turned out to be eight paces long and four wide. In the wall opposite the door a large window reached almost to the ceiling; it was barred on both sides and looked out on a wall. Later, I had my meals on the windowsill. The door had a small spy-hole, with a metal plate covering it on the outside, and above it there was a recess with a lamp inside which, under prison rules, burned all night. On the right were plank beds fixed to the wall, which, as in the cell I had been in before, left only a narrow passage along the opposite wall. Everything was painted dark red and the paint was peeling in places. For a while I walked up and down, then I took off my shoes, spread my raincoat on a bench and lay down, putting my sweater under my head as a pillow. But it was very cold, so I soon put on the sweater, and then the raincoat. I pillowed my head on my arms and gradually dozed off. I was woken up by the cold. I had to jump up and down to get warm, then I put on my shoes and curled up like a cat. (I learned later that on the night of the 14th of May the temperature had fallen to zero and stayed there for a whole week; the cells were not heated; I caught a chill, began to cough, my back ached and after a few nights I began to have a temperature.) Next morning I woke up at about six. Someone was washing the floor and the benches, flicking me with a wet rag. But I wanted to sleep for as long as possible, to shorten the prison day. As a result I missed my morning tea, and when I asked the guard – a new one, not the one who had been there the night before – when I would get something to eat, he told me I would have to wait till dinner. As a matter of fact, I wasn't very hungry. I asked to go to the lavatory. It was large, and had a washstand, a dirty towel and an empty soapbox. When, about three days later, the medical officer made his round a cake of soap was put out and a clean towel hung up, but after he had gone they were taken away again – evidently until the next inspection. Not only was there no toilet paper, there were not even scraps of newspaper. I poked my head out into the corridor and told the guard; he grumbled that he couldn't be expected to keep paper especially for 'parasites', but he gave me a piece of newspaper anyway. Subsequently other guards also gave me pieces of paper, but always grumbling about it – perhaps more out of a sense of duty than out of real annoyance at my excessive demands. In general, I was on good terms with the jailers at the P D C; they were mostly elderly men who for some reason called me 'an educated parasite' and, noting that I was evidently in jail for the first time and was well-behaved, tried to make me a little more comfortable: they brought me newspapers to read, gave me more sugar than I was entitled to, and when I told them how my neighbours had informed against me, expressed their disgust.

Back in the cell, I read the inscriptions scratched on the walls, the benches and the windowsill. Mostly, they were addressed to the prisoner's mother, wife or children, and usually they ended with the words: 'Goodbye my dear ones' and an indication of how many years they would not see each other. There were also exclamations such as 'Article 206 again!' A girl had written some loving words to a certain Ahmed adding: 'When you are back from Cairo I'll no longer be in Moscow and we shall never meet again.' This was written in pencil on the wall near the door next to the promise of some old lag nicknamed 'Lord' to be back soon in his old haunts.

Shortly before twelve the door suddenly flew open, a young policeman came in and, like a butler announcing an important guest, proclaimed triumphantly 'The Prosecutor!' The Prosecutor entered quickly, looking at the floor; he was quite unlike the judge I had seen yesterday. With his dishevelled ash-coloured hair and shabby clothes, he looked more like an elderly intellectual who had gone to seed.

'What are you accused of?' he asked me.

'Of being a "parasite".'

'The court will go into that,' said the Prosecutor, still looking at the floor. 'Any complaints?'

'No,' I said, and he walked out as swiftly as he had come in. I heard my name spoken several times, then the outer door banged as the Prosecutor went off.

Dinner came about an hour and a half later. Brought from the nearest cafeteria; it consisted of a bowl of soup and a rissole with boiled potatoes. The rissole was small but there were plenty of potatoes and black bread. The soup varied from day to day but always had the taste common to all soups in cheap cafeterias. The potatoes were sometimes replaced by *kasha* (a buckwheat mash), but there was always the rissole. Supper consisted of tea and two lumps of sugar. The tea was brewed in the pail outside and could be asked for any number of times between seven and ten. Tea was also served for breakfast, with bread but without sugar. As I have already said, I was given more sugar than my ration and one day I actually got six lumps. The prisoners were fed at the rate of thirty-nine kopecks a day, which is the highest prison rate I was ever to come across. I did not feel hungry, yet one day when, contrary to rules, the guard invited me to the next cell where two prisoners who looked like 'trusties' offered me sugar, sausage and white bread, I threw myself greedily on the bread and ate nearly half a loaf. The 'trusties' shook their heads and said that if it were up to them they would give me plenty to eat but would make me do a good day's work in return. Evidently the soft-hearted guard had described me to them as an 'educated parasite' who did no work and as a result was unused to eating his fill. It is true that on the first day I could hardly eat at all – I drank a little soup and with difficulty chewed the rissole but left all the potatoes, which astonished the guard. The following day, however, I waited impatiently for my dinner.

Soon after dinner the door opened again. It was my old friend Kiselev and the police officer on duty who told me to come out. Two other men were waiting in the guardroom for us, one in civilian clothes, the other a fat man in police uniform. Kiselev took a bunch of keys from the officer on duty and I realized that they were going to make a search of my flat. As we got into the van, I asked Kiselev whether the civilian was from the K G B. 'No, he's an old colleague of ours,' Kiselev answered grumpily. In fact, as I heard later, he was Police Captain Bushmakin, a senior officer from the C I D.

When we arrived in front of my house in Suvorov Boulevard. Kiselev asked me if I would invite my neighbours to come in as witnesses. I refused outright. Kiselev then said he would ask the caretaker, and he soon came back with two women, both of whom were in charge, in some capacity, of looking after the building. They greeted me politely, saying, 'How do you do, Comrade Almarik' (this was how they pronounced it). One immediately recalled that several years earlier I had often been late with the rent; the other noticing that a skirting board had been removed from one of the walls, cried: 'Look at that, it wasn't like that before!'

'Have you been here before?' asked Bushmakin.

'Of course, we've often been here,' replied both.

Although I had no clear recollection of them, it was probably true that they had come to remind me about the rent, or some such thing.

'We were always very nice about asking you for the rent,' they repeated several times, evidently taking considerable pride in their good manners. As to the skirting, Bushmakin at once imagined there might be a hiding place there, and promised to take up the floor.

Bushmakin next took out of his wallet a warrant for a house search signed by the Prosecutor. If I remember rightly, it said that Captain Kozlov found it necessary for Captain Bushmakin to make a search of Citizen Amalrik's apartment in order to 'find and confiscate objects acquired by means other than with money earned legitimately'. As Bushmakin and Kiselev explained, they had been ordered to find and confiscate 'abstract pictures'. The word 'abstract' – or as they pronounced it, 'obstract' – pleased them by its obscure and portentous ring and, like all words that are spoken without being understood, acquired a sinister meaning on their lips. But Bushmakin started by asking me if I had any foreign currency and when I replied no, said: 'If you have some, give it up at once or it will be the worse for you.' Then he started on the house search.

They began with the desk. Here Bushmakin was much impressed by what he called my 'book learning'. He found my old notebooks with notes of lectures on the theory of algorisms which I had attended at one time, Latin and Greek exercises, synopses of books on history, linguistics, philosophy, ethnography, and some translations from German. Sorting out this heap of notebooks and scraps of paper which told him more about my pious intentions than about my actual achievements, Bushmakin kept asking me sadly and with bewilderment how I managed to get myself into such a fix. 'You might have been teaching our children,' he kept repeating. In general his attitude towards me changed to some extent and I could see that he felt a little embarrassed about going through my things which, from the point of view of a police officer, were in no way criminal. When he came to my plays, which also lay in the desk, he asked me why I had not 'made more fuss' about being an author – since writing plays was work of a sort so how could I be a 'parasite', particularly since it took a writer time to gain recognition? Either then or when he was drawing up his report (I can't remember because he kept coming back to this again and again), he told me how in the forties when he was working at Petrovka Street* he had picked up some old woman who lived in a garret and brought her in, together with a whole heap of papers covered with writing. The head of the CID had scolded him for bringing this 'load of trash', which in any case there was no time to sort, and ordered the stuff to be sent to the Union of Writers allegedly for an expert opinion of its worth. They were astonished when after sorting it all out, the Union of Writers actually published the old woman's book, so that instead of going to jail, she was made a member of the Union! I must admit that I had little hope of anything of the sort happening to me and, as we shall see, I had more reason to keep silent about my plays than to make a fuss about them. I'm not sure whether Bushmakin had orders to confiscate them, but in any case he took several copies of four of them together with a collection of my poems, *The Seasons of the Year*. He found another lot of verse which I told him I had written during my schooldays. This was true and he showed no further interest in it. Neither did he touch my large historical work, *The Normans and the Kiev Principality*, but he took the notebook that contained Zverev's biography, and a typed copy of it. For some odd reason he failed to notice the top drawer of the desk and left

* Headquarters of the Moscow police.

it untouched – not that there was anything criminal inside
it, only notes for an article on Russian painting which I
meant to write, and several letters. In general, the search was
very perfunctory for the simple reason that what the police
wanted to find was there for them to see, i.e. the pictures on
the walls; besides, Bushmakin was a regular policeman, used
to searching the houses of real criminals, and such an
abundance of manuscripts and books discouraged him. He
only looked at the spines of my books, and never bothered at
all about the ones in my father's cubicle; I had in fact no
books from abroad except those on art. While they were
searching the desk, I happened to catch sight of the reference
given by my last employer, Smirnov, the editor-in-chief
of *Water Transport*; it stated the exact opposite of what he
had said to the police, whom he had assured of my bad
character. Six months earlier he had signed this other
reference testifying to the excellence of my character. I
took it with me and handed it together with other things to
the third police officer who had come with us, hoping later
to produce it as part of the evidence in my case.

While they were searching the desk Kiselev took no part
in the proceedings, but when they came to the pictures he
took more interest; not to waste time, he offered to search
my father's cubicle by himself, but Bushmakin stopped him :
'No, everything must be done in front of the accused.' The
third policeman did not touch anything except to look at
my monograph on Matisse, in which he saw a nude by the
painter and said : 'Now there's something ! I'd like a woman
like that.' He asked me as a 'scholar' why it was that only
fat women excited him, whereas he could do nothing at all
with thin ones, and whether there was a scientific explanation for this. I did not attempt to enlighten him.

Bushmakin began to take down the pictures from the walls
in both my part of the room and my father's. I said that
some of them belonged to my father, but no one paid any
attention. It now turned out that the policemen had instructions not to confiscate 'abstract paintings', as was said in the
warrant, but specifically works by Zverev. Several genuinely
abstract paintings were left untouched, but all those by
Zverev were taken, including some highly realistic portraits.

When they came to folders containing drawings and water colours, which lay in the cupboard, they again confiscated only those by Zverev, mainly his illustrations to my plays, though by mistake they took some drawings by other artists as well. Kiselev wanted to take some nudes which he described as pornographic, but Bushmakin said this was unnecessary. They also took three icons; they were delighted to find them and recalled the many newspaper articles about *stilyagi** giving foreigners icons in exchange for clothes. Among them was a seventeenth-century icon of the Northern School, a Virgin and Child of the Moscow School and a St Theodore Stratilatus of the Northern School, both also of the seventeenth century.

While Bushmakin, with the witnesses, was examining the drawings in my father's room, Kiselev looked through a folder containing my favourite water colours by Zverev and seemed about to take them away.

'Why are you trying so hard?' I asked him reproachfully, 'Do you want to take more than anybody else?'

'No, no,' Kiselev said, embarrassed, 'I'm not interested in them.' And he put the folder down, saying in a loud voice: 'Anyway, there are no abstracts here, only portraits.' Taking advantage of the disorder in the room, I managed to push another folder full of drawings into the pile of those that had already been examined and returned to me. At the beginning of the search I had been more or less indifferent to the outcome. But when they started taking Zverev's pictures, I became very upset. Even those drawings which only the day before I had criticized to Zverev I now found beautiful and irreplaceable. The policeman who liked fat women was astonished and asked me: 'Why do you worry so much about this stuff? You must be greedy.' Both Bushmakin and Kiselev were somewhat embarrassed at having to go through things which from their point of view were harmless. But duty was duty.

Then they prodded the mattresses and expressed astonishment at how hard my bed was; they searched the sideboard and trunk in the box-room, and finally Bushmakin sat down and wrote a report on the search in which he said that he

* *Stilyagi*: Soviet youths who dress in Western styles.

had demanded 'the surrender of all objects obtained illegally'. Why they considered that I had obtained Zverev's
pictures 'illegally' was not clear to me. Some of his paintings I had bought, some he had given me, while others still
belonged to him and were only stored in my flat. In all,
eight canvases were confiscated, including the one by Rabin
mentioned by the *druzhinniki*, eighteen sheets in tempera,
nine water colours, 133 drawings, three icons, the notebook
containing Zverev's biography, two cuttings from French
papers with reviews of the exhibition, and several copies of
my plays and verses amounting to 553 typewritten pages.
All these things I carefully packed myself for I could see
how carelessly Kiselev and Bushmakin treated the pictures.
They and the witnesses laughed at me for wasting my time,
since no one at the police or in court was going to treat them
with that much care. As we were leaving, Bushmakin
remembered at the last moment to ask me whether I had
any weapons.

Bushmakin loaded everything onto the police wagon and
drove away. Kiselev and I got into a Volga with a young
policeman at the wheel. He was evidently very new to his
job and had great difficulty getting to the 60th District
Station, though it was not far from my house. We spent a
long time cruising around the back streets, which was all to
the good, for I was in no hurry to return to my cell.

Sunday was very lonely and depressing. I walked up and
down the cell almost all day, waiting for Monday when the
lawyer might come to see me, and perhaps even the trial
would take place. I tried to console myself with the thought
that there was nothing so terrible about being exiled; it
simply meant a trip to some wild places in Siberia which
I would never otherwise have a chance to see; I remembered
the books I had read in childhood and imagined myself
going out hunting with some tough old-timer in the virgin
forest. Anticipating, I may say that I never once went hunting, though I did indeed have an encounter in the virgin
forest with a hunter and it nearly cost me my life. But more
of that later.

I was not let out for a walk, and in spite of my dislike for
such things, I did a few physical exercises and tried to

breathe as deeply as possible. I went on doing this regularly throughout my stay in prison. Apart from anything else, it was something to while away the time. Walking up and down the cell I also thought a lot about my strategy at the forthcoming trial, though I realized this was rather naïve since the verdict had already been decided in advance.

On Monday morning another prisoner was brought into my cell. He was about my age, with wavy hair and a sailor's buckle on his belt. He introduced himself as 'a young parasite'. His story was simple. He lived alone and was visited every day by friends, young men and girls, who drank and often stayed overnight; in other words, anybody could 'doss down' there. He was a trained photographer but had long since stopped working as such and only got jobs whenever he was in imminent danger of expulsion from the city. Lately he had been employed as a scene shifter in a theatre. According to his own account, his downfall had been caused by pornography. He used to photograph pornographic illustrations from French magazines and give them to his district policeman, a connoisseur of such pictures, so that the policeman would leave him alone. When he got a job in the theatre and the policeman came for his usual batch of pictures, the photographer, feeling his new-found independence, politely refused and hinted that now he had regular work he did not need to buy himself protection. The policeman said nothing, but when, shortly afterwards, the photographer was thrown out of the theatre for drunkenness he had him arrested as a 'parasite'. The trial was to take place in two days. Having told me all this, he asked me what I was in for myself. I mumbled something to the effect that I had been arrested for collecting pictures by young artists. Delighted, the photographer said that his neighbour was also a collector and he too had been arrested by the K G B three months previously. The neighbour turned out to be the well-known musician and collector Korolkov. After his arrest, there was a series of attacks on him in *Evening Moscow*, but they suddenly came to an end. There were rumours that Korolkov had hanged himself in his prison cell.

We spent half the day in such pleasant conversation. The photographer was pleased with the cell. He said that when he had served two weeks in Maloyaroslavets, near Moscow, he had been in just such a cell, but with about twenty other people sleeping on the benches. They lay side by side and could turn over only all at once at a sign from the senior prisoner. They were fed for only twenty-three kopecks a day each and were not allowed out into the lavatory: there was a slop bucket standing in the cell. This Moscow prison thus had great advantages. However, being in prison for the first time, I did not know how to appreciate any of them.

After dinner I was transferred to a neighbouring cell which had just been vacated. It was exactly the same as the first one, but like every new place it struck me as much gloomier. The previous occupant had been a woman with an unusually shrill voice. As soon as she was put into the cell she tried to get out, shouting hysterically that she was not guilty, that she had been slandered, that she would complain and 'go all the way up to Khrushchev'. The guard had reasoned with her saying: 'What can Khrushchev do? He was fired ages ago.' In the end she quietened down and even helped to take dinner to the other prisoners, peering curiously through the spy-holes in the doors. In general women were more trouble to the guards than the men. A prostitute in the end cell seized an elderly guard as soon as he opened the door, pulled him down on top of herself, and whispered: 'Come on, before it's too late.' Scared out of his wits he had a hard time breaking free; afterwards he came to my cell to tell me this extraordinary story.

Neither on Monday nor on Tuesday did the lawyer come to see me, and nothing more was heard of my trial – though Tuesday was the end of the five-day term established by law – and I started to get worried. I felt very depressed, especially as there was nothing to read and nothing to do. On Tuesday night, around eleven o'clock, a young man was brought into the cell. He had an insolent look and wore an 'Italian' cape of the sort just then coming into fashion. From the start, he treated me not so much with hostility as with scorn. He especially disliked my torn sweater, which did indeed clash with his smart get-up. When he heard that I was a 'parasite', he treated me with even greater contempt, letting it be clearly understood that he was a cut above me. It was at once evident that he was a professional criminal and such people, especially the young ones, are pathologically eager to show off.

All the same, we got into conversation. He asked me where I lived and what school I had been to, and it turned out that we had been to the same one. We talked about our teachers and found that we must have been there at about the same time. Then he had a good look at me and remembered my name. I too remembered him after a while and called him by his surname, Ivanov. We had started in the same class in the primary school and were later together in another school until he was expelled from (I think) the sixth form. We were both very surprised at this strange meeting and spent a lot of time reminiscing about our school years. Ivanov told me again with all the swagger of a real criminal how he had become a thief, at first working as a pickpocket but later specializing in shops and savings banks. Remembering the Judge's story, I asked him whether he knew Pushkin. He had heard about him but referred to him contemptuously: 'That's a man who'll get caught over a handkerchief.' He himself had also now got caught over a trifle: he had been involved in a fight on a train and did not expect more than fifteen days in prison at most. His papers were in order and he even had an engineer's diploma which he had bought for a considerable sum in Georgia. The money from his last job was being kept for him by a prostitute in Moscow, so everything was fine.

He questioned me with interest about paintings and artists, though without much idea of what it was all about. What interested him were the prices that painters got for their canvases. When I told him that my house had been searched, he asked whether there was anything among the confiscated things that could seriously harm me. I said there had been no such things and that I had managed to leave the little money I had and a notebook with addresses and telephone numbers in the safekeeping of a friend. He said that was never very safe as friends too can betray you. It would be better to destroy the notebook altogether. He offered to visit my friend when he got out and recover the notebook for me. He came back to this again and again, even after we had gone to bed, so that I began to suspect he might have been put into my cell on purpose. Careful not to betray my suspicions, I gave him a completely false address, and tried to draw him out about himself.

He boasted continually, in particular about the sums of up to twenty thousand roubles that had passed through his hands. When he first came into the cell, he had at once said that I had surely never seen anything bigger than a hundred rouble note, and now he repeated again and again that 'a hundred roubles is not money'. As a former school friend, he promised to send me money to my place of exile. But now he talked only in terms of a hundred roubles, which was evidently money after all.

'All you have to do,' he said, 'is write and I'll send it at once.' He gave me his address. He told me a lot about being in prison in the Taganka* and in various camps, where they could move around only under armed guard, and how he had pretended to have a weak heart. He made out that he was an innocent victim and had suffered all his life through the ill will of others, yet he himself told me about his thefts and must have known the risks. I realized later that to regard oneself as the victim of an unjust order is characteristic of the criminal underworld. He told me about various other thieves, especially about one great legendary figure, an old man with the strange nickname of 'Volodka Lenin' who had received sentences amounting to ninety years in all. My friend himself was a typical example of the young, semi-educated thieves such as I was to meet later, but the criminal underworld is essentially esoteric and an outsider like myself can easily make false judgments. We spent the night together protecting ourselves against the cold by huddling under the same coat. Early in the morning he was taken out and I never saw him again.

* A Moscow prison.

CHAPTER 6

The Investigation Begins;
The 'Black Maria'

ON Wednesday morning I impatiently awaited the lawyer or the summons to the court, but no one came. It was very cold. I had spent six days in jail and had caught a bad cold. I was shaking with fever nearly all the time. After dinner I lay down on the bench, keeping my shoes on. It was impossible to take them off without my feet freezing. Gradually I dozed off. I was woken up by the sound of the door opening.

A young man with an official air came in. He wore spectacles and a university badge in the lapel of his police lieutenant's uniform. With him came the duty officer and the guard. After inquiring politely whether I was Andrei Amalrik the young man asked me to follow him. We climbed to the second floor, walked along the corridor, and entered a room where there were two or three other people who paid us not the slightest attention. The Lieutenant asked me to sit down. I looked round. The room was familiar to me. I had been here once before.

In 1961 I had wanted to send my historical essay *The Normans and the Kiev Principality* to the Danish Professor of Slavic languages, Stender Petersen, with whom I had been corresponding. To send it by post seemed a senseless undertaking, so I decided to ask the Danish Embassy in Moscow to do this favour for me. I took a letter to the Embassy – again to avoid getting involved with the post – asking them whether they could forward my essay. After some argument with the policeman on duty at the Embassy gate, I managed to throw the letter into the letter-box. I was immediately arrested and taken to this room in the 60th District Police Station, where a fat major in charge of security in the diplomatic corps tried for a long time to find out from me what was in the letter. I insisted I had simply thanked the Embassy for previously giving me Professor Stender Petersen's address, and I was allowed to go. At first the Embassy agreed to send on my manuscript, and an Embassy official even came to my flat to pick it up together with a letter addressed to Stender Petersen. Later however, perhaps suspecting a provocation on my part, or simply being unwilling to get involved in the sending of any sort of manuscript, or because they had realized from my accompanying letter to the professor that it was because of this manuscript that I had been expelled from the university, the Embassy, without informing me, sent my manuscript to the Soviet Ministry of Foreign Affairs, which immediately passed it on to the KGB. Therefore, instead of discussing it with the Danish professor I had to go and explain it to the KGB. A week later the Embassy also handed over to the Ministry of Foreign Affairs a letter to the professor that I had not mentioned in my first conversation with the KGB. This did not make things any easier for me. Until this day I don't know why the Embassy, after undertaking to send on my manuscript, acted so strangely and betrayed me to the KGB instead of simply returning the manuscript to me if, for some reason, they had changed their mind. The KGB sent the manuscript out for expert comment, and, having convinced themselves that there was nothing anti-Soviet in it, that it was merely a study of Slav-Scandinavian relations in the ninth century, they returned it to me several months later with the advice that I should make no further efforts to send it abroad. All this I remembered as I now sat looking across the desk at the young official.

Seeing that I was shivering he asked me politely whether I felt all right and added that he was very much opposed to my imprisonment. There followed the usual questions – when I was born, and where I had worked – but seeing the file with my confiscated plays lying on the desk I realized that my case had taken a new turn.

Taking them out of the file, the interrogator asked me whether the plays were mine. I said they were.

'Just to avoid future misunderstandings,' said the interrogator, 'would you write on the top of the first page of each play that it is yours.'

To his dictation I wrote: 'This play belongs to me. It was confiscated during a house search on the 15th of May 1965.' Then the interrogator asked me to what audiences I had read my plays – students, writers, or any others – and to whom I had lent them to read. At first I was evasive as I couldn't understand what he was getting at, then I answered firmly that I had not read my plays to any audiences and had not lent them to anyone except the artist Zverev, who had illustrated several of them. The interrogator said he would come back to the plays, but that first he wanted to know to whom I had shown and sold Zverev's illustrations. I replied that I had neither sold nor shown them to anyone.

'But we know,' he objected, 'that several people have drawings by Zverev – not only in Moscow but also abroad.'

'That's possible,' I said, 'but it has nothing whatever to do with me.'

The interrogator didn't argue, but went on to say that in his opinion Zverev's illustrations of my plays were rather erotic. I replied that, if so, this must be explained by the nature of Zverev's art rather than of my plays. I had in mind Zverev's lack of psychological balance, of which I realized the interrogator, strange as it was, knew nothing. He asked once again to whom I had given or shown Zverev's drawings, and when I insisted that I had not given them to anyone he commented: 'You complicate my task. Now I'll have to call up all your friends and question them.'

As during my conversation with Vasilyev, I expected to be questioned about the foreigners who had been to see me; he did ask about them but only briefly, in passing, and seemed quite satisfied when I mentioned Markevich and the two Americans whom the police had found in my flat in February. He asked whether I had lent my plays to Korengold. I said I hadn't. Then, after a brief pause, he solemnly announced that I was being charged under Article 228 of the Criminal Code of the RSFSR, with the production, harbouring and dissemination of pornographic works. This was the second time pornography had come up. I was very much surprised and said that I could not regard either my plays or Zverev's drawings as pornographic. The interrogator shrugged his shoulders as though to say that what I thought or didn't think was of no importance. Then he asked me to sign his record of the interrogation. I signed without reading it, complaining that I couldn't see without my glasses and asking that my glasses should be given back to me before my next interrogation.

'I must disappoint you,' said the interrogator, 'but this will not be necessary, as you are being transferred from here to prison. I'm against this myself,' he added hastily, 'but that is the decision of the court.'

He informed me of this in a tone of sympathy and, in general, throughout the interrogation he had tried to convey that he was sorry for me and was opposed not only to my imprisonment but to my being charged with a criminal offence.

Downstairs, before taking me to a cell, the officer on duty, a police captain, let me read the charge against me and took my fingerprints. The charge stated that the People's Court of the Frunze district of the City of Moscow, consisting of Judge Yakovlev and two assessors whose names I don't remember, had examined the objects confiscated from Citizen Amalrik and found that 'his plays, besides being clearly anti-Soviet, are also of a pornographic nature, while the illustrations to them by Zverev are likewise obviously pornographic; the court has therefore decided to charge them both under Article 228 of the Criminal Code of the RSFSR, and to order both of them to be detained in custody'. I had thus become the object of a criminal charge and was threatened no longer merely with deportation but with several years in a forced-labour camp.

Late that evening I was taken to the guardroom and my things, including my spectacles and money, were returned to me. They kept only my shoelaces. Soon the Black Maria arrived. At the back of it was a door with a small barred window; inside was a platform with seats to the right and left for the guards, a narrow space between two cells, each meant for one prisoner, and at the end of it a barred door into a little compartment large enough to hold about six prisoners. I now learned, for the first time, that prisoners are obliged to keep their hands behind their back.

At first there were only two or three of us in the car, but we travelled from one police station to another and gradually picked up about ten people. It was known that we were being taken to the Butyrki prison. The people in the car were of every age, ranging from a boy of nineteen to an old man of sixty and I thought I caught a glimpse of an old woman being pushed into one of the cells; she turned out to be just over thirty but had been aged by drink. It seemed that only I was going to prison for the first time, all the others having been there several times already. This was my first encounter with people who have spent most of their lives in prison, and who look back on their few days or months of freedom as though it were a dream – beautiful but unreal. There were only a few of these, however. Most of them had spent longer periods outside prison. Nearly all were charged under Article 206, that is, with hooliganism. This is the article under which the majority of prisoners in Russia are charged, and nearly half of them go to jail because of wife-beating (as is well known, this is an old tradition in Russia). In our group, for instance, there was a shoe-maker, a man of about thirty-five who seemed very good-natured and was going to prison for the fourth time, as he put it, 'because of a woman'. It would have been truer to say that it was because of vodka. Again and again he had vowed not to drink but he still went on getting drunk and beating his wife. It was always the same pattern: she complained to the police, he went to prison and, after his sentence was over, came back to her again. This time he was in serious trouble: he had threatened his wife with a knife, and in such cases, the courts are very severe. Although he cursed her in the worst language, you could see that he loved her all the same and would return to her if ever he managed to get back to Moscow. Many of the prisoners said they never expected to see Moscow again. This did not, of course, mean that they expected to be imprisoned for life. What they feared was to be refused police registration to live in Moscow after they had served their time. 'Registration' (*propiska*) is a terrible word which I was often to hear later, so I will explain what it is for those who do not know.

Under Soviet law everyone who wishes to live anywhere, temporarily or permanently must apply within three days to the local police station, where his identity papers are marked with a permanent or temporary registration at such and such an address. Before this he must be struck off the register at his previous place of residence. In practice this bureaucratic measure means tragedy for hundreds of thousands of people. Permission to register depends wholly on the police, or rather on the numerous instructions by which they are supposed to be guided. One reason for refusal may be that the town is already overcrowded. This is the usual one in large cities. Another reason may be that there are secret installations in the district or that it is near a frontier. Or the public health authorities may decide that there is not enough room in the house where the applicant wants to live. Registration may be refused if a man has been away from his place of residence for more than six months. Apart from all this there are thousands of other pretexts invented by bureaucrats. As for a man who has been in prison, he is refused permission to register in the place where he lived before simply because he has been in prison. After endless efforts it is sometimes possible to return to your old home, especially if your family is still there, though the registration may at first be temporary. But in the case of people who have served several sentences it is almost out of the question. This is a much more dreadful punishment even than being sent to a camp, where after all you are imprisoned only for a limited period of time. Husbands are separated from their wives, sons from mothers, people who are used to living in the South have to look for work in the North, while those from the North have to move South. And what happens to a man who, after failing to get registered, decides to return home anyway and live with his relatives? He will be warned two or three times, then he will be tried again under Article 138 and sent to a camp; and when he comes out his chances of registration will be even slighter. There are, however, people who live permanently without registration and who for this alone are sent to prison again and again; they are the so-called 'attic dwellers' – people who live illegally in garrets.

Once a prison sentence is marked in one's papers, it is difficult not only to get registered but to find work. One young man who was being taken away by the police shouted to his mother: 'My papers are in the cupboard. Bring them to the police station tomorrow.' Everybody said what a fool he was, but later he explained that it was just a trick: 'Mother knew she must not bring my papers to the police station; I had carefully hidden them away.'

Sometimes it is possible to use your old papers to register somewhere in another town.

By enforcing such measures against people who have already served their sentences, the authorities only encourage them to commit further offences.

The old man in the Black Maria proved to be an acquaintance of a silent man sitting next to me. They had both been in the same camp near Moscow at the end of the fifties. The old man had managed to live in Moscow without being registered for five years.

All the rest looked at him as though he were the eighth wonder of the world. He said he might have lasted even longer, but one night he got drunk, lost the key of his girlfriend's flat where he was staying, fell asleep on the landing outside her door and was noticed by the caretaker. His acquaintance – who had been picked up by the Black Maria together with me at the 60th District Station – aroused my immediate sympathy. He was very sad and silent. This was his second arrest for hooliganism. He said he had been playing cards in the courtyard of his house with three other men who had started to cheat. He picked up his money and rose to go. They snatched it back from him. He took out a penknife and stabbed one of them in the back with it. He told the story in such a melancholy way that I was surprised he was capable of losing his temper.

'When you've been in prison for a time and your nerves have suffered like mine, then you'll understand,' he told me. 'This time at least I know what I'm going to be tried for. The first time it was for nothing at all.'

I remember one other interesting conversation in the Black Maria – about which camps are better, those near Moscow or those far away. Some people thought it was better to be near Moscow because relatives could visit you. Others objected that near Moscow you were right under the eye of the authorities and the discipline was stricter. With such talk we whiled the time away. Through the barred windows in the door I could see the familiar Moscow streets and reflected that it would be a long time before I saw them again. At last a fortress wall appeared. The car drove through a gate and I realized that we had entered the Butyrki prison.

CHAPTER 7

Butyrki

AT the end of the eighteenth century a prison fortress was built in Moscow near the Butyrki Gate by the famous architect Matvei Kazakov. In the days of Alexander I it was regarded as a model prison, in contrast to the provincial jails. In 1879 it was rebuilt and enlarged to become the largest Moscow transit and investigation prison. Many famous revolutionaries were held there and thousands of unknown criminals as well. It was here that shortly before the Revolution Felix Dzerzhinsky, who was to become the first head of the Soviet secret police, was imprisoned. The prison has never been rebuilt since 1879, though at the end of the fifties some of the fortress walls were demolished and blocks of flats built in their place to screen the prison from the street.

Today the 'Third Investigation Centre' of the Ministry of Public Order (formerly the MVD) is housed there. I believe that the investigation centre actually takes up only part of the prison, while the other part is occupied by prisoners who have already been sentenced. Some of them work in the prison workshops and others are used to help in the work of running the prison itself. As everybody knows, prison is regarded as a stricter form of punishment than the forced-labour camps. The investigation centre is reserved for prisoners whose cases have not yet been decided but whom the court or the interrogators find it necessary to keep under guard. They are not made to work, and the time spent by them under investigation counts as part of the final sentence. If, however, a prisoner is found innocent, he gets no compensation, whatever length of time he may have spent in prison. The prisons are run by the Chief Administration of Prisons and Camps, and the guards employed are not policemen but belong to the security forces.

About fifteen minutes after our arrival we were told to get out of the car and were marched in single file into a reception room with a vaulted ceiling. A notice hung over the door which struck me at the time as comic: 'To freedom with a clear conscience!' Strange as it may seem, the first thing we had to do was to 'register' our new 'address' – just as though we were applying for a permit to reside in the usual way! Then each of us was given a postcard and ordered to write down the address of his nearest relatives. When a prisoner is transferred after sentence from prison to camp, this postcard is sent to his family with the address of the camp written on it. We were then ordered to give up our papers, money, watches and keys. Spectacles and other essential items were not taken away from us. In the next room we went through a medical inspection. This meant that we each had to go up to the nurse – a squat Tartar woman of indeterminate age – and let down our trousers to the knees. My youthful appearance roused certain suspicions in her, and she peered into my anus. The inspection was completed more or less without incident, except that one of us, a powerful curly-haired man with negroid lips who specialized in robbing people in trains, was found to have syphilis. This provoked amusement rather than sympathy among the others. The nurse at first wanted to isolate him, but the warder in charge of us argued with her, saying it would be all right for the time being if he stayed with the rest of us. I don't know what they eventually decided. The man, incidentally, had inserted some small flat splints into his penis – something I had seen before only in books on anthropology.

After the medical inspection we were taken in twos and threes to have our heads shaved and afterwards to be photographed. It all went slowly, and in the intervals between the various procedures we were locked up in small cells where two could sit and another two could stand with difficulty. To while away the time prisoners again reminisced about their life outside. One told us, for instance, that while he was being questioned his interrogator had turned away for a moment, and he had grabbed his papers and jumped through the window onto a neighbouring roof; but he hadn't managed to get very far.

The prison photographer was an elderly woman in blue overalls, and it was she who also took our fingerprints. My prints were very difficult to take and several days later I was called back to have them taken again.

Next we were brought into a large room divided into two by a long, empty table. Two soldiers stood on one side of it. They too wore blue overalls on top of their uniforms. We were lined up along the other side and ordered to undress. Our things were spread out on the table and everything from jackets to socks was carefully searched while shoes were examined with the help of X-rays. The prisoner is searched not only when he first arrives, but at intervals later on, and also when he leaves. After our things had been inspected they were returned to us; in investigation centres the prisoners keep their own clothes. However, a careful list was drawn up of each prisoner's possessions. It was explained to me that this was so we should not gamble them away at cards.

After this we were drawn up in a row – about twenty or so from the various Black Marias – and marched off across a courtyard to the baths. It was now daybreak. Ever since I had been put into the Black Maria, I had felt very curious about what would come next. When the others asked what I thought of prison, as a newcomer to it, I answered frankly that I found it 'very interesting'. It was as though there were two people inside me: one who had got himself into this nasty fix and another who was just looking on, as though in the theatre, and wondering what would happen next.

Bathing was a great pleasure. We handed over our clothes to be fumigated, evidently to destroy any vermin in them, and each of us got a little piece of household soap. We washed in a big room under a shower. The water was first too cold, then too hot, but I was delighted all the same to be able to wash. Prisoners usually get baths every ten days. When we came out of the bath we got our clothes back and in addition a pair of trousers, a vest, a mattress, a mattress cover, a pillow, a blanket, a towel and an aluminium mug and spoon. Then we were lined up again and taken to our cells. In the old days prisoners were put into cells at random, but a few years ago a rule was introduced under which persons charged with the same or similar offences are to be put into the same cell. Stopping in front of a cell door, the elderly guard who accompanied us called out our names from a list, and asked each of us in turn to confirm his name, date of birth and the article under which he had been charged. When my turn came, I gave my name and date of birth, but to my embarrassment I had forgotten the number of the article under which I had been charged and simply answered that I was accused of pornography. Taken aback, the guard said nothing more and with a sad smile opened the door of the cell for me. It was just six o'clock, time for reveille. The cell was large and half dark and seemed to me to contain a lot of people – at least twenty. No one had got up yet, but everyone was awake. Some were talking, others were throwing pillows at each other. I stopped at the door and felt like a schoolboy coming to class for the first time and seeing that his new comrades are a pretty rowdy bunch. But I was greeted in a fairly friendly manner. I went forward, put my things down and asked who was the 'elder'. I knew from books that there is always an elder in each cell and thought that he would show me my place. A man with Eastern features and blazing eyes – a Persian, as I learned later – was pointed out to me. He raised himself in bed and with a thick accent asked me: 'Well, where did they fuck you at the police station, in a nice bed or on straw?' But the Persian was immediately unmasked as an impostor. I was told there was no elder in the cell and that I could take any free place. Meanwhile the more curious of my new cellmates crowded round me and asked me what I was in for. I noticed that they did not look much like professional criminals.

At that moment the door of the cell opened and a guard shouted: 'Orderlies! Come and get your milk!' One of the prisoners said to me: 'I bet you didn't get milk in the P D C, did you?' But to my disappointment the two orderlies brought in a bucket of hot water. It turned out that 'milk' was just a prison euphemism; in the same way, a rag for cleaning the floor was always referred to as a 'vacuum cleaner'. From this time onwards I had a strong craving for milk which never left me during the whole of my stay in jail.

I took a vacant bed as far as possible from the lavatory (which was by the door) and started spreading out the bed-clothes. I was not very good at it, but an elderly Georgian came up to me and quickly showed me how it was done. Later on he questioned me a good deal about the difference between collective and personal property. I couldn't tell him very much but I was curious to know which form of property had been the cause of his trouble. I learned that he was in prison for trading in narcotics. The Persian, too, was there for the same reason. Little by little I got to know the other prisoners, most of whom were in for economic offences: managers, accountants and engineers. Among them was the Chief Engineer of the Moscow Art Theatre. He had been arrested for a swindle connected with the construction of the new Art Theatre building. Although several people had already been arrested for this, the build-ing itself had not yet been begun. Other people in the cell were officials who were here for embezzlement and other kinds of abuses. They managed to keep some remnants of their former dignity, even in prison. Although I made it a rule not to ask anyone what he was in for, I was interested to know what sort of sums were involved in these embezzle-ments. One of them, it seemed, a former director of a wall-paper store had embezzled four hundred roubles for which he could expect six years in camp. Judges operate with a table of equivalents which relates the length of the sentence to the amount that has been stolen. I have no wish to justify embezzlement, but I was surprised at such a long term for such an insignificant sum. When I later mentioned this to an interrogator, he said 'Four hundred roubles is what he was *caught* with, but he must have stolen much more.' As I could see from various examples, to condemn a man not for what he has done but for what he is suspected of having done is unfortunately one of the characteristic features of our legal system.

Another large group was made up of drivers. Some were

in for having caused accidents, and others for pilfering and embezzlement. I remember one of them very well, a tall bald man with a pig-like face who had driven vegetable trucks. Together with a group of other drivers and shop-keepers, he was accused of having stolen some sacks of potatoes and a few kilograms of oranges. If the number of oranges were shared out between the accused they would hardly have made an orange a piece. The case was being handled by the Prosecutor's office of a town near Moscow. At the first hearing the Court declared that there was insufficient evidence. The same thing happened at a second hearing. Now new charges had been brought against this man. Since the start of the enquiry he had been in prison for two and a half years, although his guilt had still not been proved. He said it wasn't so bad in the common cell, but when he was kept in solitary he nearly went out of his mind. One day when a security major came to inspect the cell the driver complained to him of having been in jail so long. The Major answered: 'What do you expect? An investigation prison is like the taiga* – some people have been stranded here for five years.' According to the Soviet Procedural Code, the preliminary investigation of a criminal offence is not supposed to last more than three months.

Another group of prisoners in our cell – and the most despised – were people accused under Article 120 of corrupting minors. One of them was an Azerbaidzhanian who had taught English at Moscow University. According to his own account he had lived with a sixteen-year-old girl. He was treated fairly well, compared with a little man with greasy hair and a hypocritical smile who had been the Party secretary in some secret factory. He was accused of having had intercourse of a perverted kind with a twelve-year-old girl, and he was apparently an old hand at such matters. Prison has its own way of turning the social hierarchy upside down. A rather important person outside, he cut a very pathetic figure in jail. The butt of constant jeers and insults, he was the last to get his portion of soup, and he wasn't even allowed to read the copy of *Pravda* that was delivered daily to the cell. I think that as a former Party secretary he found

*Virgin forest of Siberia.

this particularly humiliating. He was also suspected of working as an informer for the prison authorities. On my second day in prison one of the drivers took me aside and warned me to be careful of what I said to him.

There was one other man who had, I think, been arrested for sexual offences, and who was left alone by the others. He was of enormous height and had a disproportionately small head. He once offered me some sausage, though I never bothered to conceal my dislike of him. His idea of fun was to tell an old accountant, a respectable family man who was in for embezzlement, how as an eighteen-year-old boy he had practised oral copulation with an older woman. He liked to tell this story during mealtimes so that the accountant had great difficulty getting his food down. All these people were referred to by the others as 'sodomites'.

There was one young man for whom I felt great sympathy. He was accused under Article 198, of which I have already spoken. A geologist from the Carpathians, he had arrived in Moscow as a tourist. Soon after he got there all his money was stolen from him. He reported this to the police and settled down for the night at the railway station in the naïve hope that he would be sent back home at official expense – there was no other way he could get home. The police warned him several times that he could not live in Moscow without registration. He paid no attention as it did not occur to him that in the eyes of the law he was no longer a victim but an offender. Three days later he was arrested and sent here to the Butyrki prison. The inquiry had been going on for over half a year. I could not understand why the investigation was taking all this time. He explained that part of the delay had been due to his examination by psychiatrists who, however, had found him completely sane. His investigator thought him out of his mind not to have got out of Moscow in time. When he was finally taken to court he hoped he would be sentenced to seven or eight months in prison, and since he had already been there for longer than this, that he would then be allowed to go home. Whether his hopes were fulfilled or not I don't know – I was removed from the cell before he came back from court.

The other prisoners questioned me about why I was in prison. At first I tried to tell them about Zverev's exhibition in Paris and my collection of pictures and drawings by contemporary artists, but the whole concept was unfamiliar to my listeners and they tended to misunderstand me. After a while I started to answer simply that I was in prison for pornography. Some of them called me a fool: 'Why don't you fuck women instead of looking at pictures of them?' And the Persian several times asked me to draw some naked women for him. The engineer who had embezzled funds from the Moscow Art Theatre regarded himself as being in the same boat as me, because when his apartment was searched one of the police agents stole his collection of pornographic postcards. Everybody thought I would be lucky to be tried for pornography as the maximum penalty for this was only three years. As a 'parasite', they said, I would have a much worse time. The decree about parasites was in general criticized, and many examples were given of how brutally it was applied.

It was interesting to observe the prisoners' attitude towards the régime that had put them in prison. Right from the first I came up against the most extreme views. Some people said, for instance, that they wished there would soon be a war, so that the Americans would come and free us. They cursed the Communists, saying there was nothing to choose between them and the fascists and hoping they would meet the same end. These, however, were exceptions. In our cell there were fairly frequent discussions of political subjects in the course of which the truck drivers attacked the former managers who had been thrown out of the Party for embezzlement or bribery but had remained faithful to Party ideology. The managers said that the drivers were unfamiliar with dialectical and historical materialism and could therefore not judge the merits or demerits of the Soviet system. The drivers, who had drawn their conclusions from their own experience of Soviet life, were infuriated by such arrogance. The extreme anti-Soviet camp was represented by the two dope peddlers, who said the bad thing was not that they were in prison, but the fact that life outside was very much like life in jail (though both were very anxious to be released); the drivers held more moderate opinions, the sexual offenders represented the centre, while the managers and accountants kept to orthodox Soviet views.

Life in the prison was very dreary and monotonous. We were roused at six in the morning by the strains of the national anthem. From that time on the loudspeaker continued to blare, except for two brief intervals, until ten in the evening. In the half-hour after getting up we were supposed to make our beds; after that came roll-call, for which we had to line up in two files near the door while the guard checked us off from a list. There were two further checks like this during the day and at night.

At eight o'clock we were given breakfast and were issued our daily ration of bread (half a kilogram) and sugar (fifteen grams). Breakfast, like the midday and evening meals, consisted of thin prison soup and a little *kasha* doled out to us through a serving hatch in the door at which we lined up with our small metal cans. If we were lucky, the *kasha* was made of millet; on bad days it was made of buckwheat. It was mixed with water and there was never any butter in it; even so, I ate it with relish, very slowly and with greater concentration than I ever ate outside prison. For all three meals, we were also given a brownish liquid which went by the name of tea. They gave us a kettleful which we could dilute as much as we liked with hot water freely available from a tap in the corridor.

At twelve o'clock we had our compulsory exercise: we were taken out into the yard and were supposed to walk two-by-two with our hands behind our backs (though nobody observed this rule). The yard was divided into a number of separate sections surrounded by concrete walls and covered with a wire net. Each of these sections was entered by an iron door and was about twenty to thirty metres long with a wooden bench in the middle. Each cell was allotted its own section, and we exercised here under the eye of a guard who could observe us all from a wooden platform above. There was little pleasure to be gained by exercising in such conditions, although we sometimes tried to liven things up by playing with a football improvised from a bundle of old rags.

After returning to our cell an hour later we had our lunch, which consisted of a larger portion of soup than at breakfast, and theoretically meat or fish, though there was no visible trace of either in it. For supper at eight o'clock we got even thinner soup, or sometimes salted herring, which I found impossible to eat. Lights-out was at ten o'clock.

I cannot say whether it would be possible to survive indefinitely on such a diet, because most of the prisoners got food packages from home or were able to buy things in the prison shop. The geologist from the Ukraine had neither money nor relatives in Moscow, and he had managed to live more than six months on this food, but he was emaciated. Prisoners were allowed to receive packages twice a month, though the amounts were strictly limited. Since nobody even knew where I was and it was forbidden to write letters from prison, I could not hope to get food from outside.

With the six roubles that I had with me at the time of my arrest, I was able to buy things in the prison shop. One was allowed to do this every two weeks and, luckily for me, the day on which the prisoners in our cell were able to buy from the shop came around just after my arrival. We were given a list of all the goods available for purchase with an indication of the maximum amount permitted. Sugar was limited to one kilogram per person, and butter to half a kilogram. Besides this, one could buy cheap smoked sausage, black bread, cheese, poor-quality sweets, biscuits, soap, toothpaste and cigarettes. It was also possible to get razor blades, but these were kept by the guards and were issued only for shaving in the morning, after which they had to be returned immediately. They kept a close watch on the razor blades: only a week previously a prisoner from one of the other cells who had been arrested for rape had managed to cut off his testicles.

One could fill in the time between meals simply by sleeping. I would generally sleep in the morning after breakfast because, with my weak heart, I felt very bad and feverish after nights during which it was difficult to sleep properly because of the cold. There was a library in the prison, but books were issued only on certain days at rather long intervals, so that at first I had to get along with books already borrowed by other prisoners. I re-read the comic novels of Ilf and Petrov and then started on Theodore Dreiser's *Jennie Gerhardt*, which, despite all the boredom of prison life, I was quite unable to finish. We were also allowed to play chess, draughts and dominoes. Few people played chess, but dominoes was very popular, particularly a game in which the prisoners superstitiously added up their points according to a certain system that supposedly indicated how long their sentence would be. A prisoner's mind is, of course, almost entirely preoccupied with the question of how long his sentence will be and when he will regain his freedom. At that moment there were rumours among the prisoners that, whatever the length of their sentences, they might all be amnestied on the occasion of the fiftieth anniversary of the October Revolution, in two and half years. Failing that, so the most optimistic of them believed, we would all certainly be released in 1970, on the hundredth anniversary of the birth of Lenin.

I thought at first that a day or two after my arrival in prison I would again be summoned by my interrogator, but the other prisoners laughed at me, saying that nothing would happen for at least a week – which was just as well since it meant they could not find enough evidence against me. And indeed, it was not till the end of the first week that I was summoned from my cell, and then only to see the security major whose task was to keep an eye on the mood and mutual relations among the prisoners. A fat-faced drunken-looking individual, he asked me in a tone of false bonhomie what I was in prison for. I said for nothing. 'What do you mean?' The Major was offended. 'Do you think the authorities are fools? People don't get jailed for nothing nowadays. It was different before.' We spoke a little about pornography, then he asked me what my cellmates were like and whether they treated me well. I said they were perfectly all right and nobody was unkind to me. Back in the cell I was questioned about my conversation with the Major. The former Party secretary, who had been summoned to him before me, had complained about one of the drivers and got him transferred to another cell. But the Party secretary's life hardly became any easier as a result.

On the 26th of May I was again summoned from the cell, and the guard led me down to the first floor through comfortably furnished rooms resembling Party propaganda offices where prisoners were interviewed by their lawyers and interrogators. I thought I was being taken to see my interrogator, but after waiting for a long time I was led into a room where there were two women and a man in white gowns. On the table between them lay the file with my plays and I realized that they were psychiatrists. Most of the talking was done by the women, and they seemed chiefly concerned to explore my literary tastes. They were, of course, no match for me – not only because I was better read, but also because I was myself a writer and knew the creative processes much better than they. For lack of time they hadn't even read my 'pornographic' plays but promised to do so before our next conversation. The man questioned me incessantly about my liking for Dostoyevsky. Perhaps he wanted to establish that I liked the erotic and sadistic aspect of his work. All the same I was glad of this conversation, in which for the first time in many days I could talk about things that interested me. They asked me next how I felt in prison and whether I would write about it later on. I said that I had indeed collected a great deal of material and would write about it one day or another, but that I had no inclination to do so at the moment. They also commented on my character, suggesting that I was reserved, that I liked to joke and enjoy myself, but only with my closest friends, and also that I was stubborn and always insisted on my own point of view. In the end, after much beating about the bush, they asked me if I was a 'virgin'. I said I wasn't, and we then had a brief conversation about my experience with women. After that we said goodbye, very pleased with one another. On the way back the guard said: 'You know who they were? They're psychiatrists – very important people. They could say you are abnormal and have you released from prison.' I did indeed wish that I might be pronounced abnormal, just as before I had hoped to be released because of my weak heart. As I walked along the corridor, I saw through the window that the trees were by now bright green and thought that nothing could be more beautiful than just to walk under such trees in the spring sunshine.

CHAPTER 8

Seventeen Hours of Freedom

NEXT day before dinner I was told to collect my things quickly. This was usually the signal for transfer to another cell, to the punishment block, or release from prison. The guard said that a car was waiting for me. I thought the psychiatrists must have found me a little unbalanced and I was going to be taken to a mental hospital for a proper examination. I stuffed my things into my mattress bag, wrapped up my sugar ration and the bread left over from breakfast, as well as an onion given me by another prisoner, and said goodbye to everyone. It is a prison custom for anyone who is leaving prison to be given a push by all the rest, so I positively flew out into the corridor accompanied by my cellmates' good wishes. Even though I had kept very much to myself, everyone in the cell had been kind to me.

I handed in my prison things and was again carefully searched. Then I was put in a small cell downstairs. From there I was summoned twice – the first time to be given back my personal belongings, and the second to have my finger-prints taken once more. On hearing that I had been imprisoned for pornography, the young man who came for me said cheerfully: 'I've been looking for someone who could get me some dirty pictures for a long time.' I told him I couldn't help him. I shared the cell with a mechanic who had been arrested in the winter for embezzlement and was now being released for lack of evidence. He was very upset at having to go out on a warm May day in his fur coat and winter hat. He proved to be a great admirer of Tito and kept on praising Yugoslavia, saying how much better the workers lived there than in Russia. Meanwhile I got very hungry and ate my bread and onion. Owing to the lack of vitamins, onions are in great demand in prison. From time to time I forgot about the car waiting for me and wondered whether they might not be going to release me.

At last I was called out of the cell and found myself in the large reception room under the poster 'To freedom with a clear conscience!' A major with a sheet of paper in his hand made me repeat my name, date of birth, and the article under which I had been charged, and many other details. He even asked me in what year my mother died. At the back of the room there were two young men in civilian clothes, whom I had not noticed because of my excitement at leaving the prison. One of them said: 'Yes, that's him, Andrei Alexeyevich Amalrik.' After questioning me the Major handed me a sheet of paper that bore the heading 'Provisional identity papers', but I had only just time to see my photograph and to read that the case against me had been dropped by the investigation department of the Ministry of Public Order when one of the two young men snatched the sheet from me and tucked it away. I recognized him as my interrogator. He said in a friendly voice, 'Come along, Andrei Alexeyevich,' and we went out to the waiting car. 'I have worked very hard, Andrei Alexeyevich,' he continued, 'to obtain your release. It is altogether exceptional for a criminal case to be dropped. It must be a curious feeling to be leaving prison like this.' But since I was now being driven somewhere else, I wondered whether I was really about to be freed. The interrogator told me he had taken Zverev's drawings to the Moscow branch of the Union of Artists to get an expert opinion and the experts had decided that the drawings were not pornographic but merely those of a madman. I said that since Zverev was a schizophrenic, I had not expected anything else. The interrogator then complained that Zverev had completely vanished and he could not find him anywhere. As I was told later, Zverev had been to a party at the home of Kostaki, the collector, and someone there had mentioned in front of him that whenever he tried to telephone me, he had got strange answers from my neighbours. Zverev, who was usually the last to leave any party, had immediately bolted and was not seen again for a long time. According to the interrogator the question of my plays was more complicated, as the Union of Writers had refused to give an opinion. One was finally given by

Tatyana Sytin, the literary consultant of the Lenin Komsomol Theatre, but she had been unable to say whether the plays were pornographic or not since she was not sure how pornography must be defined. She had supposedly found my plays interesting and they somewhat reminded her of Brecht. In telling me this the interrogator commented pompously: 'See how you could make a name for yourself. All you have to do is cut out everything anti-Soviet and erotic and then your plays could be put on the stage.' It was on the tip of my tongue to ask what would be left if all that were cut. The second young man in the car said: 'We have read your plays. They are very interesting. We only hope you won't be writing about us in your next one.' I replied that I couldn't guarantee it.

I was later to see these 'expert opinions' and will return to them. For the moment I need only say that because of them the accusation of pornography was dropped.

'Well, now that it's all over,' the interrogator next said in a confiding tone, 'tell us frankly, did you give your plays to foreigners?'

I repeated, as I had done during my first interrogation, that I had not given them to anyone. Meanwhile we drove on and I was by now quite convinced that we were on the way to the Lubianka and that the K G B had decided to stop dealing with me through the ordinary police and to handle my case directly. Remembering the recent case of Alexander Ginzburg, I was even pleased at this. I naïvely thought that the 'liberalism' of the K G B would be to my advantage. It's worth saying something more about this, partly because I will have to refer to Ginzburg again, and also to show what little good the K G B's 'liberalism' did him in the end.

Alexander Ginzburg is a man with a lively mind who takes a keen interest in the theatre, the cinema, painting, and literature. In 1960 he produced and circulated in typescript several issues of a magazine 'Syntax', which contained poems by young Soviet poets who had not been published in official periodicals. The K G B regarded this as almost tantamount to underground anti-Soviet activity. Ginzburg was arrested and spent several months in the Lubianka prison. The charge of being anti-Soviet could plainly not be sub-

stantiated and was finally dropped, but Ginzburg had committed an indiscretion which was now used against him:
earlier that year he had written an examination paper for a
less gifted friend of his. For this he was sentenced to two
years in camp minus the time he had already spent at the
Lubianka. In the spring of 1963, soon after he returned to
Moscow, he was once again in trouble. He had shown at his
house and at the house of his friends several short French
documentary films about artists such as Utrillo, Picasso,
and others. These films, incidentally, were later shown in
Soviet cinemas, but the authorities nevertheless regarded his
private showings as subversive. The films were confiscated
and an extremely disagreeable and mendacious article about
Ginzburg appeared in *Izvestia*. For the time being that was
the end of it. But in late 1963 or early 1964 he made friends
with one of the guides at the American exhibition of graphic
art in Moscow and asked him for American books of cul-
tural interest. The guide gave him several in Russian and
English, including some of a political nature, such as Djilas's
The New Class. I don't know whether Ginzburg realized
what sort of books they were. At any rate they were seen
at his house by various friends of his. Some of them asked
to borrow them and one – a person of the kind who has an
official job, yet at the same time frequents artistic circles out
of curiosity – reported Ginzburg to the KGB for circulating anti-Soviet literature. On the 15th of May 1964 Ginzburg's house was searched, several books were confiscated
and he himself was arrested. As he said later, his interrogators were very rough with him, stating that he would be
severely punished for handing around this kind of literature.
But after only four days at the Lubianka he was suddenly
called out of his cell and simply released without any
explanation. They continued, however, to call him in for
questioning from time to time in connection with another
case involving the circulation of anti-Soviet literature by
persons unknown. It was this relatively mild treatment of
Ginzburg that I had in mind in speaking of the KGB's
'liberalism'.

But this was not the end of the matter. Fed up with the
continual uncertainty of his situation, Ginzburg decided to

write a letter to the Central Committee of the Party asking that the KGB leave him in peace and let him get on with his work. When he showed me his draft of this letter, which contained fairly harsh comments on various blunders made by the KGB, I advised him not to send it, as I thought the Central Committee would scarcely intervene on his behalf and the KGB would certainly be furious. 'If you must send a letter to the Central Committee,' I told him, 'write one which is inoffensive to the KGB and show it to them first, as though to ask their advice about whether to send it or not. In this way, although nominally addressed to the Central Committee, the letter will in fact be seen by the KGB and will be more likely to work in your favour.' The same advice was given him by his lawyer and by the well-known woman writer and journalist Frieda Vigdorov who shortly before this had done her best to save the poet Brodsky from exile and was now taking an interest in Ginzburg's fate. I had known her for several years and took Ginzburg to see her in an office where she received people in her capacity as a deputy of one of the Moscow district Soviets. I mention this because by an odd coincidence these were the same premises, situated opposite the Ministry of Public Order, where one of my neighbours, my childhood friend Valeri Zhakovsky, had not long before been recruited to spy on me. Since the room was used both by deputies of the local Soviet and for recruiting and interviewing informers, it was certainly equipped with a hidden microphone and recording apparatus.

After this meeting Ginzburg redrafted his letter several times, but he still showed a certain lack of proportion. This time he went to the other extreme and in his final version wrote that, if need be, he was even willing to give an official reply to his 'well-wishers in the West', assuming that this suggestion would be taken as a mere rhetorical flourish. It is a sad thing that people who are more or less in opposition to the official line on art and literature, and who are therefore unrecognized in our country but arouse interest abroad, are apt in their dealings (whether enforced or voluntary) with the authorities to put on a wheedling tone and plead: 'If only you would pay attention to us and our art we would at once forget all about foreigners.' The authorities of course are not deceived by this transparent ploy, which apart from being very ugly is also unwise, since the interest taken in the work of young Russian artists by foreigners – whatever they may be like as individuals – is of great help. To some extent, then, Ginzburg fell into this trap, and by the time he came to his senses it was too late. The KGB seized upon that particular passage in his letter and said: 'Excellent, you will reply through one of the Soviet papers.' Without refusing outright, Ginzburg managed to stall for nearly a year. I did not see him during the last months before my arrest, and I assumed that he would either avoid writing a letter to the papers at all or that he would write one, on lines we had discussed, which would fail to satisfy the KGB.

Later, however, I heard that just a week after my release from the Butyrki prison the newspaper *Evening Moscow* published a letter from Ginzburg and that in tone it was exactly what the KGB wanted. (I haven't read it myself and don't propose to.) Its appearance was, I trust, the result of direct threats and pressures on Ginzburg. Many of his friends turned away from him, and he found himself in a very false position. That autumn Sinyavsky and Daniel were arrested and their trial took place in February 1966. Regarding the verdict as unjust and the trial itself as having been rigged for political reasons, Ginzburg began to collect information about the case in order to make it known to the Soviet public and thereby help Sinyavsky and Daniel. I think he must also have done this partly to rehabilitate himself in his own eyes and those of his friends after his unfortunate letter to *Evening Moscow*. He put all the material together as a White Book, copies of which he sent to the Supreme Court, the Central Committee and the KGB, and which he evidently intended to circulate among the Moscow intellectuals. By some unknown means a copy of the manuscript got abroad, where I have heard that it is to be published.*

* The record of the Sinyavsky-Daniel trial was published in Great Britain under the title *On Trial*: The case of Sinyavsky (Tertz) and Daniel (Arzhak), ed. by Leopold Labedz and Max Hayward, Collins and Harvill Press, London 1967.

The authorities treated Ginzburg with the same stupid callousness as they used on Sinyavsky and Daniel. On the 17th of January 1967, his house was searched and on the 23rd he was arrested. The way in which he was arrested was pretty vicious and in the best 'cloak and dagger' tradition: he was seized outside his house at about midnight and all his mother heard was a stifled cry under her window. As I write these lines, he is being held for interrogation in the Lefortovo prison.

Several more house searches took place in Moscow at this time, and about ten other people were arrested. There was a lot of talk about this police action in the city, where people assumed that the arrests were a political purge undertaken by the authorities before the fiftieth anniversary of the October Revolution. If this is so, it was a strange way of celebrating the anniversary of a revolution whose aim was to put an end to all oppression of the weak by the strong.

None of this of course was known to me on this spring day in 1965 as I was being driven with two young interrogators in what seemed to be the direction of the Lubianka. One thing I could be sure of: unlike Ginzburg, I would not be pressed by anyone there to make a public repudiation of my work and my friends since neither I nor my plays were known to anyone. As it turned out, however, we were not on our way to the Lubianka.

The car stopped outside the building of the court where I had had my conversation with Yakovlev. I realized that, having escaped prosecution as a criminal, I was reverting to my old status of 'parasite'. We passed Yakovlev in the corridor, and he even bowed to me and went quickly on. As I heard later, he had got into trouble for starting a criminal case without sufficient evidence and was in fact subsequently dismissed from his job and replaced by another judge called Chigrinov. It was Chigrinov whom I was now taken to see – though this was before his promotion to Chief Judge. My interrogator went straight into Chigrinov's study while I waited in a small courtroom with the other man. He asked me what was in the bundle in my hands. I said it was bread and sugar which I was keeping in case of emergency. He said something to the effect that a man must have been reduced to a pretty state if even when he was released from prison he took his prison rations with him. But looking at the policeman who was sitting nearby, ready, if need be, to take me back to the detention cells, I said to myself that my prudence was amply justified. We talked a little more about life in prison, then I was called into Chigrinov's office.

Chigrinov, a burly man of about fifty with an artificial arm covered in black leather, sat at his desk facing my interrogator, who had evidently been having an argument with him. Nearby, sitting primly on a little sofa, were an elderly man who looked like a worker and a younger one with the bland face of a Komsomol activist.

'When I read your plays,' Chigrinov said to me, 'I kept wondering what kind of man could write such stuff. I couldn't imagine what you were like. I was told that you were reserved and apparently no fool, although,' the Judge unexpectedly added, 'you do wear your hair like Kerensky.'

This comment surprised me very much. I had worn my hair short ever since I was fifteen simply so that it wouldn't get in my eyes, and without a thought about Kerensky, but I soon found that Chigrinov was very fond of this kind of insinuation.

I don't remember all the details of our conversation. He spoke not about whether I had been working but mainly about my plays which he referred to scathingly and described as anti-Soviet. Much to his annoyance I denied that they were. In my view, as I told him, they were Soviet in the sense that they were written by a Soviet citizen and hence, for better or for worse, were part of Soviet literature, not political tracts for or against the existing order in our country. The Judge then switched to painting and said that one of the pictures in my collection entitled 'One Rouble' was anti-Soviet because it showed a Soviet rouble falling into the sea. I replied that it was not falling into the sea (this was what the semi-literate *druzhinniki* had said during the search of my flat) and that the artist had to some extent been influenced by Pop art which depicts ordinary everyday objects in an unusual way and exaggerates their size. The Judge seemed to accept this explanation.

I was upset by the loose way in which the Judge used the

word 'anti-Soviet'. As a lawyer he should have known better. In our country this is not just a description of a political attitude but a legal term used to define actions or utterances punishable by prison sentences of up to seven years. Either the Judge ought to have based his case against me on these grounds or he should have avoided the use of the term. My plays had earlier been described as 'anti-Soviet' by Judge Yakovlev, but in the proceedings he had started against me I had been charged with pornography. In other words, I was being accused of one thing (writing 'anti-Soviet' plays) while under preliminary investigation, but was actually being formally charged for other things: pornography and failure to get regular employment. There can be no rule of law in conditions where such chicanery is allowed.

Next the Judge asked me what I thought should be done with me now. I replied that I thought I should be released at once. 'And what I think,' Chigrinov said, 'is that you should be sent to Siberia to look at things with your own eyes, not from inside somebody else's pants.'

Apart from the boorish way he put it, I was surprised that, without any court hearing to establish whether or not I was liable to exile under the 'parasite' decree of 1961, the Judge should tell me his verdict beforehand – a verdict based not even on the evidence collected by the police but on the fact that he (and perhaps other people higher up) had read my plays, which was not relevant to the question of whether I was working or not. After this I realized that if Chigrinov were to settle the case himself, and if no outside forces intervened, as had happened with the accusation of pornography, he would sentence me to the maximum penalty of exile for five years.

As I had suspected, Chigrinov now calmly announced that he was going to deal with me. I said I had asked for a witness and for a lawyer.

'Oh, yes,' he said in a peevish voice, 'I see that in your application to Yakovlev you said something about a lawyer and calling some woman as a witness.' Then he mentioned the name of a lawyer, though I had not asked for anyone by name in my application. It now struck me that I had better not insist on having a lawyer as he would certainly not help me and my insistence on one might only turn the authorities against me even more. For such defiance they would simply slap on the maximum. I therefore told Chigrinov that I didn't need a lawyer, but would still like to call a witness: it was simply a way of letting people outside know what was happening to me.

'Then write an application for a witness and say that you don't want a lawyer,' said the Judge. 'Otherwise you will be asking for one again before long.'

He rang up the superintendent of the 5th District to ask him to produce the witness for the following morning. The superintendent apparently raised some objections to this, and Chigrinov replied that the accused was a tricky fellow who wrote all kinds of appeals, so they'd better do everything according to the rules. He then told me that as I was asking for a witness for the defence, he might call some of my neighbours as witnesses for the prosecution. Next he turned to the two silent men sitting on the sofa and told them gruffly that they could go. In silence they got up, bowed respectfully to him and went away. I had thought they might be former prisoners, but they now turned out to be the two 'people's assessors' with whose assistance Chigrinov was trying my case.

My interrogator, who with his silent companion had been listening to my conversation with Chigrinov, now asked me to leave the room and began to argue loudly with the Judge. As far as I could make out they were quarrelling about my trial. After a short while the two young men came out, telling the Judge over their shoulders that they would phone their superiors, and went off without saying goodbye to me. They looked very angry. The Judge called me in again and, turning to a dreary looking woman, evidently the Clerk of the Court, said: 'Fill out a form that Amalrik undertakes to appear in court tomorrow at 11 a.m. and let him sign it.'

'We haven't got a form like that. I don't know how to write it,' said the Clerk, displeased at the idea that someone was being released, even if only for one night. But I was so eager to enjoy a few hours of freedom that I wrote out a statement in my own words and handed it to her. The Judge sent the waiting policeman away and said I was free to go but must be sure to appear at eleven o'clock the next morning. This show of leniency was evidently intended not for me but for the two young interrogators with whom he had just had a row.

I left quickly. There was a shoe shop next to the court building and I decided to buy myself some shoelaces. The salesman, a bald Jew who rather reminded me of Korengold, looked at my unlaced shoes and my shaven head and said with a friendly smile: 'I'll get you the very best ones I have.' This was the only time anyone had ever been nice to me in a shop.

I walked home along Aleksei Tolstoy Street with its green trees. I had a sensation not so much of happiness at being free as of dreaming a beautiful dream. When I reached Nikitsky Gate the clock on the square showed 6 p.m. I had exactly seventeen hours of freedom ahead of me.

The first to welcome me when I got home was the neighbour who had informed against me. Surprised though he was to see me, he met me with a broad smile and outstretched hand. I cut him short by telling him that I had read his evidence. He tried to excuse himself by saying that the interrogator had tricked him into making this statement. To this I replied that if he was called as a witness next morning he must retract his previous evidence, and so must his wife. 'If you don't do that,' I said, 'I'll get up in the courtroom and expose your connection with the KGB.' He looked frightened and agreed.

I didn't feel like staying in my room, where everything was still upside down from the house search. I thought of going out of town to see my father, but decided not to. It was better not to upset him, and I hoped he knew nothing of what had happened to me. Instead, I went to see the girl whom I had applied to have called as a witness in my defence and found several other people at her flat, including my future wife. They were all amazed to see me. Kiselev had already been to see the girl and given her a summons to appear in court. They had been looking for me for two weeks, but without success. The police had refused to give any information about me. My friend Yuri Galanskov had inquired at all the prisons. At the Lubianka they were told that nothing was known of me, and the same at the Lefortovo prison. Through my neighbours they had found the witnesses who had been present at the search of my flat, and through them they had contacted Captain Bushmakin. Bushmakin admitted he had conducted the search but said he knew nothing of what had happened to me subsequently. Finally my uncle, who also became involved in the search for me, had managed to find out the interrogator in charge of my case (his name was Novikov, as I now learned). One of my friends was supposed to be seeing him the next day, but with the termination of criminal proceedings against me there was no longer any need for this.

Not wishing to go home, I spent the night with my friends. Contrary to prison habit, I went to bed late and could not fall asleep for a long time. The first thing I saw when I woke up in the morning was a large jug of milk standing on the table. I had longed for milk all the time I had been in prison, but now, perhaps because of the pain in my stomach, I could not bear to look at it. The first time I was to see milk again was a month later.

CHAPTER 9

The Trial

THE next morning at eleven o'clock I went to the court-room. Judge Chigrinov was already there. The room was divided into two. On one side were benches for the public; on the other, a table and chair for the Judge and the People's Assessors, to the right of them the desk of the Clerk of the Court and on the left a door that led to the consulting room. Before the hearing began I asked permission to make a further application to the court: I wished to summon several more witnesses and also, as my friends had insistently advised me the day before, to ask for a lawyer. The Judge merely shrugged his shoulders and showed me to my place in the dock, facing the court and with my back to the public. I had no guard. There were about fifteen people in the courtroom: a few of my friends, Captain Kiselev, Gon-charenko, the KGB officer from the Frunze district, and a colleague of his – they sat inconspicuously in the corner by the door, looking as though they were there only by chance. There was also another man who, I gathered, really had come in by chance. The Judge went into the consulting room and a moment later came out accompanied by the assessors and the Clerk of the Court. He said 'Please rise' and everyone stood up. Then he took his seat and said 'Please sit down'.

In a bored voice he read from a piece of paper that these were administrative proceedings in the case of Citizen Amalrik, charged under the decree of the Praesidium of the Supreme Soviet of the RSFSR of the 4th May 1961. Then he asked me my name, date of birth and whether I had ever been in court or under judicial investigation before. I replied that I had been under investigation. The Judge said sullenly: 'You mean that last case. That doesn't count.' Then he read the charge. I was accused of having for many years 'sys-tematically avoided socially useful work'; if I did work anywhere, I did it very badly, and for the last year I had not had any job at all; my pretext was that I had to look after my father, but in reality I did nothing of the sort – he was either looked after by the neighbours or not at all; as a result I had a lot of spare time which I spent on dubious meetings with foreigners and on writing anti-Soviet plays; in spite of being warned by the police, I had not taken a job.

As soon as he had finished, I again asked to be allowed to summon two more witnesses and to have the reference from my last place of work produced in court. As I have already mentioned, the editor for whom I worked had given me a good reference, but later supplied a bad one to the police. I wanted both to be produced to show how much these references were worth. After consulting the assessors the Judge refused to admit another reference on the grounds that there was already one in the record. The day before I had asked for the good reference to be included, but the Judge had evidently got rid of it. As to the extra witnesses, he agreed to hear them if they were already in court. I said they were, so two more witnesses for the defence were allowed. Unfortunately, I had not had time to contact any of my father's friends, and the Judge refused to delay the hearing to make it possible for me to do so. After sending the witnesses out of the courtroom he asked me whether I pleaded guilty to the charge and what explanation I could give of my conduct.

I was told later that I spoke throughout the hearing in a strained, unnaturally clear voice, but did not allow the Judge to put me off my stroke. I said I did not plead guilty to any of the charges, since I had worked steadily since 1956. The Judge, I added, had taken account only of the jobs that were recorded in my work-book, but I had also worked as a cartographer, a proof-reader and a translator for payment and under contracts, of which I could supply evidence to the court. Besides this, for two and a half years I had studied at the university, which the court seemed also to regard as an evasion of socially useful work. It was true that in May 1964 I had given up all permanent employment, because my father was very ill and I had to look after him, but I had continued to do part-time jobs. The evidence of the neighbours was false and would be denied by my witnesses. Equally false was the statement that I had got bad references from my employers wherever I worked. I instanced a case in which I had at first been taken on temporarily by the magazine *Water Transport* and then given permanent work there. After being warned by the police I had twice tried to get work – with a magazine that had not given me a definite answer and in a library where they had not managed to consider my application before my arrest. As for the foreigners who were allegedly always visiting me, bringing paintings and taking them away, this was obviously a misunderstanding. It was based on the evidence of the neighbours who knew no foreign languages and mistook artists from the Baltic States and the Caucasus who came to see me for foreigners. Anyway, even if I had had foreign guests this was no reason for trying me. The case against my plays, which the Judge had just called 'anti-Soviet', had been dropped and was not relevant to the present hearing. I denied that they libelled the Soviet way of life or any other way of life, and pointed out that an author often uses the life around him only in order to construct his own world.

All the time I was speaking the Judge kept interrupting me, saying for instance that I could have worked an eight-hour day and still had time to look after my father; that my aunt was not 'a member of the family', so there was no need for me to look after her; that the neighbours 'can always tell a Soviet citizen from a foreigner'; that in my plays I libelled the Soviet people and described them as having spy mania; that I promoted anti-Soviet painting (here the 'rouble falling into the sea' was brought up again), and that I must, therefore, be made to learn the facts of life. His general attitude was that I was a spoilt young man from a well-to-do family who had had an easy life and had never mixed with anyone except a small clique of intellectuals like myself. Yet there was plenty of evidence before the court to show how difficult my life had been since the beginning of my father's illness, and particularly since my mother's death, and the extent to which I had met all kinds of people in my various jobs and travels around the country. But the Judge was less concerned with my working career than with my pictures and plays, about which he kept trying to engage me in discussion. He evidently thought he was well qualified to do so. But after answering one of his questions about my plays, I refused to be drawn any further into this subject, and confined my replies strictly to the essentials of my case.

'Well, I see you don't want to talk about that. But all the same, I hope you may still tell us what your view of literature is,' the Judge said pompously. He then asked me how I spent my free time. I said usually at home or at the library.

Having finished with me, he proceeded to the examination, or rather the discountenancing of the witnesses. After taking down their names and addresses, he asked them: 'Well, what have you got to say?' This confused them as they had expected to be questioned and it was very difficult for them to answer without knowing what had gone before. I now regretted not having a lawyer who might have helped to draw them out. The woman witness whom I had called said that I was not a 'parasite', that I had looked after my father, whom she knew well, and that the neighbours, far from looking after him, were always trying to browbeat him. The Judge listened with a bored and sceptical air; sometimes he yawned ostentatiously and at other times he rudely interrupted the witness, trying to turn her every word inside out. Thus, when she mentioned that I often went to fetch her little girl home from the kindergarten, intending this as an illustration of my good nature, the Judge took it as proof that I could not be looking after my father all the time. When she said I was fond of painting and that she enjoyed going to museums with me, the Judge asked which painters I liked and she replied: 'Of the classics, Rembrandt.' There was nothing objectionable in describing an old master as 'classic', but the Judge seized on it to deliver a lecture on the history of art, proudly concluding: 'You didn't think I knew so much, did you?' (But he had avoided haranguing me in this way for fear I might put him in his place.) Next he asked her whether she had read my plays, and she said she hadn't. 'How odd that he should not have shown them to you,' said the Judge. 'I myself wrote something the other day, and couldn't wait to show it to my friends.' He put the same question to my other witnesses, but they all gave the same answer. I had called one of them chiefly because he was a member of the Party and might therefore expect to get a better hearing from the Judge, but none of them were even asked whether they were Party members or not.

After the questioning of the witnesses there was a short recess. I asked Kiselev how he thought things were going. He said it was all a farce, since the verdict had been decided beforehand. 'And yet the criminal charge against me was dropped,' I said hopefully. 'Yes, but they made rather a mess of that,' said Kiselev.

After a quarter of an hour the session was resumed. The Judge asked me once again to give some explanation of my conduct and to make my final statement, giving me to understand that I must now comment on my plays and pictures. He evidently expected me either to express regret and condemn my writings or, conversely, to make a provocative speech in defence of my views on art and literature. I was firmly determined not to make things easier for him in this way. A recantation would not have helped me but only made my position more humiliating. A defiant speech, on the other hand, would simply have untied his hands – if indeed they were in any sense tied. Besides, I am not a propagandist by nature and I believe that loyalty to one's convictions does not consist in arguing with fools but in being faithful to them in your work. Therefore I spoke only about the formal charges in the case. I said I did not regard myself as a 'parasite', and had worked and studied consistently since the age of eighteen, though this had been particularly difficult for me during the past year owing to my father's illness. Perhaps in the past few months I had shown less determination in looking for a job, but I asked the court to give me a chance to find work and to continue looking after my father. I hoped that this short speech would be enough, but the Judge still asked me whether I had anything to say, hinting once again that I should talk about my plays. I replied that I had just made my final statement, and the court thereupon withdrew to deliberate.

They deliberated for forty minutes, though usually, when a 'parasite' is being tried, it takes them no more than five and sometimes they don't even bother to leave the court-room. The Judge and his assessors were not completely isolated from the outside world during their deliberations; several times I heard the phone ring. Although I expected the maximum sentence, somewhere at the back of my mind I still hoped I might be acquitted, or at least be given a lighter sentence. Much depended on the attitude of the Moscow department of the KGB which, through Goncharenko, had been in charge of my case from the outset. It was even possible that the two assessors might take my side against the Judge, though they had sat silent and passive throughout the trial, only once asking a minor question. The fact that the court was taking so long also gave me a little hope, and I waited in tense expectation.

At last the door opened and, ordering everybody to stand, the Judge read out the sentence. I was sentenced to two and a half years' exile in a specially designated area and to obligatory physical labour, but not to confiscation of my property. The sentence was not subject to appeal. The Judge added that I could be released for good conduct after serving half my term, and ordered me to be removed under guard.

In my opinion Judge Chigrinov had behaved throughout in an unfair, prejudiced and illegal manner. He had, for example, virtually told me what the sentence would be the day before in the presence of the interrogator, the assessors and the Clerk of the Court.

Throughout the trial he behaved less like a judge than a prosecutor and, instead of concentrating on the case, devoted most of his time to the expression of his own opinions on literature and art. I doubt if such a man should ever have been appointed judge, yet soon after my trial he was promoted Chief Judge for the district, and in December of that year *Evening Moscow* published an article praising him as one of the most cultured of the Moscow judges.

Both before and after my trial I found myself in court several times as an onlooker, and each time I was amazed by the extreme rudeness of the judges, their bias and utter contempt for the due processes of the law. I don't, of course, mean that all our judges are like this but such behaviour is evidently quite commonplace. A court sentence ought not to be an act of vengeance but the expression of a generally acceptable idea of justice. The educational value of a trial lies in convincing the defendant and everyone else that he is being judged in strict accordance with the law and with the ethical standards that mankind has arrived at during its long history; it certainly does not lie in the judge tediously haranguing the court or in his crudely defaming the defendant and witnesses. There is even less educational value in trials staged for avowedly propaganda purposes – as an object lesson to others. This is not a way of enlightening people but only of intimidating them, and it brings nothing but discredit on the courts. When a man is charged with one thing but then accused of something else during the actual trial, this may help the police in achieving their limited aim, but it also results in a still further deterioration of the whole system of justice.

It seems that nowadays the Soviet authorities are very worried about the rise in the crime rate. But the struggle against it is impossible without an effective judicial system that enjoys people's respect. What we need is not the passing of new and ever stricter laws, but the proper application of the existing ones, which are already quite harsh enough as it is. Furthermore, a man who has served his term should be given the chance to live a normal life, instead of being restricted in his choice of residence and always having his criminal record held against him. This ought to be taken into account only if he commits a new offence, not if he wants to get a job or go back to his family.

Finally, not all our laws are really valid. How can we put up with the fact that some articles of the Criminal Code plainly contradict the Soviet Constitution? Thus, Article 70* is an obvious violation of paragraphs a, b, and c of Article 125 of the Constitution. How, then, can it be right to put such a broad construction on the term 'anti-Soviet' as at

* Article 70, under which Sinyavsky, Daniel and other Soviet intellectuals have been tried in recent years, makes it an offence, punishable by up to seven years' imprisonment, to disseminate 'slanderous inventions defamatory to the Soviet political and social system'. Article 125 of the Constitution guarantees freedom of speech.

the trial of Sinyavsky and Daniel? 'Anti-Soviet propaganda' should be understood as incitement to the violent overthrow of the régime, but when the term is applied to an article about 'socialist realism' one is all too vividly reminded of the year 1951, when my aunt's husband got five years for not liking the novels of Sholokhov and Fadeyev.* Those in high office ought surely to reflect that without a proper rule of law they themselves may one day share the fate of Sinyavsky and Daniel. As long as we live in a State that violates its own laws, nobody, from the rulers of the country down to unregistered attic-dwellers, will have any sense of responsibility for their actions or feel assured of their personal safety.

* Alexander Fadeyev: Soviet novelist and President of the Union of Writers in the last year of Stalin's rule; committed suicide in 1956 after Khrushchev's 'secret speech' about Stalin's crimes.
  Mikhail Sholokhov: author of *Quiet flows the Don*.

CHAPTER 10

Krasnaya Presnya

AFTER the trial I was taken to the cell in the 5th District, where I had been detained two weeks previously. There were two other prisoners in the cell. One of them, a short dishevelled man who looked like a worker, was drunk and walked up and down, sometimes banging his head on the wall and shouting: 'Not again!' It appeared that he had recently been released from a prison camp and had been refused permission to live in Moscow. It was not clear why he was in again now – he kept muttering about a window he had broken in a workers' hostel, and presumably he had been arrested for hooliganism, or possibly for theft. He kept hammering his fists on the cell door, but at last a burly guard came in and hit him in the face. He fell onto a bunk and was quiet after that. The other man was also frantically pacing the cell and kept clutching at my sleeve, apparently soliciting my sympathy. He had a speech defect that made him quite incomprehensible and he was obviously mad. My nerves were so tense after the trial that I thought I too would go mad if I didn't get out of there soon.

Fortunately, after about an hour I was led out and put into a police truck. Kiselev was sitting inside it. He was astonished at my getting only two and a half years and not five. He thought the Judge must have felt sorry for me after all.

A little later a bedraggled, haggard woman of about forty was pushed into the truck. She was cheerfully defiant and shouted as she came in: 'Fuck you! Catch me working for the Communists! You wait, in five years I'll be back, then I'll show you.' Evidently feeling quite at home here she then leaned out of the door and bawled at the police superintendent who had just come out into the yard.

She had been tried as a 'parasite' immediately after me

and had got five years. As she told us, she had been brought up in an orphanage and had been sentenced for banditry at the age of fifteen while she was still there. Since then she had had only eight years of freedom. Somewhere in another orphanage she had a son of fifteen. Her name was Zina.

We were driven to the 60th District where I was welcomed like an old friend. Next day Kiselev came by and took me home to collect my things. I asked whether I could say goodbye to my father, but he said it was impossible. I took a raincoat, an old suit, a padded jacket, rubber boots, several shirts, a pillow, a blanket, two sheets, two towels, a knife, spoon and fork, soap, toothpaste and a toothbrush. The only neighbour who had not given evidence against me presented me with a metal cup to take with me, as well as a packet of sugar and some sausages and boiled eggs; later on I was very glad I had them. Besides my belongings, I had twenty-five roubles, which my friends had given me after the trial. This was as much as prisoners were allowed to take with them. Kiselev told me I was being sent to the Tomsk region, but he didn't know exactly where.

That evening a Black Maria came for Zina and me. Before we left Zina sang a song for the policemen; she referred to the prison as a hotel, to ourselves as tourists and called the sergeant who helped carry her things 'my valet', which he found very funny. 'We shouldn't let her go,' said the policeman, 'we'll miss her.' We then departed in style. Zina was put in the cage at the back while I sat in front next to a sullen curly-headed youth with a gypsy face. On the way we picked up a girl of about nineteen; she too was being sent to Tomsk as a 'parasite'; her name was Nina.

I knew that we were going to the transit prison of Krasnaya Presnya, but on the way we stopped at the Moscow police headquarters to pick up someone else. It was dark inside the truck but the man's face seemed familiar. Indeed, it was my old friend the photographer who had been my cellmate two weeks before. He had been tried as a 'parasite' by Chigrinov the day after we parted and sentenced to three years, although the Public Prosecutor had only asked for two. Since then, however, he had for some reason been kept in a cell at police headquarters. No one had questioned him or explained anything to him, but today he was told to take his things with him and had been put in this truck on the first stage of his journey to the Altai region.

In his ten days at police headquarters he had heard all kinds of things from his cellmates. I particularly remember a story about a taxi-driver who had got involved with a gang that worked outside the railway stations. Using prostitutes as bait, they made their money by robbery and extortion. Usually the girl would entice a prosperous-looking traveller into a taxi. As soon as it started, two of her companions would climb in and, pretending to be *druzhinniki*, blackmailed the wretched provincial into giving up all his money. Sometimes the girl, her accomplices following in another taxi, drove her victim to some faraway, lonely street where they threatened to beat him up or murder him, and robbed him of all he had. There were seven youths and two girls in the gang. The amount they made each time was probably just enough for a night's drinking, and the following evening out they went again to the railway stations, as though going to a regular job. The driver got a cut of five or ten roubles, depending on the wealth of the 'client'. It was a crude way of working and very soon they all got caught. As he told his story to the photographer, the taxi-driver kept whining that he was a family man and a Party member, and that only the day before his arrest he had meant to go to the police and inform on the others, but his nerve had failed him.

We made our last stop at the Butyrki prison where we picked up a talkative criminal of about thirty. He had been summoned from Vladivostok to Moscow for a confrontation with another man involved in his case, and he was now going back. The journey had taken nearly two months. The reason it had lasted so long was that prisoners are not sent straight to their destination, but in stages, via a series of transit prisons. The system goes back to the days when prisoners were marched to Siberia on foot and they and their guards needed to rest on the way. As a result, all along the great Siberian prison highway, transit jails where the convicts could rest and be regrouped had been built.

During my several days at Krasnaya Presnya I gradually got to know my companions in misfortune. All were 'para-

sites' and all had been undone by drink. A youth with a red
face and strong hands who looked like a manual worker had
spent the two weeks before his trial with D Ts in the prison
hospital; instead of being sent away for treatment, he was
sentenced to exile. Another was a little man of uncertain age
who liked to tell stories about homosexuals in the camps and,
to everybody's delight, sang dirty songs with great gusto; he
said he had been tried three times – twice they let him off,
but this time they had decided to deport him. He was a
stovemaker from somewhere near Moscow and, as such
naturally worked on his own account – sufficient grounds
for being classed as a 'parasite'. Another cheerful and kindly
man was a cobbler who for some reason was nicknamed
Mobutu; despite lack of materials he managed to mend
people's shoes even here in the cells. Unfortunately, he took
a dislike to me for my 'conceit'. There was an old man who
looked as though he were sixty or seventy and who shook
so badly that at mealtimes he could scarcely hold his spoon.
In reality he was only fifty-five and he was being sent away
for five years because by the time he came back he would
qualify for an old age pension. I was to meet several other
people of this kind: the court sentenced them for just the
number of years left before their old-age pension because
after that a man can no longer count as a 'parasite'. There
was also an attractive, modest man who I learned was a
retired major and had once been a school teacher. He
suffered from drinking bouts and had not been working for
the past few years; he was supported by his wife, who was a
shop manager. None of these people ever had enough
money for vodka, so they drank whatever they could get,
including furniture polish.

The population of the cell kept changing as new
prisoners were brought in and others were taken away.
Among those who were later sent to Tomsk with me, I
should mention three more: Boris, Leva and Tolya.

Leva, when he was first brought in, looked like an old man
of sixty, but deprived of liquor in the cell, he soon began
to look his real age: thirty-five. Before he had taken to drink
he had been a trade union official, and he still couldn't understand what had happened to him. Every time the key turned

in the door, he rushed over to it, certain that he was about to be released, as 'a good Soviet citizen', at the request of his trade union. I was often to meet people who had been exiled for being unemployed for only a month, but Leva had been given a number of chances over several years. He had been warned a number of times about absenteeism, or leaving his work altogether, and he had spent more nights in the 'sobering-up stations'* than he could remember. All this was brought up at his trial, but even so he got only three years. He was a very difficult person to get on with and was always provoking quarrels. I had a terrific row with him over the toilet. All the drunks in the cell had filthy habits, and I made a great effort to get them to flush the toilet after they used it to lessen the stench in the cell. Most of them reluctantly obeyed, except Leva. He denounced me as a snooty intellectual who would 'have to smell even worse things one of these days'. He and the others were upset by the fact that I was so different from them.

Boris was a burly man of about forty who had worked somewhere as a loader or a watchman but had then been fired for drunkenness. He ran through several more jobs, until it became very difficult to get work because of the entries in his work-book. Even so, he thought he might not have been deported if it hadn't been for his wife, whom he always referred to as 'my whore'.

Tolya was a soft-spoken young man with a sad, weak but agreeable face. He was being exiled for the second time, so everybody wanted him to describe how 'parasites' fared in Siberia. He said that at first the local people, being themselves former exiles – kulaks, Vlasovites, Latvians† – had welcomed them, but when they saw what a wretched lot

* These exist in large Soviet cities for the overnight detention of drunks picked up in the streets. They are released in the morning on payment of a fine.

† Kulaks: Rich peasants. Vlasovites: P.O.W.s who had fought in the army formed by General Vlasov, a captured Soviet general, in Germany during World War II. Many were handed over to the Soviet authorities by the Allies at the end of the war, and were sentenced to long terms of forced labour. Latvians: There were mass deportations to Siberia from Latvia and the other Baltic States at the end of the war.

of drunks had been sent them their attitude changed sharply. Tolya himself was, I thought, a basically decent fellow who could be influenced for either good or evil. But he had an unfortunate childhood, dropped out of school, fallen into bad company and begun to drink. In 1962 he was exiled for two years. At the sawmill where he was put to work he drank more than ever. When he returned to Moscow he no longer had a room: according to the existing law anyone who is absent for more than six months loses the right to his living space in Moscow. In theory the authorities were nevertheless obliged to register him but in practice they said they could not do so. In the end he was registered temporarily at his mother's flat for six months, but this meant that nobody wanted to give him a permanent job. At the end of the six months his registration was not renewed, he was again tried as a 'parasite' and this time sentenced to five years. It was clear that he would now become a hopeless drifter.

On the eve of our departure about six or seven new 'parasites', who were being sent north to the Komi region, were brought into our cell, and one of them, a boy of eighteen, told me something of his story. He had finished school the year before and then got a job, but he didn't like the work and left after about four months. After another job that lasted only three months he just began to drift, loafing around with other youths of his own age. One would have thought it would be better to help young people of this type rather than arrest them. Now he had been sentenced to a further three years, and it would be the usual vicious circle: in exile he would pick up criminal ways and then be refused registration when he returned to Moscow. Soon he would be in jail again. The same thing would happen to the nineteen-year-old Nina in our group. How can these youngsters be classed as 'parasites', even under the inhuman decree of 1961? Together with the old people nearing pension age, these children are the saddest cases of all.

Time goes even more slowly in a transit jail than in an investigation cell, and to make the wait more bearable, the prisoners told stories about their life outside. Mostly it was about their drinking exploits: how they would hang around outside a shop until there were enough people to put their money together and buy a bottle of furniture polish or some 'B F' glue (affectionately known as 'Boris Fydorovich'). Then they would go to some backyard and sit drinking it until they eventually managed to get home or were picked up and put in a 'sobering-up station'.

They all cursed Nikita Khrushchev with great bitterness, holding him responsible for the 'parasite decree'. They said that under the Tsars only political prisoners were sent to Siberia, but Khrushchev had started doing it to simple drunks. They always called him 'that bald pig', and I now heard for the first time a song which I subsequently often heard the kolkhozniks* sing:

> Once there were three bandits,
> Hitler, Stalin and Nikita.
> Hitler hanged us, Stalin beat us,
> Nikita made us starve.

Finally, on the 3rd of June, seven of us were told to collect our belongings. Before we left, the dull resentment that the other parasites felt against me came into the open. It happened over the question of shaving. We hadn't shaved all the time we were in prison, but now someone managed to cadge a razor, a cake of soap and a brush from the authorities. I would have been glad to have a shave but I have a sensitive skin and had therefore always used an electric razor, which I hadn't taken with me because I wasn't sure of finding electricity where I was going. To shave with a blunt razor and someone else's dirty brush did not appeal to me, so I said I wouldn't shave. This infuriated the others: 'Look at him, he won't shave like everybody else! He thinks he's better than us.' I was surrounded by an atmosphere of hostility but I had never believed in being 'like everybody else' and I refused to give in. This incident estranged me still more from those with whom I was to travel to Tomsk.

In the evening our personal belongings were returned to us and we were given our food ration for the journey. One day's ration consisted of two pieces of sugar (fifteen grams), a hunk of black bread (one kilogram), and half a salted herring.

*Collective-farm peasants.

Since we were given enough for two days we figured we must be going first to Sverdlovsk. Next we were taken to the cell intended for prisoners about to be transported. Among the people already there I recognized the man from Vladivostok and the gypsy-looking youth whose head had now been shaved. In fact he really was a gypsy. He had stolen some money in Izhevsk and come to Moscow where he had wandered around for a week, spending the nights at railway stations, until he was arrested. He was now being sent back to Izhevsk for trial.

At ten o'clock we were checked off from a list and our papers were handed to the officer in charge of the armed guards who were to accompany us. These papers were in sealed envelopes to which our photographs were affixed on the outside; the envelopes also showed our names, date of birth, place of exile and length of sentence. On my envelope they had mistakenly written 'two years'. We were now searched once again, this time by the young conscript soldiers of the internal security forces who were to be our guards on the journey. My knife and fork were taken from me once more and I never saw them again.

CHAPTER II

The 'Stolypin' car; Sverdlovsk

THROUGH the tiny window of the Black Maria we could see that we were being taken to Komsomol Square, where the three main stations of Moscow are situated. We stopped in a side street where we were asked to get out and walk in single file through a gap in a fence to the railway line. All around there were guards with dogs. It was a gloomy evening with a light drizzling rain. We were ordered to follow our escort at a distance of fifteen paces and warned that leaving the column would be regarded as an attempt to escape. We stumbled along the tracks to some closed carriages standing about three hundred metres away. Carrying our bundles, we looked less like prisoners than a gang of black marketeers from Civil War days when 'bagmen' used to go out by rail to the countryside and sell scarce goods from the towns.

We clambered up into the carriages with difficulty and, except for Nina and Zina, we were all pushed into a compartment divided from the rest of the carriage by a grille. There were already a few people there sitting on the upper and lower bunks. The neighbouring cages were crammed full. This was a so-called 'Stolypin' car, specially constructed for the transport of prisoners. Later on, during the journey, there was an argument as to the origin of this name. Some people said the cars were called after their inventor, although 'invention' was scarcely the word for them. In fact, they are named after the Tsarist Prime Minister and Minister of the Interior who introduced them after the first Russian Revolution of 1905, so the name had been preserved in oral tradition for sixty years. Of course, our car was quite new, but the principle was just the same. It was like an ordinary railway carriage, except that there were cages instead of compartments and a corridor down one side for the armed guards.

Each cage had seven bunks: three on each side and an extra one that could be pulled down in the middle between the two second-tier bunks, leaving a gap by the grille through which one could climb up to the top bunk. There are no windows in these cars except a barred one in the door.

There was a fearful din in the car. First we were all just pushed into the cages at random, but then they started calling us out one by one, searching us and assigning us to cages in accordance with the article under which we had been charged and the length of the sentence. Nearly everybody was here on criminal charges. A few people were taken out of our cage and we had a little more room. The man from Vladivostok started offering to sell his suit and watch. He said the suit was worth a hundred roubles and would fetch even more in Siberia. (He said it was of no use to him because he was going back to prison, whereas we were going to exile and would thus have use for the money.) He was now offering it for ten, and the watch for five roubles. After much hesitation Leva bought the suit and Boris bought the watch. The man from Vladivostok now had nothing but his shirt, but somebody gave him a pair of tattered trousers. He soon spent all fifteen roubles on drink; the guards carried on a secret trade in vodka at five roubles a bottle and in tea at a rouble a packet. Eventually, we seven 'parasites' were all sorted out and put in a cage to ourselves, so that we could look forward to travelling in relative comfort. Each of us had his own bunk, and I managed to get one of the top ones.

After two hours our two cars were hitched on to a passenger train, and we began to move. In the daytime, one could glimpse distant grey fields and Tartar villages through the barred window in the door of the car. We were going to Sverdlovsk via Kazan.

We all wondered what would happen to us when we got to Tomsk and where we would have to work: in a kolkhoz – this everybody feared most of all – or in a lumber camp. Somebody who had been in Tomsk before frightened us with stories about the terrible swamps in the west of the region where we would all certainly perish. He told us how, during collectivization when lots of peasants had been exiled there, certain local inhabitants used to offer to help them escape for large sums of money, and then led them into the swamps where they died.

I soon felt hungry on a diet of nothing but herring and black bread, and the herring made me feel very thirsty all the time. The guards would occasionally hang small cans of tepid dirty water on the grille, but it didn't last long.

We were taken out to the toilet, one by one, four times a day. There was a barred window in the toilet, and we were not allowed to close the door. There was no water in the basin so that we couldn't wash our hands, greasy from herring. The guards gave us very little time, since every prisoner had to have his turn.

When Nina and Zina were taken to the toilet the other prisoners raised a tremendous din, pressing up against the grilles as the women were led the whole length of the corridor (they were kept in a cage with several other women at the opposite end to the toilet) and shouting obscenities the like of which I had never heard before. 'Zina,' one of the prisoners would shout, 'want a bit of lard?', and would even show her a piece. Then: 'Do you want to fuck?', and the whole car would roar with laughter. The same thing happened when Nina, or one of the other women went through. They also made scathing comments about Zina, saying that she was old and 'ready for the garbage heap'. When she snapped back at one fellow and said he'd be only too glad to have her right now, he replied: 'Yes, but outside I wouldn't have you even for nothing.' There were one or two completely pathological types, such as one man who begged Zina to lend him her panties and brassière – which, taking pity on him, she did through one of the guards. Despite all the attention paid to Nina and Zina, nobody found he had any need for a woman; life in jail took away the sexual appetite. When Boris – as could be seen through his trousers – once had an erection in his sleep, it was regarded as so extraordinary that all the other prisoners got quite excited, and even the guards came to stare.

There was an even greater uproar whenever a policeman came through the car. This happened at the frequent stops when prisoners were taken off or new ones brought on by the local police. As they hastened along the corridor in their dark blue uniforms with envelopes under their arms they were followed by hoots and howls from the cages.

The young guards, unlike the police, walked up and down with imperturbable expressions, as if nothing could ever surprise or upset them. But even they were put out by the photographer, who had formerly served in the Navy. He kept asking them reproachfully what sort of soldiers they were to spend all their time just transporting prisoners. They were embarrassed and didn't know how to reply.

On the evening of the third day we arrived in Sverdlovsk, where we had to go through the same procedure as in Moscow: we were driven by Black Maria to the transit jail, and after a long wait in the cells we were searched and taken to the baths. Here, incidentally, we had a disagreeable surprise when we were told we must shave off the hair around our private parts. We were given clippers to do this and standing bashfully round the locker room we did as we were told and were then carefully inspected by the bath attendant and a doctor. After this, we were issued mattresses, spoons, and a mug, while all our own things, with the exception of foodstuffs, had to be handed over for safekeeping in the prison storeroom. When they took us to our cells at about two in the afternoon, I was soon longing to be back in the old prison. I had never seen anything as oppressive as this; the cell was between twenty and thirty square metres in size and it was crammed with people. There was a fearful stench. The door was made of thick iron bars, like the entrance to a cage in the zoo; this was in order to keep the rooms ventilated. There were two tiers of bunks which would hold approximately thirty people if the mattresses were placed right next to each other. At the moment this was about the number of people in the cell, but two days previously there had been more than fifty, and the number rose to forty-six while I was there. As a result some people had to sleep on the floor under the bunks. Tolya told me this was nothing compared with conditions when he had been exiled the first time, just after the decree came into force in 1961, when there had been so little space that people had to lie on top of each other. Then there had been no toilet or basin in the cell, only a slop bucket near the door. It

was only possible to urinate in this, and the men were therefore taken out twice a day, morning and evening, to a place
where there was a stone gutter over which they all squatted
in a row. It was very hard on people who had trouble
with their bowels.

I was surprised to learn that a large number of the people
in the cell were 'parasites' who had run away from their
places of exile but had been caught and were now being sent
back again. Most of them were from Sverdlovsk itself and
had been deported to places between six hundred and nine
hundred kilometres to the north of the city. Almost all of
them had run away from kolkhozes. I had naïvely supposed
that life was easier in the kolkhozes if only because there
was sure to be enough food, but people just laughed at me.
I was soon to learn myself what they meant. People who
got away rarely remained at liberty for more than a few
months, and when they were caught they would be sent to
forced-labour camps for up to a year. After this they would
still have to complete their term of exile. But this was no
deterrent, and they often ran away again – because they
were homesick, or hated the work, or didn't have enough to
eat (particularly in the kolkhozes), or because they thought
they had nothing to lose anyway. Thus it could go on for
years, a duel between hopeless despair and senseless cruelty.

I remember especially two of the fifteen recaptured 'parasites' who came to our cell during the ten days I was there.
One of them, who looked like a fairly well-educated person,
lay silently on his bunk all the time, scarcely ever speaking
to anyone. This was the first time he had run away and
when I asked him why, he said: 'If you get to a kolkhoz,
you'll run away too.' When I asked him what he would do
when they took him back, he said tonelessly that he would
run away again. The other one, Volodya, a professional
criminal of about thirty, was a completely different type
who loved to talk. He said this was his eighth escape since
1960, so that he had spent scarcely any time as an exile but
had been in forced-labour camps almost all the time. He
was now going to escape again as soon as he got some money
from his girl-friend. For him the status of 'parasite' was
rather like that of a slave in antiquity, and whenever he was

sent back to his place of exile he always greeted the police commandant with the words: 'Here's your slave, Chief.' Among the many interesting things he told me was the story of how the police in Sverdlovsk had arrested all the criminals there on the day before Nehru had been due to visit the city. This was because they were not used to coping with visits by important foreigners. When Nehru left they let them all go. When Castro visited the city they didn't bother to do this, and Volodya, who had just escaped from his place of exile, was himself among the crowds that greeted him.

As well as 'parasites' there were quite a lot of other prisoners who had been sentenced to exile by way of an additional punishment after doing time in a labour camp. They were better off than we were because every day they spent in prison counted as three days of exile; in other words, their sentences could be shortened by three months if they spent a month in transit prisons on the way. On the other hand, we had an advantage over them in that we could get a remission of half our sentence for 'good conduct', but I will have something to say later about how this worked out in practice. Most of these other exiles were common criminals. The most colourful among them was an old pickpocket nicknamed 'Grandpa'. He was a small, scruffy, red-bearded man who always walked around in his pants and vest. He slept on the floor and muttered to himself all the time about a sum of four hundred roubles, some gabardine cloth and his mistresses. 'I don't fuck 'em any more, I just write 'em letters,' he kept on saying. The other, younger criminals laughed at him and pulled his leg. It wasn't clear whether he was really crazy or just putting it on.

Four days after we got to Sverdlovsk we were joined by another band of 'parasites' from Moscow – all either old men or youths of about eighteen or nineteen. One of the old men joyfully greeted Leva – they had both always bought furniture polish at the same shop in Moscow. The old man related sadly that there had been a big round-up of drunks, and that he himself had been picked up when he was found sleeping on Gorki Street.

All the 'parasites' I saw on the journey, and later in

Siberia could be divided into four categories. The largest consisted of drunks, both chronic alcoholics who were no longer capable of work and needed treatment and people who had been dismissed from their work because they had got drunk for some particular reason and failed to appear at work as a result. There was, for example, a young taxi driver from Leningrad who had gone on a binge for four days when his mother died, and was then arrested a month later for failing to find a new job. These people, of course, drink even more in exile. In the same category are the drug addicts who, in their places of exile, spend all their money on opium or other drugs which they buy from the local veterinarians. I got to know one of these addicts in the Sverdlovsk jail; he was only twenty-eight years old, but he already had a very bad heart and several times was taken ill in the over-crowded cell. He was being deported from a small place near Moscow to the Amur, where he hoped he might get the doctors to pronounce him unfit for work – as long as he could conceal from them that he was a drug addict!

A second, smaller category consisted of people who were not in any sense 'parasites' but good workers who carried on their own individual business as carpenters, stovemakers, and such like, but who from an official point of view were not regarded as having regular employment. I got to know one of these 'parasites' in Sverdlovsk. He was a carpenter from Pskov and was very kind to me, lending me his spoon when mine was stolen. He cursed the drunks and the criminals and wanted only to get to his place of exile as quickly as possible in the hope that he might get lodgings with some decent people, and work at his trade again.

There was a third group of 'parasites' who were really professional criminals with police records, but because the police had nothing particular on them at the moment, they were simply being deported under the 'parasite' decree. Volodya, of whom I have just spoken, belonged to this category; most of them always wound up in the labour camps.

Finally, in the fourth group, there were religious sectarians, intellectuals, and various people who had got here completely by chance, for no particular reason. The one type of person I never saw (except for the professional criminals) were people who were real 'parasites' in the sense of wanting to live at the expense of others.

Most of the 'parasites' in our cell were from the provinces. I was curious about how many times they had been warned before being deported, whether they had had a medical examination, and how long their trials had lasted. Some of them had been warned once and some twice, but others had been sentenced without any warning at all. As regards medical reports on their fitness to work, none of them had even heard of such a thing. The judge would simply say: 'So you don't work? You want to have a trip to Siberia?' and then sentence them on the spot.

Every day we waited impatiently to be sent on our way. By law, prisoners are not supposed to be held more than two weeks in a transit jail, but there were people in our cell who had already been here for nearly three. Sverdlovsk is the largest transit centre, which is evidently why one had to wait there so long. About twice a week a few people were taken out of the cell to be sent on the next stage of their journey, but new people were brought in almost daily, generally late in the evening. Among these I particularly remember a Tartar from Syzran who was being deported for two years to the Irkutsk region because he had sold the meat of a cow he had bought. He was not saved by the fact that he had regular employment as a watchman in a school. He was clearly quite shaken by what had happened to him, and at night he talked excitedly in a strong accent about how on the way here the guards had made them all go down on their knees when they were checking their numbers and how, when the police took his fingerprints, they had said: 'Now take down your pants, we're going to take prints of your prick.' In the cell they all laughed and told him that this was a standard joke in police stations.

This dreary period of waiting was enlivened somewhat by endless arguments between Leva and Boris. Once, for instance, Leva started telling how he had fought in Korea in 1951: the whole of their unit had been put in civilian clothes, they had been taken into the country across a river on rafts, and told not to tell anybody about it. Here Boris interrupted him: 'Why are you telling us then – you're giving away a State secret.' Leva said it didn't matter because it was a long time ago. He had, incidentally, retained no impressions of the Korean War except a visit to a brothel. On another occasion he began to talk with emotion about what a good mother he had: not only did she feed him, she even gave him thirty kopecks a day to buy furniture polish. Boris immediately began to reproach him, saying: 'How much longer can a grown-up drunk like you expect to be supported by your mother?' 'Why not?' Leva replied in all seriousness. 'She didn't know how to bring me up right, so now she can support me.' Another time they had an exchange that went like this:

'Ever drunk furniture polish?' Boris asked Leva.

'Yes.'

'Ever drunk Eau de Cologne?'

'Yes,' Leva replied.

'Formic acid?'

'Yes.'

'Anti-dandruff lotion?'

'Yes.'

'Brake lubricating fluid?' Boris went on relentlessly.

'Yes,' Leva replied triumphantly, and all the prisoners guffawed.

To while away the time we played dominoes nearly all day; there were two sets of them in the cell. Since it was strictly forbidden, the criminals played cards out of sight on the top bunks. They made the cards out of newspaper with the help of an indelible pencil, bread, sugar and water, tracing the patterns on them with stencils cut out by a razor blade. Some people literally lost their shirts, and the winners would put on several of them, one on top of another.

At last, on the 14th of June, after nine days in Sverdlovsk, all of us who had been brought from Moscow were ordered to gather our belongings and were then taken to the cell for prisoners about to be transported to their further destinations. Here there were not only people being sent into exile, but others of different categories who were now on the way east to prisons or camps after being tried and sentenced. There were some pretty rough types walking around the cell, many of them with tattoo marks in typical criminal fashion. Some of them had obscene sayings tattooed on various parts of the body; one, for instance, had on his arm: 'Happiness is not a prick. You can't take it in your hand.'

I remember also a boy of about sixteen with a completely crazed expression on his face. He was going to be tried for stealing a bicycle. He walked up and down all the time muttering incoherently to himself. The others said he was a 'goat' – the camp slang for a passive homosexual, and the most insulting thing that a man could be called.

In the evening we were taken to the baths, and our possessions were returned to us. After another night in the cells we were taken off in the morning and loaded into Black Marias. It was very difficult to breathe because they had crammed so many of us inside, and the weather now had become very warm. This time we were not so lucky in the train, either: in each cage of our Stolypin car they now put fourteen, instead of seven, so that Boris and I had to share a narrow bunk, while two other people slept on the floor. However, it got a little easier after Omsk when several prisoners were taken off the train.

CHAPTER 12

Novosibirsk, Tomsk and Krivosheino

AFTER another night in the train we arrived in Novosibirsk on the 16th of June. The Sverdlovsk transit prison, like
the one in Moscow, had consisted of a square block with an
inner courtyard, but in Novosibirsk the prison is a series of
quite separate buildings. After giving up our belongings we
were first taken to the baths, where we had to wash out of
buckets because there were no showers. After that we were
taken to the prison shop, which could be used only at the
time of arrival or departure. There was, however, very little
to buy except black bread, sugar, cigarettes and chocolate.
By the time we left the prison all the cigarettes and chocolate
were gone too. Then we were all taken to our cells. I found
myself together with a few old acquaintances, such as the
Tartar and the drug addict whom I had met in Sverdlovsk.
There was also a card-sharper I had got to know there; all
told there were twelve of us. Two of the new ones stood out
from the rest. One was a man of just over fifty who must
have been a high official since, as appeared from his conversation, even his deputy had had a personal automobile.
By training an economist, he had spent eight years in 'strict
régime' camps for large-scale embezzlement. He was now
being deported to exile in the Tomsk region where he would
have to stay indefinitely. The second man was about forty
years old and had an Asian type of face. He was covered all
over with tattoo marks so that, as he told us, he was
embarrassed to bathe in public. He and the economist argued
all the time, generating more heat than sense, about philosophy, politics, literature, art or anything else that came into
their heads. Both of them talked with the excitement of
people once in touch with the world of learning, but the

economist, as a former high official, tended to patronize the Asian-looking intellectual, who, small and bird-like, reacted furiously and accused the other of having been in his time a 'poor leader'. The ex-official was very hurt. The other prisoners, mostly uneducated people, just laughed at them. Shortly after we had been put into the cell they had a violent argument about Marxism in which the economist invited me, 'as an educated person', to take part. But I refused, saying I didn't believe in Marxism and knew little about it. The former official was taken aback. 'How old are you?' he asked me and, learning that I was twenty-seven, expressed his astonishment: 'It didn't take you long. I don't believe in Marxism either, but I only got disillusioned at fifty.' He then began to question me about the verse of Esenin-Volpin,* wanting to know whether it was like that of his father, of whom he was a great admirer.

The card-sharper had brought with him to the cell a packet of tea bought from the guards on the train. I now saw how they make *chifir*, an exceptionally strong brew of tea, which is the most wide-spread drug used in the camps. Some people become so addicted to it that they cannot do without it, and have no need at all of vodka. The fifty gram packet of tea was emptied into an aluminium mug full of water, and the mug was fastened to a stick. Then one of the prisoners, perched on the toilet in a corner of the cell where he could not be observed through the peephole in the door, held the mug over the toilet bowl while others twisted pieces of newspaper into thin spills and burned them under the mug until the water boiled. When the supply of newspaper ran out one of the criminals, a young Jew, gave up his personal letters at the request of the *chifir* drinkers. At last it was ready and six prisoners sat in a circle, each taking a sip in turn from the mug. It was all rather like a ritual. The same tea can be brewed a second and a third time, and experienced drinkers use these brews of different strength in various combinations.

* Alexander Esenin-Volpin: son of the famous Soviet poet Sergei Esenin, who committed suicide in 1926. Esenin-Volpin is a distinguished mathematician and poet who in recent years has become one of the leaders of the dissident Soviet intellectuals.

The next day a few people, including me, were taken out and put into another cell for prisoners in transit. After yet another day we were called out, one by one, in the morning and given back our personal belongings; my watch was not returned to me, but I was handed a receipt to enable me to reclaim it when I reached my place of exile (it took the watch a year to get there). Next we were all lined up in the corridor and made to squat while they called our names from a list. One by one, we went up to a desk at which prison officials were sitting, took off our caps, and replied to the same old questions: 'Name?... date of birth?... length of sentence?...' After this we got our rations for the journey: bread, salted herring and a tiny packet of sugar, which I ate straightaway because I was so hungry. In general the food in Novosibirsk was better than in other prisons; on the first day I found a little bit of meat in my soup – this was something quite unheard of in prison! – and the tea they gave us, though weak, was at least the real thing. With all these procedures, it was evening when at last they took us to the railway in the usual Black Marias. The carriage in which they put us this time might really have been used to transport prisoners in the days of Stolypin himself, or even in the time of Yaroshenko, whose painting had made such an impression on Judge Yakovlev. Several of the cages were full of juvenile delinquents. At the sight of me in my spectacles and black beret they pressed up against the grille arguing among themselves as to whether I was a musician or a geologist, and made a terrific din, shouting for cigarettes and money. I was put in a small cage for only three persons together with Leva, an old carpenter from the Kuban, and a criminal. The case of the old man from the Kuban was rather strange. Despite the fact that he was a war invalid, and contrary to all the laws, he had been deported as a 'parasite'. When we later arrived at our destination, the police Commandant was very surprised and said he had no right to keep him there, but even so he sent him to a kolkhoz. He was given the job of watchman in a cowshed and it was several months before he was able to get permission to go to the local hospital. At last, in the spring, he managed to obtain a document certifying him as an invalid, and was allowed to go home.

I slept almost all the way to Tomsk, where we arrived on the morning of the 19th of June. At the prison there we were to be told which areas in the region we would be sent to. Our reception was very friendly, almost as if we were long-awaited guests, and I believe someone even suggested that we rest from the journey. We threw down our things in the prison yard, and wandered around for a while.

Later, after a visit to the baths we were taken to our cells, which for some reason were in the women's wing of the prison, so that we had female guards. The cell was large with white-washed walls, and the windows had bars, but the panes had been removed because it was summer.

We were taken out to exercise in a rather pleasant yard where there was even a tree growing. There were two posters on the wall. One of them showed a sad woman in a long dress sitting with a handkerchief to her eyes in the middle of a ransacked room; underneath was written: 'Burglars bring Sorrow to the Workers'. The second poster showed another woman of similar appearance sitting at a table with a letter in her hand and a sickly child at her side. The inscription on this one read 'Your Family awaits You', and the prisoners found it particularly irritating.

The food was exceptionally bad here. In Tomsk, I gathered, there was nothing to make *kasha* of and for all three meals we got only soup; in the evenings it looked like soapy water in which underwear had been washed. I just couldn't touch it. I had lost my bread ration on the way, and things would have been very bad for me if another prisoner, who had spent a long time in the camps, had not noticed my hungry look and given me some biscuits. The next day I bought sugar, butter and biscuits in the prison shop, and was thus independent of the food supplied by the prison. After the usual initial depression in a new prison, I got used to the cell, and I now remember those three days in Tomsk as by no means the worst. Here too, the time was passed in the telling of stories, and one old prisoner who had previously been in exile in Yakutia described the peculiarities of the local population. The Yakuts, it seems, are very fond of dogs and he told us how a Yakut had shot a Russian for throwing his dog out of his car – not immediately but a year after the event. He explained that the Russians there behave badly and throw their weight around, while the Yakuts are rather timid. He also told us how the Yakut women stop their children from crying: when a baby begins to cry they pick it up by the legs and pitch it into the snow where it will soon quieten down. As soon as it stops the mother picks it up and takes it into the house, but the treatment is repeated if the child cries again.

On the 21st of June we were told where we were being sent. We 'parasites' – the Major, Leva, Boris, Tolya, the carpenter, a young tractor driver from the Kuban, and myself – were assigned to the Krivosheino District, not far from Tomsk itself; Nina, Zina and two other women 'parasites', both about forty years old, were also going there. Most of the criminals were being sent to districts farther down the Ob where, they were told, they would be taken by plane.

In the afternoon all the 'parasites' were taken to the prison Governor for a roll-call which was rather like a graduation ceremony at a high school. The Governor opened our envelopes, looked through our papers and gave us each a friendly smile. Then, for the last time, we were given travel rations and an hour later were taken in a Black Maria to the wharf to be put aboard a steamer for the journey down the Ob to the village of Krivosheino, 150 kilometres south of Tomsk.

In the hold of the steamer, next to the engine-room, there were two enclosures, divided from each other by iron grilles and a central passageway, one for men and one for women. One could catch an occasional glimpse through a port-hole of the low, scrub-covered banks of the Ob. On the wall I noticed a bullet-hole near which somebody had scrawled in pencil: 'Here died Sasha Korolev, age 22, shot by a guard'. I asked our guards what had happened. They said a young guard had been fooling around with a revolver in the hold crammed with prisoners, and it had gone off accidentally, killing Korolev. I asked whether he would be tried, and they said they did not know but had recently seen him at liberty in the barracks.

We arrived in Krivosheino at about ten in the evening.

Under the curious glances of other passengers, we disembarked at the village, a row of small houses along the top of a high, sandy ridge. An open truck was waiting for us and we were greeted by a young police lieutenant whose almost childlike face had a friendly expression. The police station was not far from the pier. We piled our things in the corridor there and were given some nasty-tasting herb tea to drink before being put in the cells for the night. It was very crowded and stuffy in the small cell into which three or four of us were put with about five local prisoners. We were squeezed in like sardines and Leva had to lie on the floor. I was rather taken aback by the easy-going relations between prisoners and guards here. One of the local prisoners shouted: 'Sasha, put out the light!' and the policeman on duty did as he was told, although it was strictly against the rules. This would have been quite unthinkable in the larger jails. All the others in our cell were in for a few days on charges of petty hooliganism. Strictly speaking, they were not local people at all, since most of them had been deported here as 'parasites' some years before. I asked how long they had been here and whether it was easy to get the remission of half one's sentence provided for in the decree. One of them said it was a good question. He was from Yaroslavl and had been sentenced to three years' exile in 1960. Since then five years had gone by and he had no idea whether and when he would get back. His wife had come out here to join him. Neither he nor the other prisoners in the cell had ever heard of a 'parasite' being released on completing half his term.

In the morning we were all let out into a grass-covered courtyard where there was a young lieutenant (not the one of the day before, but another with a hare-lip and pompous manner) who introduced himself as the 'officer in charge of exiles' or, as he was generally called, 'The Commandant'. Each of us was then summoned in turn to his office, and this took up almost all day. While waiting we walked around the village, looking at the restaurant and the shops. I went to the river and had a swim. At last I was out of prison, but I cannot say I took any special pleasure in wandering about the dusty streets of Krivosheino.

Krivosheino is a biggish village, dusty in the heat and – as I was to discover – unbelievably muddy when it rains; it has wooden sidewalks and stunted trees growing along its two main streets. Before collectivization, which in Siberia started five years later than in Russia, it was a very small village, but later, especially after the war, when it was made into a district centre, its population grew considerably: people flooded in from the surrounding villages because they didn't want to work in the kolkhozes. Now it has a butter and a flax factory and a light-industry co-operative. The houses are made of wood and are mostly one storey high; the only brick building is that of the district Party committee. There is a shop in the main street where everything from fur jackets to gramophone records is sold; there are also a post office, a savings bank, a chemist, a hairdresser, three food shops, a bakery and a restaurant. It was here I had my first meal in exile – quite decent though expensive – and a glass of wine. My companions showed less restraint and most of them were drunk by the middle of the day.

Around four o'clock I was summoned by the Commandant, who had my file lying open on the desk in front of him. The conversation was brief. He asked me how I could have got in such a fix as this. I replied drily that there it was, I had to lump it. 'Well, don't worry,' he said. 'If you work you'll be released when you've served half your term; if you don't we'll give you a longer sentence.' He added that on the whole his district had a 'good record'. The figures, according to him, showed that only a third of his exiles had tried to run away or committed other crimes for which they were sent to camps, nearly half had served their sentence in full, and the rest were released halfway through. In other districts, it appeared, things were even worse. He gave me two papers to sign; one informed me that if I left the region without permission I would be prosecuted under the relevant article of the Criminal Code, the other that if I refused to work I would be tried under another.

We were told that the men were being sent to the Kalinin kolkhoz, which people said wasn't too bad, and the women to a fishing village on the river Ob. A truck was to come for us that evening. But by then one of my companions, Leva, was blind drunk and had had a fight with some peasant in the yard of the police station. Another, Boris, also drunk, had pushed one of the women parasites so that she fell on top of the sleeping police sergeant, and there had been a blazing row. Tolya and the tractor driver from the Kuban had also had a fight. The women had walked drunkenly about the streets singing and demanding money from passers-by. As a result the Commandant had ordered everybody to be returned to the cells, except the Major, the sick old man and myself.

Towards seven a truck came for us and we three got in; the rest were to be kept until the following day. At the very last moment the Commandant noticed a bottle of brandy sticking out of the Major's pocket; he took it from him and broke it against the fence. The same thing had happened earlier in the day to a bottle of spirits that Leva had bought.

On the whole, however, the police in Siberia made a much better impression on me than those in Moscow; in Siberia they are more civil and humane. I think the reason is that they are recruited locally : the local population respects them and they try to live up to its respect. In Moscow, on the other hand, the police are mostly provincials who have come out of the army or the security forces; finding themselves in an unfamiliar environment, they feel that people are hostile to them and react accordingly.

CHAPTER 13

The House with a Curse on it

THE village of Novokrivosheino, where the kolkhoz had its main office, was about ten kilometres away. The road, running between steep slopes overgrown with pines, was quite picturesque in places. But this was exceptional. The whole of western Siberia is an enormous marsh, overgrown with virgin forest in the south and treeless in the north. We drove past fields surrounded by taiga and, in an exceptionally grey and gloomy village, we stopped in front of a small hut where the office was housed. A man in a dark cap came out. This was Zharkov, the deputy chairman of the kolkhoz; he looked at a piece of paper and said that two of us were staying here and the other two were going on to Malinovka, a big village which was also part of the Kalinin kolkhoz. As luck would have it, I was left behind with Leva, which surprised him and annoyed me because he was now getting on my nerves. The truck drove on, and Leva, Zharkov and I went into the office. There were several people working at desks in the front room; sitting at a filthy table under a crude portrait of Lenin in the back room was the chairman; he was wearing a dirty black suit and had a rather prim look about him. As I heard later, he had been Party secretary in this same kolkhoz and since then his face had set once and for all in this expression which came from pretending to listen to people with understanding, and then laying down the law to them. He was short and hunchbacked. Like many people with physical defects who have grown up in a brutal environment where such things are laughed at, he had a look of suppressed anger and resentment. But he greeted us politely and asked us to sit down. His name was Gerasimov.

Zharkov had previously been chairman in Malinovka but later, by a decision of the district Party committee, the two kolkhozes were joined together and he became deputy. The

Malinovka kolkhozniks were highly displeased by the merger
because it very considerably reduced the value of their
'labour-day'* Soon after our arrival the decision was reversed
and Zharkov once again became chairman in Malinovka. He
had begun as a factory worker and had been sent to the
kolkhoz in the course of one of the periodic campaigns to
'tighten up discipline'. But the kolkhozniks had some respect
for him, whereas their attitude towards the chairman, Gerasimov, was indifferent if not contemptuous; 'neither fish
nor fowl' they said of him.

Neither Zharkov nor I took much part in the conversation
that now began, leaving the talking to Leva who was still
tipsy. What he said was on the whole true, but this was
scarcely the place to say it, and he kept repeating it over
and over again. He said that our agriculture was a shambles,
the collective farms were wretchedly poor, and what they
wrote about them in the papers was all lies. Gerasimov
replied that since the towns were getting food supplies and
Leva himself ate every day, the kolkhozes must be doing
their business. Leva then went on to insist that he must have
a job as a mechanic: that was all he knew how to do and if
they made him do anything else they need not expect him to
be any good. Zharkov said that farming is easy to learn and
asked me where I had been working. I said chiefly with
magazines. Both he and Gerasimov looked bewildered; a
mechanic might possibly be some use to them, but short of
starting their own newspaper, what were they to do with a
journalist? Leva went on arguing drunkenly while I went
outside, bored by all this futile talk.

I wanted to find out whether I could rent a room from
one of the local people and also get some idea of what life
in the village was like.

'God knows why I've been sent out here,' I said to the

---

* 'Labour-day' (*trudoden*) is a unit calculated from the amount of
work a kolkhoznik has done. Each kolkhoznik is paid, partly in kind
and partly in cash, according to the number of labour-days he has
earned. Advances may be made from time to time, but the general
settlement comes only at the end of the year. In recent years the
kolkhozes have been converting to a system of paying wages in
regular cash instalments.

first person I met, as though making fun of my own uselessness. He looked like a sullen peasant.

'I'm in the same boat as you,' he replied. 'I've been here three years now.'

The second person I spoke to was also an exile. The third looked like a cowherd, judging from the whip handle stuck in his belt. He was very glad to talk to me; he too was an exile and he suggested there and then that I should stay with him and several other 'parasites' in a kind of hostel they had fixed up for themselves – a 'gypsy shack', as he called it. Meanwhile several exiles had gathered around a low barn, which was used as the kolkhoz storeroom. A few minutes later the storekeeper drove up on his motorcycle. Out of curiosity I looked inside to see what the 'parasites' were being given. They each got a bottle of sunflower oil and several loaves of coarse bread; as far as I could see that was all there was to be had. Everything looked so poor that I felt more wretched than in prison.

'Well, so long, I must look after the cattle,' said my new acquaintance and I went back to the office, reflecting on the fact that the first three people I had met were all exiles.

By this time Leva had obviously got on Gerasimov's nerves to such an extent that, on the pretext that there was no room for us, he had decided to send us to a small village called Guryevka, about eight kilometres farther on. 'There's a good pond there,' said Zharkov, 'you'll be able to fish.' We were taken there by truck.

The first thing we saw on arriving was an unfinished or perhaps half-ruined house and a worn-out old woman taking bricks from a pile and carrying them inside. Nearby a tough-looking man of about fifty was loading some of the bricks on a cart. This was the brigade* foreman Shapovalov, a good-natured and shrewd Ukrainian who was to be our boss. He greeted us in a friendly way but said he could not find lodgings for us. For the time being he took us to his home, saying that his 'old woman' was away for a few days. The house was pretty cheerless, perhaps because the stove was broken – the foreman was now getting the bricks to build

---

* 'Brigade' is the term for a kolkhoz work team.

a new one. Leva whispered to me that we ought to get something to 'treat' him. I gave Leva two roubles, with which he went to the village shop and bought half a litre of vodka; the three of us drank to our arrival, eating pickled cabbage and indigestible bread that had been baked by the foreman's wife and looked like clay. Shapovalov cheered me up by saying that in his village several people had been released halfway through their sentences, adding that it all depended upon his recommendation.

Hearing that a film was to be shown that night at the village recreation room, Leva immediately decided to go, first looking in at the shop and having another good drink. I stayed at the foreman's; for a while I helped him to stack the bricks, then I went for a walk through the village. Late at night Leva and I spread our coats on the floor of Shapovalov's house and lay down to sleep, forgetting all our worries till the next day.

The main problem was where to live. Leva was very anxious for us to stick together and wanted to live with me, but I was firmly against this. During my evening walk I had got into conversation with the watchman outside the cattlesheds. He assured me that no kolkhoznik was likely to rent a room to an exile. In the morning, however, the foreman told me that Vera, the woman in charge of the recreation room, had agreed to let me live in her house. Vera was the old, tired-looking woman I had noticed the day before. Shapovalov also promised to arrange for Leva to lodge with a woman called Aksinya, who lived alone, as soon as she returned from the neighbouring village.

On the first day the foreman let us rest and I was able to look round the village. It lay on two ridges along the sides of a shallow ravine; a stream had once run at the bottom but it had been dammed in the middle to form a pond. In the summer people went there to swim and do their washing. Once there had been more than eighty families in the village, but now there were only thirty-two left. Many of the wooden houses along the sides of the ravine were in ruins, and of some there was hardly any trace left.

Most of the houses were old. Only a few of the more substantial ones had slate roofs; the rest were thatched. The

private plots * were fenced in and fairly large – an acre or
a bit more. Only potatoes were grown on these plots, and a
few onions, carrots and cucumbers next to the houses; the
cucumbers here ripened in August and were large and taste-
less. No fruit or berries were grown, but there were plenty of
wild currants and raspberries in the woods nearby. The fruit
trees that had once grown on the plots had been cut down
and potatoes planted instead, so now the kolkhozniks bought
expensive raspberry jam in the village shop and were very
glad to have it! Two old men in the village kept bees – five
or six hives each; the honey cost two and a half roubles a
litre. Inside the houses the walls and ceilings were white-
washed, and the better ones had painted floors. The windows
were very small and could not be opened. Every house had a
large, vaulted stove, but it was lit only on the days when
bread was baked; on the other days the houses were kept
warm by small portable iron stoves. In summer they were
often taken out into the yard, as they made the house too
hot. In winter they gave a lot of heat but needed constant
attention. The furniture was mostly mass-produced: round
tables, dressers and iron bedsteads, the latter being regarded
as the first sign of prosperity. Only in a few houses had the
old home-made wooden beds and square tables been kept.
One house had a leather divan which everyone else joked
about but secretly envied. No one ever sat on it, however – it
was covered with a clean white cloth and was intended only
for show. As a rule the houses are divided into four rooms
The first is where the cooking is done (and fodder prepared
for the livestock) and the family have their meals. The
second is the bedroom which in the daytime serves a purely
ornamental purpose: bedspreads are put on the beds and
pillows are piled one on top of the other. On the wall, except
in the poorest homes, there was always a cheap print: swans
swimming on a lake in front of a white castle, or a knight
in shining armour riding out of the castle gates while a lady
in a white dress waves goodbye. Such pictures were sold in
Tomsk at ten roubles apiece. Icons hung in almost every

* Private plots: the peasants on collective farms are allowed to
grow vegetables and rear chickens and other livestock on small
plots of land near their houses.

house, but the attitude towards religion was one of utter in-
difference, and the old men would ask: 'Who can tell if God
exists or not?' Only one of them went regularly once a year
to Tomsk to pray in a church – the Krivosheino district had
no church of its own. The houses had outbuildings for livestock, but newly born calves and pigs were kept in the house
itself. Many houses had radio sets, but half of them didn't
work because the strength of the electric current kept changing. Electricity had been brought to the village three years
earlier; two dynamos in Novokrivosheino supplied the current, chiefly at milking times – early in the morning, at midday and at night until eleven o'clock.

The village was built after the construction of the Trans-
Siberian highway; the first settlers came from Byelorussia
(where the land is just as marshy as here) and the local people
still speak with a Byelorussian accent. They started by building individual farmsteads, but after the collectivization of
the land in the early thirties they began to cluster in the
village, which continued to grow until after the war; then
people began to move out so that by now there were only
fifteen able-bodied men left. In the neighbouring village of
Ivanovka, half the peasants came from Latvia; New Istam-
bul, ten kilometres away, was inhabited by Tartars, and a
little farther away there were Poles. The region was thus
thoroughly varied from an ethnic point of view.

The day after my arrival I wrote to my father; we had not
been allowed to write letters during the journey. Even by
airmail the post was very slow and his reply came over two
weeks later. He wrote that he was living in the country and
was often visited by my friends. He had had another stroke
but was better now. He also wrote about what had been
done to try to obtain my release. Immediately after my trial
my friends had hired a good lawyer who, after studying the
documents in the case, had complained to the Moscow City
Prosecutor's office. As I heard later, at that time everybody
believed I had been deported on the initiative of the Frunze
district branch of the KGB who, my lawyer thought, were
surely exceeding their powers by flouting the law like this.
The impression that it was a local initiative was confirmed
by something said in the offices of *Evening Moscow* when

Ginzburg was taken there by a KGB official the day before his unfortunate letter was to appear. The official started boasting that the KGB was using new methods: they no longer imprisoned people or deported them but 're-educated' them instead. Ginzburg interrupted to say he had heard of the recent deportation of a certain Amalrik, and that KGB agents had had a hand in it. The official got excited and rang up various KGB departments. Finally he reached Goncharenko, the KGB officer in charge of the Frunze district, who confirmed the fact of my exile. So my friends concluded that the decision to deport me was a purely local one and that it would therefore not be too difficult to get it changed. I myself was certain, however, that the decision had been taken by the heads of the Moscow KGB and, as it turned out, I was right. My lawyer's application was turned down two months later by the Moscow Prosecutor's office, which gave no reason for its action.

Our next problem in Guryevka was food. The foreman gave Leva and me vouchers for supplies from the kolkhoz storeroom, which duly issued us eggs, sugar, bread, sunflower seed oil, and even a little butter. (All this was available only because the storeroom had to stock provisions for a day-nursery opened during the summer months when the kolkhoz women were all out working in the fields.) I asked when there was likely to be meat. It would be available, they said, only when students and workers came down from Tomsk to help with the harvest. The food was supplied to us against our future earnings in the kolkhoz at market and shop prices. The storekeeper had no idea what these prices were and in her monthly returns to the kolkhoz office she simply recorded the amount we took. Neither did she know the maximum we were entitled to receive, so she gave us as much bread, sugar, oil and eggs as we asked for. We could get milk from the cowsheds, but it was rationed to one litre a day. When I asked if I could have two litres to avoid coming back the next day I was told rudely: 'We know your sort, if we give you two litres today, you won't go to work tomorrow.' The milk was sold to us at twenty kopecks a litre, i.e. at the market price, whereas the State bought it from the kolkhoz at twelve kopecks.

On the evening of the second day I moved to Vera's. She was forty-six, recently widowed, and the mother of four boys and a little girl. The secretary of the Krivosheino Party committee, Pupov, who had been a friend of her husband's, had got her the job of looking after the recreation room in Guryevka. Officially, she also managed the one in Ivanovka, eight kilometres away, but she hardly ever went there. Her salary from the two jobs was seventy roubles a month. Most of her life she had lived in the town, where she worked as a telephone operator, and she felt very uncomfortable in the country. Naturally, she was glad to have a lodger, who could help her with the household chores. The village soviet had given her a ramshackle house that she was now busy repairing; she filled up all the cracks with clay she mixed herself, and a stovemaker was putting in a new stove for her. While I helped to carry sand for the mortar, I talked a bit with the stovemaker. I learned that it was very profitable work. To build a stove took three days and brought in as much as fifty roubles, so he made some three hundred a month, about ten times more than a kolkhoznik. I now realized why so many stovemakers in Russia prefer to work privately and as a result get rounded up as 'parasites'.

I can't say that life with Vera suited me very well. The eldest boy was away at school, but the other four children were constantly fighting and quarrelling among themselves and with their mother. A small, exhausted, irritable woman, she was always shouting at them: 'You wretched vermin, I wish you'd die! Good children die, but not these vermin!' They only laughed at her. When we sat down to a meal and she put out a saucer of sugar with the tea they immediately grabbed it all and ate it; and if she gave me an egg, the smaller children stared at my mouth and whined: 'We want an egg too.'

Leva was much better off at Aksinya's and kept urging me to move in with him, saying that I could live in comfort instead of having to carry buckets of water to the garden and chop firewood on top of a hard day's work. I was almost persuaded that it would perhaps be better to live with Leva than with Vera and the four children, but Vera was highly offended at the idea of my moving. She was very much afraid of having to live alone, particularly in winter, and besides, I think she had some designs on me for the future. Her hopes faded, however, when the village soviet summoned her and asked how it was possible for a woman in her position to allow a 'parasite' into her house. Very upset, she tried to telephone the secretary of the Krivosheino Party committee who alone could give a ruling on such a question. It took her three days to reach him, but meanwhile our relations began to deteriorate and I decided I had to get out. I thought I would move to Aksinya's, but it seemed that, despite her sixty years, she had designs of her own on Leva, so that I would have been very much in the way. When nothing came of her plans, she later asked me several times to move in with her, but by then I had firmly resolved not to lodge with anyone.

The foreman had mentioned that there was a house beyond the pond that had once been inhabited by 'parasites' but was now derelict. I went to look at it and liked it very much. Despite the heat, it was cool inside. It consisted of one large room with three small windows, and a lean-to with a connecting door. It was well protected against the winter winds by a solid, windowless wall facing south. There was no stove, but it had a cooking range made of brick. By way of furniture there was a rickety wooden bed like the one Van Gogh slept on at Arles, and a large table carved all over with names such as Sasha, Vanya and Nadya, not to mention a four-letter word in letters a foot high. The timbers of the house were rotted right through, several windowpanes were missing, and the electricity had been cut off, but it was quite possible to live in it – at any rate in the summer. A remarkable feature was a large outdoor lavatory with a cesspit in the ground adjoining the house. The village had four or five of these at most; people usually just squatted down where they pleased. The foreman helped me to put corrugated iron over the windows where the panes were missing; he promised that the electricity would be switched on as soon as the electrician arrived in the village, so I moved my things from Vera's and settled in. The woman in charge of the storeroom gave me two buckets, a washbasin, two aluminium bowls, a spoon, a fork, an axe, a saw, a saucepan, a kettle, a small frying pan and two sacks sewn together which I filled with hay to make a mattress; the foreman brought over an old iron stove which I put in the yard. I bought a milk-can and a knife in the village shop, and soon settled down to live by myself.

As I learned later, the house had quite a history. It had once been the stables of a farm belonging to a kulak; when collectivization came, it was taken away from him and people were put to live in it. The kulak thereupon cursed all who should ever live in the house, saying they would never be happy. Sure enough, Lyubochka, the woman who moved in, was deserted by her children and, to make matters worse, the devil started visiting her at night. So she left the house and moved to town. The house was then offered to Aksinya – the woman Leva was now living with – when she first came here from another village, but she turned it down. After this, it was always given to exiles, and at the beginning of the sixties there were about fifteen of them living in it. Later some of them landed in prison, others finished their sentences and left, and the rest moved to neighbouring villages or went to live with local women.

One of the exiles who had lived in the house was a seventeen-year-old girl who belonged to a religious sect. She astonished the local inhabitants by refusing to work for the Soviet régime, saying: 'I'll work for any private master, but not for the Communists.' The chairman of the kolkhoz came to reason with her, and the police threatened her, but she kept on saying: 'You can do what you like with my body, but my soul is not subject to you.' At the end of a month she was taken away somewhere else. There were several sectarians at Krivosheino in my time. But as a rule they stayed only until the first elections.* When they refused to vote, as they invariably did, they were sent farther north, down the Ob. For the past two winters the house had been deserted; in the late summer, people from Tomsk who came to help with the harvest were billeted in it.

* i.e. elections to the local soviet. As the author later points out, such elections are only nominal, since they offer no real choice of candidates, let alone of political alternatives. 'Voting' is, however, virtually compulsory, and sectarians boycott them on principle.

There was a persistent rumour in the village that the house was haunted. A woman said she had seen the devil coming out of it; a tractor driver had gone in to it for his midday rest on a hot day and felt someone trying to strangle him – he had only just got away in time. In winter, when I lived there alone, I used to hear someone walking along the windowless south wall behind my bed and clanking chains. One might well have imagined it was the former owner of the stable being marched away in fetters, but in fact there was a smithy not far away where old iron often clanked in the wind.

CHAPTER 14

Work; The Exiles

I HAD already started working in the kolkhoz on the 24th of June. At eight in the morning Shapovalov, the foreman, had come to Vera's to tell me what I had to do. He made a good impression at first meeting. He was called Peter or, as he preferred to pronounce it in the Ukrainian way, Petro, and he was sixty years old. It was said in the village that his father had been a bandit during the Civil War in the Ukraine, and had been deported to Siberia after his son had informed on him, but that when famine came to the Ukraine because of collectivization, Peter had followed his father voluntarily. The collectivization was his most vivid and terrifying memory. He recalled how at the beginning of the thirties a small boy, catching sight of a piglet running along a Ukrainian village street, shouted: 'Grandpa, come and look at this funny animal!' and it had made the old man weep to think that there were now children growing up who had never seen a pig. This story was typical of that time when millions of peasants starved to death. He told me how thousands of people were put in prison, and kept without food or water, so that hundreds died in the police cells without ever coming to trial.

Shapovalov had hardly settled in Guryevka when collectivization began in Siberia as well; there was nowhere farther he could go. But the shrewd Ukrainian kept his wits about him. He worked in the kolkhoz, first as a blacksmith, then as storekeeper, and after the war he was made chairman on the strength of his war service. In those days the kolkhoz was small: there was only one village in it. The local people had very bad memories of Shapovalov's days as chairman and one old man said it was because of his brutality that so many people had left Guryevka. But I think it was due more to the cruelty of the times – in the post-war years the

peasants were paid nothing for their work on the kolkhoz
fields and were obliged to pay a huge tax on their private
crops. Two words from that period still remembered with
terror by the collective farmers are 'tax' and 'lumber'. Each
winter the kolkhoz was obliged to send all its able-bodied
men to cut wood at the nearest lumber camp. They lived
behind barbed wire, like common prisoners, and if they tried
to escape they were sent to forced-labour camps for several
years. Only in the spring were they released for work in the
kolkhoz, and then their place was taken by all the unmarried
and childless women for the job of floating the logs down
the river. It was Shapovalov's task as chairman to supply
the labour for the lumber camps. At the beginning of each
winter he was waylaid and beaten up several times, but
nobody ever got out of this corvée until it was abolished
after Stalin's death. When the collective farms were
increased in size, Shapovalov remained as foreman in
Guryevka and people said that his character improved. Some
five years before I arrived he had joined the Party, of which
he was very proud.

My first task was to dig pits and put in supports for the
poles that carried the electric cable from Novokrivosheino
to Guryevka; many of them were leaning over and threatened
to fall down. They had to be pulled out of the ground and
the supports fastened to them with wire. At the moment,
however, there was no wire. The foreman took me to a
large ploughed field outside the village – the row of poles ran
down the middle of it – and gave me a spade and a measuring
rod: I was supposed to dig to a depth of nearly five feet.
The soil was exceptionally hard; two feet below the surface
it was solid clay; besides, I had no experience of digging, let
alone skill at it. It was unbearably hot and there were clouds
of midges; at the bottom of the pit it was cooler, but there
were still more midges. (As I mentioned, the whole of
western Siberia is an enormous marsh.) By evening my face
was all swollen and the midges made it impossible for me
to relieve myself until it occurred to me to do so from the
top of a tall birch tree where there were fewer of them. I dug
one pit and then just managed to walk to a wood at the edge
of the field where I could rest a little in the shade and light

a fire to keep the midges away. But the moment I sat down huge Siberian ants started crawling all over me; they stung even more painfully than the midges. That first day I dug three pits, cheating a little by making them slightly shallower than they were supposed to be, and one of Vera's sons helped me to fix the supports; after that it was an easy job to fill in the pit. Later on, in good soil, I managed to dig four pits in as many hours. It amazed me that the blocks of wood which served as supports had not been treated to prevent'them from rotting. I soon realized that this was the usual style of work on collective farms: who cared if the poles fell down in a couple of years as long as they stood up today!

A day or two later the foreman sent Leva to work with me; until then he had been working on a silage pit. We each started digging, but Leva soon came over to me and, while I got on with the job, complained of the heat, the hard work and of having to do it for 'ticks'. He just managed to finish one pit by the evening and he asked me not to do more myself out of 'solidarity'.

It must be said that his grievances were well founded. The expression 'to work for ticks' has been current ever since the establishment of the kolkhoz system. The point is that the pay for obligatory work on a kolkhoz is calculated not in money but in 'labour-days', an arbitrarily defined unit. The half-literate accountants used to put down 'ticks' corresponding to the number of 'labour-days' earned. Nowadays figures are put down instead of ticks, but the system is basically the same.

At the end of the year the amount set aside as the kolkhoz wages fund in cash and farm products is divided between the kolkhozniks according to the number of 'labour-days' they have earned. In earlier times no cash was paid at all: each kolkhoznik got, say, half a kilo of potatoes or two hundred grams of grain for every 'labour-day'. This meant that he had to be credited with five hundred 'labour-days' by the end of the year to get a sack of grain or three sacks of potatoes for his year's work. Three years ago our kolkhoz had gone over to the system of paying cash advances on the year's earnings. These are based on an estimate of what the year's output is likely to be and each month the kolkhoz-nik receives in cash half the amount due to him for the previous month. The accounts are made up at the end of the year when any balance due is paid in cash and in kind. According to the previous year's plan, for instance, each 'labour-day' was calculated to be worth sixty kopecks and a kilogram of grain. Every month the kolkhoznik received an advance of thirty kopecks per 'labour-day', of which he earned an average of forty to sixty a month in summer and twenty to thirty in winter (slightly more if he worked with the livestock). But since actual output fell short of the estimate for the year, they received a balance of only fifteen kopecks (instead of thirty) per 'labour-day'; the estimated kilogram of grain per 'labour-day' they received in full, and this is most important for the peasants as they need it not only for baking bread but also for feeding their private holdings of livestock. Any grain left over could be sold in the market at Krivosheino, where it fetched twenty-five to thirty-five kopecks the kilo, compared with the State's price to the kolkhoz of twelve kopecks.

This year the advance was again thirty kopecks per 'labour-day' – enough to buy a litre of milk and one egg from the kolkhoz stores. In July, when I took no days off, I earned sixty 'labour-days' and in August forty; on the average this was what all the others earned as well. It was very difficult to live on this pay. One day I bought a kilo of butter for three roubles sixty kopecks – the advance on twelve 'labour-days'. This meant that I had worked a ten-hour day for almost a week to buy one kilo of butter. As we got no meat and were allowed only one litre of milk a day, butter was quite essential to keep up our strength. My daily litre of milk cost me six roubles a month, i.e. between a third and a half of my monthly earnings, but in the heat it was only too easy to drink it all up at one go. While supplies in the kolkhoz storeroom lasted we exiles took as much as we needed on credit, thus getting more and more deeply into debt. Even at the end of the year, when we were paid the rest of our money and got grain that we could sell, we were still unable to settle with the kolkhoz. In the old days, if anyone was released halfway through his sentence, debts of up to a hundred roubles were simply cancelled, but now this practice had been abolished. Our difficulties were increased by the fact that prices are higher in these remote areas. For industrial workers this is compensated for by correspondingly higher wages, but for agricultural workers there is no such bonus. In Moscow a bottle of vodka costs two roubles seventy-five kopecks, but in Guryevka you pay thirty kopecks more; sugar costs fifteen per cent more in Guryevka than in Moscow. The same is true of all foodstuffs not locally produced. Although nearly all the kolkhozniks kept livestock, the price of meat was very high in the Guryevka district: a kilo of mutton costs as much as three roubles in the summer, bacon fat four roubles and about a rouble less in the winter. It wasn't easy to manage on fifteen roubles a month, unless one had a private plot.

The simplest solution for an exile was to find a local woman and live with her. This was strongly encouraged by the police who realized that the exiles were not getting a living wage on the collective farms. There were four exiles in the village, beside Leva and myself, and they had all 'married' in this way. I got to know one of them, Fedya, the day I started work. He was fifty and had been exiled as a 'parasite' for five years, of which he had already served two. Quickly sizing things up, he moved in with a local woman, Katya; she was a hopeless drunkard with two daughters of school age, but she had her own house, a cow and some piglets. In winter Fedya worked on the kolkhoz and in summer he herded the cattle that the peasants kept on their private plots: it had been Katya's job to do this, but she now handed it over to Fedya. I was surprised at how little a herdsman was paid: a rouble a month for each cow, forty kopecks for a sheep plus a little milk and grain – roughly sixty roubles a month altogether. In European Russia a herdsman in charge of a much smaller herd gets a hundred and fifty roubles and all his meals from the owners of the cattle. But Fedya was satisfied with what he got – it was more than he would have earned by working for the kolkhoz alone.

Another 'parasite' from Krasnodar, Sanka, about thirty years old, was in charge of the calves owned by the kolkhoz. He lived with one of the dairywomen, the forty-year-old

Nadya Kabanov who was as big-boned as a work-horse and had two teenage children.

Another exile, Lenka, also about thirty, a tall youth, curly-headed like a gypsy, had served ten years in camps for banditry; he was sentenced immediately after leaving an orphanage and was now doing his additional two years of exile. The woman he lived with was ten years older, had two children and a very domineering character. Lenka was a stableman, but he never did a stroke of work; the horses wandered around the village like tourists. In August he came to the end of his sentence, had a row with his mistress and left. The woman was upset, of course, but she was soon going around saying: 'Why should I worry? I won't be alone for long, Khrushchev will send us some more "parasites".'

Luckily for me, digging pits turned out to be a profitable job; I was credited with one and a half 'labour-days' for every one I dug. Altogether, during June and July I earned seventy 'labour-days'. In spite of the shortage of labour on the farm endless effort went into cutting the supporting blocks of wood and bringing them to the field. When they were at last ready and six had been fastened to the poles, we ran out of wire, and the whole business was dropped; neither that summer nor the next did anyone go near the poles again. Fortunately none fell down although they leaned more heavily than the Tower of Pisa. This way of working is very typical of the kolkhozes: a tremendous expenditure of energy on a job never finished. To dig the pits using nothing but a spade was very hard, a hand drill would have made it ten times easier and quicker. There was a drill that needed repairing, but nobody could be spared for the job at the height of the harvest (though people were diverted to other, less important work). Then, nobody bothered to treat the supports to prevent their rotting ('What's the point? If these rot we'll put others in.') In the end all the work was wasted anyway because there was no wire!

Several years previously they had started building a garage for tractors in Guryevka; it was still standing unfinished, and the timber was gradually pilfered for firewood. The summer I arrived the foundations were laid for a day-

nursery, but it was still unfinished a year later and looked as
if it would suffer the same fate as the garage. Leaving the
nursery unfinished, the kolkhoz next started building a new
barn. By the following summer this too was unfinished, yet
next door to it a space was already being cleared for a drying shed. I imagine these things happen mainly because
labour is paid so little that nobody thinks it worth economizing. There is also perhaps the mentality of the kolkhoznik:
he has ceased to be a peasant but has not become a labourer,
and hence cares nothing about what happens to the results
of his work. Finally, though the kolkhoz is a big unit, the
methods of running it are more appropriate to a small family
farm: things needing attention are done in the same spirit
as that in which a fence is mended on a smallholding.

My next job was preparing silage. In the morning Leva
and I and about fifteen women, girls and boys gathered in
front of the village shop. A tractor with a cart attached to it
took us some five kilometres into the forest; there, in a clearing too small for a reaping machine to manoeuvre in, the
women cut the grass for silage by hand. The girls then raked
the cut grass together into heaps, a truck drove up and the
boys used pitchforks to throw the grass on top, where one of
them trampled it down. We loaded four or five trucks a day,
working from nine in the morning till ten in the evening
with a two-hour break for the midday meal. There were no
days off. Sunday was counted as a 'voluntary' workday. It
was assumed that on Sundays we worked not out of a sense
of duty, but out of sheer enthusiasm. 'Labour-days' were
credited according to the number of loads and averaged out
at two a day per person, but there were endless squabbles
about who had done most of the work. Leva and I were
always in trouble because however hard we tried we were
not as quick as the villagers who were used to this work
since childhood. One truck counted as a ton load but in
reality it held more. This was a typical example of how the
kolkhoz officials were always trying to keep down our earnings, pitifully small as they already were.

The day I started on this job I walked behind the women
raking up the hay, but I could soon scarcely see anything in
front of me: clouds of midges got into my eyes, my mouth

and my nose, so that I raked with one hand and fought off midges with the other. No remedies against them were supplied or could be bought. Gradually I somehow got used to them, but I still could not keep up with the women; they even took pity on me and raked a few heaps of hay for me themselves. After a couple of days I changed over to loading; this was heavier work but it required less skill. It amazed me that work which a tractor could have finished off in a day was done by hand and took two or three weeks. If the kolkhoz had possessed a small mechanical mower, a lot of labour would immediately have been saved. But why buy a mower when labour costs nothing? The lack of small labour-saving devices is a misfortune for the villagers which no amount of combines or heavy tractors can remedy. Yet the kolkhozniks or rather the kolkhoz authorities appear unwilling to simplify their work even by such small mechanical gadgets as could be made in the kolkhoz repair shop.

Haymaking started in mid-July and for this mechanical mowers, both tractor and horse-drawn, were used. Young boys cut and raked the hay, using horse-drawn rakes. Leva and I helped to heap it up into piles. Here again we were no match for the women. By midday my back ached unbearably and in the evening, after ten hours of unfamiliar work, I felt as if I had been pounded all over. Eventually the piles we had made were gathered together into haystacks for the winter. When the stacks were high enough they were hauled off by tractor and set up in a row somewhere near the village. The hardest part of all was 'topping up' the stacks. This was done by throwing up hay with long pitchforks while a woman on top built it up into a cone. Much of this very laborious process of stacking could also much more easily have been done by machines.

Owing to my lack of experience, I had a small accident and I had to spend two days in bed before I could walk again. I was so tired that I slept almost the whole time.

After this I got the job of cleaning and repairing the barn used for drying and storing grain. Inside was an enormous drying drum that was heated by birch logs. The barn itself was so ramshackle that it was in danger of collapsing –

indeed, as I have already mentioned, the following summer other building projects were abandoned in order to put up a new one. Most of the grain was sent straight to the State granaries, but seed grain and grain meant for distribution to the kolkhozniks was dried and stored on the spot. Most of the work in the barn was done by women and by students sent from Tomsk. The drier was operated by the kolkhoz blacksmith and another man who was too lazy to keep up the necessary temperature in the drum so that the grain soon began to rot. Several times I drove with our grain truck to the State granary, twenty-five kilometres away. Our grain was of very poor quality and was mixed with grass, but it was nevertheless accepted. Trucks from other collective farms were turned away, so ours was evidently not the worst!

CHAPTER 15

The Kolkhozniks

GRADUALLY I became familiar with life on the kolkhoz. I learned, for instance, that it was made up of four work teams ('brigades' as they are called) – one in each of the four villages of which the kolkhoz consisted. The brigade in Guryevka, which worked under the overall direction of Shapovalov, was a so-called 'complex' one subdivided into three sections: the field workers (who were directly responsible to Shapovalov), the drivers and mechanics (who had their own foreman) and the cattle hands (herdsmen, milkmaids, etc.).

The field workers were paid least of all, especially in winter; but, except during sowing and harvesting, they had more free time than the others. The drivers (of trucks, tractors and combines) and the mechanics are the aristocracy of the collective farms. In Guryevka their monthly cash advances are paid in full – sixty (instead of thirty) kopecks per 'labour-day' – and in the general settlement at the end of the year they received two kilos of grain per 'labour-day', while everybody else got only one. As a result, during the sowing and harvesting seasons their earnings are relatively high – sometimes over one hundred roubles a month. But in winter they make only a fourth or fifth of this amount – which is why fewer people want to became tractor-drivers nowadays. Of the fifteen able-bodied men in the village, ten belonged to this 'aristocracy': eight drivers, the blacksmith, and the man in charge of the milking machinery. Of the five others, one, Shapovalov, was foreman of the brigade, two were herdsmen, and one was a bookkeeper whose job was to calculate and keep a record of everybody's earnings. In summer the cattle were looked after mostly by women, except for the two herdsmen and the man who operated the milking machinery, but in winter men were employed to clean the cowsheds and cart fodder, etc. Work with the livestock was much better paid than field work, and in winter it was even several times more lucrative than being a driver or a mechanic. The cowsheds were managed by a wily, energetic woman of forty whom everybody called Steshka.

Although earnings on the kolkhozes have gone up in recent years, they are still not enough to live on, and, as before, the peasants rely chiefly on their private plots. They all keep a cow or two and some sheep. The sheep are killed for meat and also provide very poor-quality wool from which the kolkhozniks make socks and mittens. If a kolkhoz cow ceases to give milk, it will occasionally be sold to an individual member of the kolkhoz at a low price, though the normal price is close to five hundred roubles. Bulls can be owned only by the kolkhoz, but no charge is made for serving privately-owned cows. Calves are usually reared for sale to the State or, much more rarely, in the market. Pigs are bred for their lard; a two-week-old piglet costs ten roubles. Nearly everyone kept poultry; eggs could be sold to the State at eight or nine kopecks each.

Unlike the peasants of Central Russia, the peasants of Guryevka had no great problem about feeding their livestock. When the kolkhoz had finished haymaking, the kolkhozniks were allowed to cut hay for themselves. The only problem was to find the time. The milkmaids, especially the unmarried ones, did not always manage to cut enough hay for themselves before winter came, but it was always possible to buy some in winter; and the grain they received at the end of the year, as well as the potatoes they grew on their plots, provided them with enough fodder for their pigs and hens.

As I was later to see, things are very different in the Moscow region. The kolkhozniks are no longer forbidden to keep cattle and they are not taxed, but the days of Stalin are remembered almost with nostalgia. The taxes may have been crushing and the peasants paid nothing for their work on the kolkhoz, but at least they had enough fodder for their own livestock. Thus, while the kolkhoznik is no longer forced to deliver eggs to the State, he needs two hundred of them to buy a hundredweight of fodder. In a village on the Oka where I went to stay after my exile there were only five cows among thirty households, and not everybody was able to keep pigs. In this respect, therefore, the kolkhozniks are much better off in Siberia.

The peasants work on their private plots just as inefficiently as they do in the kolkhoz, and they haven't the slightest idea of how much an egg, a litre of milk, or a kilo of pork costs them to produce. Since they don't pay money for them, they have the illusion of getting them for nothing. They put the value of their own work just as low as does the kolkhoz or the State. They don't starve but they are, as it were, slaves to their own livestock. The moment they have finished their work on the kolkhoz they rush home to milk the cow, feed the pig or tend the potatoes they are growing for fodder.

They often complained about their life, the hard work and the hated 'ticks'. But when I asked them how they would like to live, they would reply: 'What other life is there? We've forgotten how it was without those ticks.' I was interested to know what those who still remembered private farming thought of the kolkhoz system. A few were full of praise for the days when 'each man was his own master'. Others said that work on the kolkhoz was easier and also used the curious argument that they no longer had to keep the Church fasts. All, however, were agreed that it was impossible to return to the past: the peasants wouldn't want to go back to individual farming and, what is more, wouldn't know how to do it. Stories were told about how the rich peasants lived before collectivization – how, for instance, they kept bees on a large scale but never tasted the honey themselves because they sent it all to market; and how their houses were almost bare of furniture, whereas now even the poorest peasant was eager to buy an iron bedstead and a radio. The mentality of the peasants has evidently been quite revolutionized by the fact of not being their own masters and the general precariousness of their situation: what little they have can so easily be taken away. Now that they are allowed to keep their own livestock, receive payment in grain and money for their work, and no longer have to pay taxes on their private lots (not to mention the abolition of obligatory labour service in the lumber camps), the collective farmers say they are much better off. Yet in the same breath they complain of the hard work and the low pay.

I think that these are people with whom you can do anything. If tomorrow the authorities decided, out of some mysterious political or economic consideration, to go back to individual farming, each man would meekly accept his share of land and start to sow wheat or flax on it; but if the Government decided to abolish private plots and private houses, herding the peasants into barracks and feeding them in mess halls, this too could be done without the slightest difficulty. In other words, the authorities are free to experiment as they wish; wages can be raised or lowered, private livestock can be allowed or forbidden. But in my opinion nothing will come of any such experiments unless the kolkhozniks learn to respect themselves and stop allowing themselves to be played around with – only then will they start to work properly

The present kolkhoz system is based, in effect, on forced labour, and the peasants are totally without rights. They have no right to move except to another kolkhoz; their identity papers are kept at the kolkhoz office and never handed to them. Occasionally a sick man, a cripple, or a woman on her own who can no longer work is allowed to leave. For young people there are only two ways out of the kolkhoz: not to return home after military service (this is how most of them escape) or to go and study – those who have finished school and have managed to get into technical colleges are given their identity papers.

Nor do the peasants have any rights in administering the farm: they have no say whatever in the so-called 'election' of the chairman, the merging or separation of neighbouring kolkhozes, the fixing of their rates of pay, or anything whatever. They are subject to a system of prohibitions and monetary fines, and they cannot sue the farm in case of a dispute. Just as the kolkhoznik knows that he is not allowed to leave the farm, so he also knows that he will not be expelled, however badly he works. He may be transferred to another job, or he may be fined, but he has so little money anyway that this makes little sense – paupers do not worry about fines. Moreover, fines are imposed so unjustly that far from raising the peasant's sense of responsibility, they destroy whatever remains of it.

Very few families in Guryevka were well-to-do by kolkhoz standards, and these were mostly the families of tractor-drivers. The worst off were women without husbands, who accounted for nearly half the village. Eight of them lived with their children, the others were old and their children had left. Some were widows or divorced, and some had never married – this was because so many men of their generation had been killed in the war. If they had children, they had been fathered by exiles, or by local officials who in the days of Stalin paid for their favours by lowering their taxes or exempting them from work in the lumber camps. Because abortions are now allowed, women under forty have fewer children than used to be the case in the villages, where it was customary to have three or four. One old man in Guryevka told me he had twelve children, but that now the women went to the district hospital in Krivosheino where their unborn babies were, as he put it, 'scraped out with a poker'. Trips to Krivosheino for an abortion could never be concealed and were always the subject of much gossip. Medical service in Guryevka was limited to a weekly visit (in winter it was only monthly) by a young nurse from a neighbouring village. People preferred to be treated by her rather than go to the district hospital, about which all kinds of horror stories were told: somebody, for instance, swore he had seen a patient suspended by hooks from the ceiling to be roasted by the doctors on a slow fire. Another story was that the doctors took your blood and sold it for large sums until you eventually died. All this was explained by the fact that some of the doctors were 'not Russian' – evidently an echo of the rumours deliberately spread in the last years of Stalin's rule that Jewish doctors killed off their patients. Despite these stories, however, all the kolkhozniks went to the hospital if there was anything seriously wrong with them.

Regardless of the many illegitimate children and the frequent affairs with exiles, the village had its own firm moral standards which the women did not dare to break. It was not done, for instance, for a woman to go into a man's house, whether he was a local or an exile. 'Manka,' I once said to one of the milkmaids passing my door, 'come inside!' 'I certainly won't.' 'Why not?' 'I know your tricks,' said Manka, a woman of forty with two illegitimate children. She might have had no objection to my visiting her at home, but she lived with her sister.

The children were brought up very strangely, as though they were midget adults and from early childhood they were initiated into all the most intimate problems of the grown-ups. Everybody used filthy language – neither men nor women could say a sentence without it – and nearly all of them swore in front of their children, whether they were three or sixteen years old. You would hear a boy of four who had only just learned to speak using the same choice expressions as an elderly drunk. No one stopped him. Teenage girls also used the same remarkably coarse language.

The village had two institutions for children: a day-nursery and a primary school. The nursery was for children of pre-school age and was opened only during the harvest. It was run by a children's nurse and a matron who also cooked for them. The matron that year was a little woman of fifty, Auntie Prosa, who before that had looked after the calves – work which she much preferred to caring for children. However, she was on the whole a decent woman and never used bad language in front of her charges. The nurse was Polya, a hunch-backed woman of sixty who never stopped cursing the children in a thin, high-pitched voice. In winter she sometimes looked after the children of the milk-maids while they were busy with the cows. The nursery was housed next door to the recreation room, in what had been the kolkhoz office before Guryevka was merged with the neighbouring farms.

The four-form primary school started in September. It had twenty pupils and one tall thin teacher in his forties who held a degree from a technical college and, apart from Shapovalov, was the only other Party member in the village. For a short season in winter, he was assisted by a girl who had just finished the ten-year school in Krivosheino. Most of the children learned very slowly and were often kept behind in their class for an extra year, or sometimes three or four. About two-thirds of those who finished primary school went on to the eight-year school in Novokrivosheino where there was also a boarding school. But some left after a short while and returned home. The ten-year school, which also took boarders, was in Krivosheino, but only one little girl from Guryevka went there.

The peasants disliked the teacher – not because he was a bad teacher or a bad man, but because he was outside the system of compulsion within which they themselves were confined. They resented the fact that his work was lighter than theirs, that he was paid more for it and yet also, like them, had his private plot as well. For the same reason they disliked his wife, who managed the village shop, and Vera who ran the recreation room. In general the attitude towards 'city people' was unconsciously resentful, the peasants feeling that in the cities people just had a good time, while the kolkhozniks waded around in muck all day long – it was a kind of inferiority complex.

Nearly all the villagers were related, but they quarrelled ceaselessly among themselves, keeping a close eye on each other's earnings and resenting one another's good fortune more than their own setbacks. They did not like the exiles either, but their attitude to them was more one of contempt, though they often said that they themselves were little more than 'exiles for life' here. The exiles were regarded not only as outsiders, but also as people whose lives were even more degraded than theirs and who had even fewer rights; if so far the kolkhozniks had been the lowest form of life in the Soviet social scale, they now found that there were people even worse off than themselves; used to regarding the kolkhoz chairman almost as a god on earth and incapable of imagining anything higher than the district authorities, they now had people they could look down on.

'Parasites' are indeed in the worst position of all. They are assigned to jobs that nobody else wants, and they can easily get a couple of years added to their term of exile just for taking three days off work; they didn't even have to be consecutive days – it was enough to take one off this week, another in a month and a third a year later. If the foreman reported this to the chairman there was every chance of the police being informed and of a trial being held. In summer there were no days off in the kolkhoz, and in the cowsheds, where most of the exiles worked, there were none in winter either. To work without respite for several years on end is truly unbearable, and the peasants complained of this as much as the exiles. Theoretically, everybody was supposed to get one day off a week and two weeks' holiday a year, but instead of this the peasants were given a minimal addition to their pay – as I remember, it was around a fifth of a 'labour-day' for a Sunday. They did, however, get a few days after the sowing season and after haymaking to enable them to plant potatoes on their private plots and cut hay for their own livestock. In winter, as I have already said, there was an actual shortage of work: the field workers had little to do and got every Sunday off, and the drivers were completely idle unless they helped to bring in silage. But none of this applied to the cowsheds, where many of the milkmaids worked without a holiday for years on end – only on some very rare occasion would a neighbour replace them for a couple of days. This was why nobody wanted to work with the cattle, in spite of the high earnings.

Strange as it may seem, the exiles had a slightly better chance of getting a holiday than the kolkhozniks. If a 'parasite' had worked for two years and had a faultless record, he could get a month's vacation in winter and spend it at home – but only if he was not working in the cattlesheds. These, however, were very exceptional cases, and I myself met no one to whom it had happened. Every exile hoped for the remission of half his term for good conduct. As a result, he was more dependent than anyone else on the local authorities, since his release would be granted not so much as a reward for good work as for his good relations with his masters: the foreman, the chairman, the commandant, the district police chief and the local judge on whom the final decision depended. If the 'parasite' had annoyed any one of them, he could say goodbye to his chance of a remission. Even those who got their release could not leave during the busy season and had to stay on till it was over.

The peasants' life was remarkably dull; all their free time was spent working on their private plots. Their main distraction was drink, especially in winter, when they drank nearly every day. Ordinary vodka bought in the village was kept for special occasions; they usually drank the home-distilled variety. Made from rye, this is singularly unpleasant to the taste, muddy green in colour and about 70° proof. Not every villager had his own still. In preparation for a holiday or to repay a neighbour for some good turn people borrowed a still from someone and made an extra supply. Homemade beer, on the other hand, was brewed by everybody and all year round. Boiled water is poured into a bucket, three – or if the brewer is mean, two – kilograms of sugar are added; yeast is put in when the water has cooled, and sometimes tea for colouring and hops for taste. Hops are always added if the beer is going to be offered to guests, so they should get drunk quickly and drink less: a characteristic feature of village hospitality. The beer must ferment for at least three or four days and after that it still goes on getting stronger and stronger. Three mugs of beer are enough to knock a man out, so the peasant finds it cheaper to brew a bucketful of beer than to buy half a litre of vodka in the shop. Illicit brewing is an offence punishable at the very least by a fine of one hundred roubles but it can also lead to forced labour for several years. Many of the villagers had paid fines, and one had spent a year in camp, but this deterred no one.

While the older people drank, the teenagers went to the recreation room. In summer there was dancing almost every evening, especially when students arrived from Tomsk to help with the harvest, and once a week there was a film show. The films and the projector had to be brought from Krivosheino by two mechanics on motor-cycles; in winter there was nothing but the cinema, and in spring and autumn, when the roads turned to mud, there was nothing at all. The films were old and after each reel the lights went on while the projector was reloaded. Older people sometimes went to see them too and occasionally made comments. One day, when a film about the horrors of daily life under the Emir of Bokhara was being shown, one old man said to me with interest: 'That's about the old days when everyone was his own master.' The film was followed by dancing, but there was no gramophone and the local accordion player knew only three tunes – the waltz, the Charleston and a local folk dance accompanied by clapping and stamping of heels. The recreation room was not very large; the four benches around the walls were moved into the middle for film shows. The village women competed for the work of cleaning the place, as it paid twenty-six roubles and released them from farm work.

My friend Vera, who was in charge of the recreation room, had little to do with arranging entertainment and she was, indeed, hardly ever there. Her job was to write slogans on posters, such as 'Tractor drivers! Bring the harvest in on time and without waste!' These texts were provided by the district Party committee and she wrote them in chalk on strips of red material that she hung up in various places in the village for the edification of the kolkhozniks. It was also her duty to issue bulletins written on special sheets of paper with a letterhead design which showed a peasant boy and girl in profile with a flying sputnik in the background. If the foreman told her that X and Y had worked well during the haymaking, she wrote: 'Honour and glory to collective farmers X and Y who have worked well at bringing in the hay.' Or if he said that such and such a herdsman had worked badly and should be criticized, she wrote 'So and so is bad at his job and is too fond of vodka.' All the names and facts were invariably mixed up, and there were many grammatical errors.

Another recreation room of a sort, chiefly for the women, was the village shop, where the customers exchanged the latest gossip – who had quarrelled with whom, and what people's drinking habits were. This, for some reason, aroused great interest and the amounts consumed were discussed in detail. The shopkeeper was particularly well informed, since she knew who had bought how many bottles of vodka, and how much wine and sugar.

To the credit of Siberia, it must be said that every village there had its own shop – presumably because of the great distances between places. Our shop was open in the morning and in the evening when the villagers were not working.

It sold vodka, wine, sugar, grain, biscuits, sweets, vegetable oil, tinned food, household utensils and a small selection of men and women's clothes; occasionally bicycles and pieces of furniture could be obtained on order. Thanks to the efficiency of our shopkeeper, we were well supplied by village standards.

CHAPTER 16

The Students

BUILDERS, carpenters, stovemakers and suchlike who seek private employment are labelled 'parasites' and are exiled, jailed and in general harshly dealt with by the authorities. But this creates a problem for poor collective farms like Guryevka, which cannot afford to maintain their own building teams. A strange solution has been adopted: during the summer vacation students are recruited for the work and sent out to the collective farms where they work under contract, like the private builders denounced as 'parasites', though they are paid a little less. The students rarely have any experience and their work is always of very poor quality: the cattleshed they had built in Malinovka fell down as soon as an attempt was made to use it, crushing one milk-maid to death and injuring several others. This was not the students' fault but that of the system by which unskilled labour is employed, building plans are made without regard to local conditions and the wrong materials are provided (even so, it is a devil of a job to find them). I watched the students building the new day-nursery. They did their best, but the only ones who knew their job were their team leader, an unpleasant red-haired fellow who had grown up in a village where he had learned carpentry, and another student from Eastern Siberia. Most of them had come out to Guryevka under pressure from the Komsomol.* One of them did nothing at all, just idly tapped his axe, while the rest appeared to work with a will, even though clumsily and unproductively. It took them a month to put up the wooden frame.

The idea of employing students and giving them a chance to earn something extra is all very well. But it is no solution for the urgent building problem on the collective farms.

* Young Communist Youth organization.

Guryevka alone needed a day-nursery, a recreation room, a grain drier, barns, a cattleshed, a garage and several new houses for the villagers. There were four other villages like Guryevka in the kolkhoz, and there are many thousands of similar kolkhozes throughout the country. In lots of them things are even worse – to the extent that the peasants are forced to keep the kolkhoz cattle in their own homes. All this while skilled carpenters, bricklayers and masons get jobs as watchmen for fear of being exiled as 'parasites' if they take jobs as private individuals! It must also be said that if students are to be employed, their services could be used much more wisely: those from technical colleges could help in the task of mechanization, while those studying social sciences could do research on village conditions, thus helping to bring about a scientific approach to the reform of agriculture. If a man has spent three or four years of his life in college, it would seem more sensible to use him for his brainpower rather than as a manual worker.

Ten students who arrived in mid-July to build the nursery, together with a woman student to cook for them, were billeted in my house. Aged between twenty and twenty-four, they were in their fourth year at the Tomsk Electronics Institute, students from which – as I gathered from its initial letters carved on my table – had been to Guryevka before. They were to stay until the 2nd of August. They at once shared out their chores: two were assigned to help the cook, carry water and chop wood for the stove; I brought milk for them every day from the farm. I had no choice but to eat with them, since there was only one stove for cooking, and they used my saucepan, frying pan and kettle. Under their contract with the farm they were each paid close to one hundred and fifty roubles, so they ate well, buying all they needed in the way of meat, eggs and margarine from the village shop. Trying to keep pace with them, I was soon up to my neck in debt to the kolkhoz. Even so, I was unable to contribute my fair share and found myself living partly at their expense. I remember the meals we took at a long table placed outside the house, and our majestic fair-haired cook – she was the tallest among us – doling out *kasha* into our bowls.

At the end of July some fifteen men arrived from a factory in Tomsk. They were used on various jobs, such as digging pits. Like the collective farmers, they were paid by 'labour-days', but they received a guaranteed minimum of ninety kopecks a day. They too bought their supplies from the shop and by the end of their stay had no cash left to take home with them, though they were not in debt either. They had been sent at an odd time, between haymaking and harvesting, so they had little to do. I am not sure what economic sense it makes to send factory workers out to the collective farms in summer and autumn.

The students undertook privately to build a small shed for one of the tractor drivers and in return he allowed them to use his bathhouse once a week. I went with them, and this was my first experience of a Siberian bath, until then I had washed in the lake. The bathhouse was a small timber hut with a stove, just like the one which, according to the ancient Russian chronicle, so astonished the Apostle Andrew in Novgorod. It was a so-called 'black' bathhouse (i.e. without a chimney) and its walls were covered with soot, so one had to be careful not to come out dirtier than when one went in. You could steam yourself on a ledge fixed close to the ceiling on one of the walls. To make the bath birch logs are lit several hours beforehand in the stove; pieces of iron are put in with the logs and become red hot. When the bathhouse is properly heated, it is ventilated to let out the fumes, and then completely closed, except for a small window high up in the wall to let in the light. The red-hot pieces of iron are thrown into a bucket of water which immediately turns to steam and fills the bathhouse. From time to time hot water is splashed over the red-hot stove. The bathers lie on the ledge and slap themselves with sprays of birch twigs to open up the pores. The steam heat is so intense that a novice cannot stand it for very long. The first time I ran out into the fresh air several times before I could start washing. It is very bracing, after steaming yourself, to dive into the cold water of a pond, or in winter to roll in the snow. After the bath you feel as if you were newly born.

Owing to the trouble I have already described with the poles that bore the electric cable, power was switched off throughout the village for a month. When it came on again (the poles, incidentally, were never fixed to the supports for which I had dug pits), the students installed electricity in our house. Meanwhile we spent the evenings by the light of an oil lamp, several of us usually playing cards. One evening we had an argument which I am sure would have been impossible five or six years earlier, when I was a student; no one would even have dared to raise the question then. We argued about which was better·: socialism or capitalism, and which system created the best conditions for economic development? I said that within certain limits free private enterprise was much more favourable to progress than a system of strict regimentation from above. Two or three of the students firmly contradicted me; others were very confused in what they said – they were evidently extremely interested in the problem but had no answer of their own to it. Not that I had one myself. I stood up for capitalism only because someone had to take its side in the argument. One student, who was not in the least hostile to socialism as such, attacked the Communists, saying that if they were deprived of their privileges there would be 'less stink'. This infuriated the only Communist in the group. We also talked about forced labour. Although the students were well disposed towards me personally, the majority thought it right to deport 'parasites' on the ground that if a man won't work he must be forced to. Some of the students held almost openly Stalinist views and stressed at every point that Stalin had been an outstanding man, unlike Khrushchev or our present rulers.

Still more Stalinist were the ten students – five boys and five girls – who arrived to help with the harvest in September and were also lodged in my house. They came from various villages and small towns in Siberia and were only in their first year at the medical school in Tomsk; they were thus quite new to student life and had preserved intact the militant provincialism of their last year at school. I heard them say that Khrushchev had 'spoilt the people', so that nobody worked properly any more, and that a strong man like Stalin was needed to keep everyone in hand. Unfortunately, the idea that nothing can be achieved except by force and coercion is deeply rooted in the Soviet people. Yet some of them, who had not only studied but also worked, cursed the conditions in the factories, the low pay and the bad housing. But for all this they blamed the Jews who, they said, had taken the best jobs. Nearly all the students in this group were anti-Semites (of a most disagreeable Ukrainian variety, furthermore). I don't know about the first group; one of them was Jewish, so the question never came up directly.

I was on bad terms with the second group from the beginning. This was partly because of an incident that took place when they first arrived. Wishing to play the gracious host, the secretary of the district Party committee, the very same Pupov who had installed my former landlady as manageress of the recreation room, came with them to inspect their billets. The first group of students had drunk a lot during their stay and a whole battery of empty bottles had been left behind. Pupov and his retinue – Shapovalov and the students – arrived while I was out at work. 'Who lives here?' Pupov shouted at the sight of all the empty bottles. 'A parasite? Throw the drunkard out at once.'

Next morning Shapovalov came and told me to move into the half ruined building of the old recreation room where some factory workers from Tomsk were already billeted. It seemed that it was wrong for a 'parasite' to live with students, but all right for him to be put in with workers! However, I refused to move out, and Shapovalov gave up, thinking that it would be a long time before Pupov turned up again.

CHAPTER 17

Horses and Cows;
The Vladivostok-Moscow Express

AT the end of July, when the haymaking was over, I was able to have a little rest. Though the foreman still assigned me daily jobs – putting up posts, taking grain to the granary, etc. – this work, for the most part, took up very little time. One day in the middle of August I was told to drive to Novokrivosheino and fetch some seed grain. When I went over to the barns where the truck should have been waiting for me, I saw the foreman surrounded by a group of kolkhozniks and arguing with Sanka, one of the exiles. Sanka was a thin, hook-nosed fellow with straggly flaxen hair who had been deported from somewhere near Sochi in the Krasnodar region (which in general accounted for the highest proportion of 'parasites' in the whole country). He later told me his story which was all very confused: he had worked as a driver, a carpenter and a shepherd; he had been in Kolyma* and done time in jail ... I noticed that he was not averse to embellishing his tale, but only for its own sake, never for reasons of personal advantage to himself. He claimed he had been deported because of a drinking bout after the death of his mother and sister. He often got drunk out here too, but his girl-friend Nadya Kabanov, kept a firm grip on him. To hear him talk, he would stop at nothing, but in actual fact he was very weakminded and totally unreliable. In the summer his job was to take the kolkhoz heifers out to pasture. During haymaking I had often seen him with his herd, on horseback like a Texas cowboy, a whip in his hand and a mosquito net over his head. Sanka was now shouting at the foreman that he could no longer stand doing his work alone,

* One of the main concentration camp areas in Eastern Siberia under Stalin.

and that unless he was given an assistant, the heifers would have to stay in their paddock. Things were indeed very tough for him: he had to look after a hundred heifers all by himself. A similar number of cows would have been tended by two herdsmen, and heifers were much more difficult to manage. 'Where can I find a second man?' the foreman was saying, waving his arms. 'I don't have anyone.' 'What about him?' said one of the kolkhozniks, pointing at me. They all laughed, but the idea of becoming a herdsman was not exactly new to me. When I was still at school, if I got bad marks, my mother always used to scold me by saying that I would end up grazing cattle. So now I said: 'All right, I can do the job.' Everybody was very surprised. 'But how will you manage?' asked Shapovalov, very pleased. I shrugged my shoulders, since I didn't really know what the job entailed.

'Take this one,' said Sanka, handing me the bridle of his mare, 'and I'll go and get myself another saddle and horse.' I had great difficulty in climbing up on the mare – up to that moment I had never had anything to do with horses, or with cows for that matter. She ambled slowly down to some low ground where the other horses were grazing. When I looked round there was no sign of Shapovalov or Sanka. 'Gee-up,' I shouted at her and jabbed her flanks with my boots, giving her the 'touch of the spurs' I had read about in books. But she just went on at the same slow pace till she reached a patch of dried-up swamp where, in full view of the whole village, she began to munch the grass. However much I shouted and dug my heel into her side, she refused to budge. To make my shame complete, a foal came up to her and began to suck at her teats. I had no choice but to dismount and lead her by the bridle back up the hill where Shapovalov and Sanka were waiting. I demanded another horse. Sanka let me have a young gelding called 'Buri', and we rode off together to take the heifers out to pasture.

They had got tired of waiting in their paddock and were mooing from hunger, butting the gate with their horns. They had been served by the kolkhoz bull and were pretty big already – nearly all of them were expected to calve in the coming winter. They were in a paddock with a low fence around some old, half-ruined stables, and stood almost up to their bellies in thick mud mixed with dung. Sanka climbed through a gap in the fence and started driving them out, while I watched on horseback to make sure none of them got into the wheat field at the back of the stables. We – or rather Sanka, since I had little idea of what to do – drove them, squelching through the mud, around the back of the village. As we went by, the students building the day-nursery threw down their axes and saws and looking at me in amazement, shouted 'Hurrah!'

I had now been given a young horse, but the saddle was an old one that had seen better days. As we were going through a wood it slipped and I was thrown to the ground, with one leg stuck in the stirrup. Fortunately 'Buri' stopped almost at once. However, after another mishap during which the saddle was ruined completely, I decided to go back to the more placid mare with whom I soon established a reasonable relationship.

The main problem about grazing the cattle, as I discovered on the first day of my new job, was the lack of good pastureland. Most of it consisted of narrow strips between land sown with wheat or oats. This meant a constant danger of damage to crops. We were supposed to keep the cattle out at pasture from nine in the morning to nine at night (though we sometimes cheated and brought them home earlier) and, since the grass in August is no longer much good, the heifers were tempted all the time by the scent of ripening wheat carried on the wind. As we made our way through the low brush and swamps of the taiga, where it was hard to keep track of them, they would make for the wheat fields, and it was a devil of a job to round them up again. No wonder nobody wanted to do this work, especially since any damage had to be paid for in full by the herdsman responsible for letting the cattle roam. He was also made to pay for any that died, which could happen, for example, when a heifer got into a field of clover and over-ate. One dead cow could cancel out the whole of a herdsman's earnings for the season. Sanka had lost two cows before I joined him, but the kolkhoz authorities had decided to forgive him because he had had to look after a hundred head all by himself. But another herdsman,

Kritsky, who was in charge of the milch-cows and had someone to help him, was told that he would have to pay for
several that had died. On hearing this decision he got blind
drunk and chased after his wife with a knife, threatening
to kill her and then hang himself. Events such as these did
nothing to cheer me up.

However, I gradually got used to the work and the terrain,
though sometimes I would lose part of my herd in the taiga
or get it mixed up with another one. But despite a number
of misadventures, I was lucky during the whole time I did
the job: no crops were damaged by my heifers, and none of
them died. (I will tell later what happened when two died
after I had been switched to a new job.) Sanka and I went
out with the herd on alternate days, so that we could each
rest every other day. In fact, however, there were days when
Sanka was so drunk he could hardly sit in the saddle, and
I had to take over from him. The village people were always
laughing at me for my clumsiness in the saddle, and I swore
I would never take on this job again, if I could help it.

In Siberia grazing goes on until the first snow in about
the middle of October, and I was counting the days until
this time. But deliverance came earlier than I expected. The
foreman, Shapovalov, had been unhappy for some time at
the sight of one man resting every other day, particularly
now that the kolkhoz was very busy getting in the flax, and
he decided that Sanka should once again graze the heifers
by himself. In the middle of September, when it was time
to harvest the corn for silage, Shapovalov sent me back,
despite all of Sanka's protests, to my old job on the silo....

Coming home from work one day a couple of weeks after
this, I was met by the son of the village postman who said
there was a telegram for me. Wondering what it could be, I
opened the yellow envelope and read the following: 'Your
father's condition extremely grave. This certified by doctor.
Pavel.'

In my first letter to my father I had asked him to send
me a telegram such as this towards the middle of October,
hoping that it would help me to get a permit from the police
to visit Moscow and make some sort of arrangement for him.
I reckoned that until then he could stay in the country with

his woman friend and also that in October, when the harvest was over, it would be easier for me to get leave. It was now the beginning of October, and I could not make out whether my father had asked his cousin Pavel to send the wire earlier than we had arranged, or whether his health had indeed taken a turn for the worse. I had mixed feelings of anxiety for my father and pleasure at the vague hope of seeing Moscow again soon.

I went straight to Shapovalov. He said he could do nothing: I must go and see the chairman of the kolkhoz. He promised, however, to have a word with him on the phone. Next morning I got a lift by tractor to Novokrivosheino, thinking that if I got the permit I would be able to come back to Guryevka for my things. The chairman was quite friendly; he asked how old my father was and whether twelve days' leave would be enough. I said the journey alone would take eight, so he gave me eighteen. The next problem was money for the journey: I hadn't a single kopeck in cash. The chairman ordered the accountant, a disagreeable old man with a goatee, to pay me an advance of thirty roubles. With this money and a note authorizing me to take leave, I walked to Krivosheino. The first person I saw at the police station was the Commandant.

'What on earth are you doing here?' he asked.

I said the kolkhoz had given me leave.

'What do you mean?' the Commandant asked in astonishment. 'Parasites have to work for two years before they get leave.'

I explained about my father and showed him the telegram.

'What of it?' he said, but all the same went off to see the Chief of the station.

A lieutenant-colonel with a bald patch on his curly head came in and looked through my file.

'You say you want to go and look after your father,' he said at last. 'But the trial verdict says you neglected him and that he was looked after by the neighbours.'

I said that the neighbours had lied, that they had persecuted my father and informed against me.

'Oh, well,' he said, turning to the Commandant, 'let him go.' He then gave me a sheet of paper which allowed me to travel to Moscow, via Tomsk, Novosibirsk and Sverdlovsk between the 25th of September and the 12th of October 1965. If I failed to keep to the prescribed route, the permit would automatically lose its validity. The Commandant advised me to return to Guryevka on time (otherwise I might forfeit my chance of release at half term), and not to make trouble for my neighbours in Moscow (or I would make things even worse for myself). He also told me that the next steamer was leaving within half an hour. I decided to waste none of my precious time and to leave at once without going back to Guryevka.

At the police station I had seen a familiar face: that of Boris with whom I had travelled from the prison in Moscow to Krivosheino. It turned out that he too was off to Moscow – but for good. This is what had happened to him.

He and Tolya, who was being deported for the second time, arrived in Novokrivosheino a day later than the rest of us. Tolya immediately got drunk and started a fight with one of the local peasants who cut open his thigh with an axe. He was taken to the hospital where he was joined almost immediately by Boris who had been drinking in the restaurant and got talking with another exile, a criminal type from a provincial town. Boris put on airs about being a Muscovite. The other said nothing, but as they were leaving the place, he stabbed Boris in the back. Unconscious and bleeding, Boris was taken to the hospital and underwent an emergency operation. The man who had stabbed him got two years.

In the hospital Tolya had made friends with another criminal, a fellow patient who was being treated for stomach trouble caused by the food in the labour camp where he had been held. As soon as they were released, the two of them raided the village shop. The whole thing couldn't have been more stupid: they stole a few bottles of vodka, some coffee and condensed milk, hid in some nearby bushes, got drunk and went to sleep. In the morning they were woken up by the police. Tolya was later sentenced to three years. There was nothing much wrong with him – I think he was simply weak-willed and too easily influenced by others. I don't mean that he was innocent or that he was sentenced unjustly, but it seems to me that the ceaseless pressure brought to bear by the authorities on people once they fall foul of the law creates in them a feeling of being doomed and drives them step by step to still more serious crimes.

Boris came out of hospital with a certificate exempting him from work. For want of something better to do, he hung about at the hospital and at the police station where he created such a good impression that he was even asked to become an informer. After several weeks he induced the surgeon who had operated on him to certify that he was now an invalid permanently incapacitated for physical work. The police, as was usual in such cases, handed the certificate over to the court. There Boris claimed that he had criticized his would-be murderer for breaking the law by bringing his own vodka to a restaurant, and that this had been the reason for his being wounded. It was immediately proved that he was lying, for several people had seen the two men drinking together, but in view of the doctor's certificate the Judge nevertheless decided to release him. Boris was overjoyed, especially at the thought of settling accounts with his wife who, he believed, had informed on him and caused him to be deported in the first place. 'I won't say anything to begin with,' he said, 'but once I've got my residence permit, I'll let her have what's coming to her.' But his immediate problem was to reach Moscow. Like myself, he had earned nothing at the kolkhoz and had got into debt with the kolkhoz store. The chairman let him off paying what he owed, but he still had no money for his fare. All he had was seven roubles that he had obtained by a trick : he had taken eggs on credit from the kolkhoz store and, pretending he was doing so out of good will and patriotism, sold them cheap to the shop in Krivosheino. For a long time he tried to beg money from the police, the local Soviet and the Welfare Department, arguing that 'parasites' were similar in status to old-age pensioners, but nobody would help him. The police advised him to present his certificate of release to the ticket inspectors in the hope that they would allow him to travel free, 'for the sake of Christ', like a beggar. To make matters worse he had to lug with him two huge bundles of warm clothing, which his wife, not suspecting he would be back so soon, had sent him for the winter.

Boris was seen off to the boat by Sanka, who was a friend of his. The day before Sanka had received all the grain he had earned in a year, but he had already sold it and spent the money on drink. His friendship with Boris had started with his purchase of Boris's watch: as a herdsman, Sanka needed a watch and the kolkhoz had advanced him fifteen roubles to buy it. Boris got ten, and the remaining five they had spent on drink. By next day Sanka had sold the watch and drunk away the proceeds, as did Boris his ten roubles.

On the boat neither of us took sailing tickets. They cost three roubles and I had no idea how much I would have to pay for my ticket from Tomsk to Moscow. Boris said that if there was an inspection he would produce not only his certificate of release but also a paper showing that in 1947 he had worked for several months as a steersman on the Moscow-Volga canal and was thus in some sense a former workmate of theirs. We sailed slowly up the Ob, often stopping at small river stations; it grew dark and lights began to blink on navigation buoys. The boat gradually became crowded and I went to sleep, my head between somebody's feet and a large bundle.

We reached Tomsk in the middle of the night. As the other passengers started to disembark, giving up their tickets at the gangway, Boris and I clambered over two empty barges moored beside the boat, climbed ashore some distance from the pier and emerged into an empty street, where there were tramlines. Tomsk at night struck me as attractive in its provincial way, rather like one of the ancient small towns near Moscow with their wooden pavements.

The first tram arrived a couple of hours later and we crossed the town to the railway station. The through train to Moscow left only in the evening, but we could take a Trans-Siberian local train to Taiga, where trains to Moscow often stopped. As soon as the ticket office opened I bought the cheapest possible ticket to Moscow. Luckily, it cost only twenty-three roubles, which left me with seven for my food on the way. Waiting for the train to Taiga we sat in the buffet and got into conversation with a grey-faced man of about forty-five. He had been sitting alone, drinking wine – he had no money left for vodka. The waitress told us he had spent twenty years in a labour camp. As soon as he came out he had drunk away the money he had earned, lost his identity papers, and was now getting through his last bottle of wine, having given up all hope of reaching home. Judging from the fact that he had been in camp ever since 1945, he was probably a former member of the Vlasov army or Bendera Partisans.*

When the train arrived, Boris slipped in among a crowd of students who were coming back from work on kolkhozes and many of whom were also probably travelling without tickets. In Taiga, however, he was too nervous to board the Moscow train. I advised him to buy a ticket to the next station, get into the first train travelling West, stay in it until he was thrown out, and then board the following one. He took my advice and left before me on a train going to Kiev. He was reluctant to part from me, and hoped we would meet later on during the journey, if he was thrown off the Kiev train. As for me, I was glad to be left alone; I had had enough of him.

Just before the train arrived I was stopped by a policeman. With my town jacket peeping from under a padded coat, my muddy rubber boots, black beret, beard and glasses I looked very suspicious to him. I showed him my travel permit and he was satisfied. In the coach I managed to install myself on the wide shelf at the top usually reserved for luggage; using my padded coat as a pillow, I was able to sleep there during the three nights spent on the train. I had tea morning and evening, and one meal in the restaurant car. My return journey to Moscow was thus considerably more comfortable than the one from Moscow to Tomsk. Strangely enough, however, I felt no joy at the thought of going home, but rather a vague anxiety.

We arrived on the evening of the 27th of September. My face pressed against a window, I could see the familiar suburban platforms. When I got out at the Yaroslav Station in Moscow, I went to a kiosk and spent the last of my money on a glass of milk. I had been away only four months, but how much everything had changed for me!

* General A. Vlaslov: see footnote on page 123.
Stepan Bendera: leader of anti-Soviet Ukrainian Partisans.

It was nearly eleven, too late to go to the country to my father's. I didn't feel like going to our flat, so an hour later I knocked on the door of friends who were astounded to see me.

CHAPTER 18

My Father's Death

M Y friends knew nothing about the telegram. They had seen my father the previous week and had found him no worse than usual in health, but very worried about his future: he could not stay on in the country and was afraid of living at home in Moscow alone, in constant terror of the neighbours.

Next morning I set out with one of my friends to see him. We took the wrong train and had to walk the distance between the last two stations. I well remember that sunny September day and the pine trees along the edge of the road. I had often been to see my father here in former years; usually he sat waiting for me on the verandah or at a window. This time I didn't see him. I thought he must be in bed, but suddenly I felt a sharp foreboding. At the sound of our footsteps the woman whose house it was came out into the hall and threw her arms around me. I realized that my father had died. He had died without regaining consciousness on the 23rd of September, the day I got the telegram about his illness. My uncle had sent me a second one, but I had left before it arrived. Not hearing from me, they had buried him while I was still on the way.

I should like at this point to say a little about my father and about the history of our family which he had often told me when I was a small boy.

Our surname is evidently of ancient Semitic origin and even occurs in a distorted form in the Bible. It appears again at the time of the Crusades when two kings of Cyprus bore the name Amalric. It was also the name of a Papal legate who, when asked during the campaign against the Albigensians how the soldiers were to tell good Catholics from heretics, made the famous reply: 'Kill them all, God will tell which is which.' There was also a famous mediaeval philosopher, Amalric of Bena, a pantheist whose teaching was condemned by the Church, and whose remains were disinterred and burned. He had, however, many followers, especially in the South of France where there was a sect named after him, and it is possible that we are descended from one of its adherents. At any event, my great-great-grandfather Jean Amalric, came to Russia from Avignon in the middle of the nineteenth century.

He came to Moscow with the intention of making a fortune and started a lace factory. But he was too fond of the bottle and one day when he was drunk the house caught fire; the factory burned down and he and his wife died in the blaze. By some miracle his four-year-old son was saved; this was my great-grandfather, also christened Jean but called Ivan Ivanovich in Russian. The French colony in Moscow looked after the child and one old craftsman who grew very fond of him passed on to him before his death a secret method of making dyestuffs. Thanks to this knowledge, Ivan Ivanovich later rose to be a master foreman at Huebner's cotton factory which still exists today. He eloped with the daughter of a rich Moscow merchant, Belkin, and had three sons and a daughter by her; the eldest, Sergei, was my grandfather.

My great-grandfather was a stern, ill-tempered man. If he came home and found his wife giving tea to a friend – something he didn't approve of – he threw the cups and saucers out of the window. He treated his workers in much the same way, constantly flying into a rage and beating them with a stick. True, he would immediately afterwards give them money so that some of them deliberately tried to make him lose his temper. But in general they respected him and when there were strikes he was the only foreman who did not get the customary treatment of being trundled out of the works in a wheelbarrow. His views were socialist, but he was a follower of Proudhon and greatly disliked Marx. His end was tragic. He went blind and had to go and live with his sons. For a man of his pride and independence this was intolerable. Furthermore he had until then been very fond of reading and so one day, in despair, he cut his throat almost in front of his small grandson, my father.

My grandfather, Sergei, was in many ways less remarkable than his father but he was a man of extraordinary willpower. Wishing as a child to prove that he was afraid of nothing, he once lit a bonfire in the yard, stood a barrel of water on it and climbed inside. He was pulled out only just in time. Physically very strong, he served in the Preobrazhensky regiment and Emperor Alexander III, who was also known to be exceptionally strong, was so impressed by him that he bent a silver rouble with his own hands and gave it to him as a present. The rouble was long treasured in our family but it was lost during the last war. Grandfather was never ill and perhaps because of this his first illness proved fatal: he died of typhus in 1921 in the Ukraine.

My grandmother was ten years younger than her husband but had a very masterful character. She was unhappy in her marriage and lavished all her love first on her only son, then on me, her grandson. As a result I remember my childhood as divided into two: happy until grandmother's death in 1947, and less happy after it. She too had an interesting family history. Her grandfather was a minor Ukrainian nobleman. Shortly before the liberation of the serfs in 1861, he found that his serf mistress had a lover; he killed both of them with an axe and bricked up their bodies in the walls of his house. But the crime was discovered, and he was stripped of his title and sent to forced labour in Siberia. He must have been a real brute – both his sons ran away from him as children and went to America. I don't know what happened to the younger but the elder one, my great-grandfather, worked as an engineer on the railway there. Later he returned to Russia just when the railway boom was beginning and became stationmaster at the Kursk Station in Moscow.

On the way back to Russia he went to Sweden where he married the daughter of a Lutheran minister in a small village. All the people in this village, including the minister and his daughter, suffered from lethargy, and it is said that my great-grandfather came across the minister's daughter sleeping, half-frozen, in the snow and struck by her beauty, he saved her from death. When he was a child my father once slept for a whole week and his cousin still always carries around with him a card to say he is not dead but asleep – just in case people might mistakenly decide he is dead and want to bury him. There were three children from this Ukrainian-Swedish marriage: a son, Nicholas, and two daughters. The elder daughter, Claudia, my grandmother, was born under the wheels of a train. Her mother, about to give birth, was crossing the railway line near the Kursk Station and to avoid going all the way around a freight train decided to slip under one of the cars. Just at that moment the train began to move and while the cars were passing over her head she gave birth out of sheer terror. From her earliest years grandmother was noted for her difficult character; she quarrelled with her mother and for several years lived with another woman. She married my grandfather when she was twenty-one. He had met her at a dance in the Noblemen's Assembly Rooms, danced a waltz with her, and then snatched her up in his arms and drove her off in his carriage.

In 1906 they had a son, Alexei, my father. He grew up in an atmosphere of comfort and ease in his parents' house in the Moscow district of Razgulyai. It was a life marked by liberal conversation and winter visits to grandfather in horse-drawn cabs right across Moscow, past the Spassk Gates of the Kremlin where one always remembers the well known lines:

> Who can lift the Tsar of bells
> Who can move the Tsar of cannons
> Who is too proud to doff his cap
> By the Kremlin's hoary gate?

At the age of eight my father was sent to a commercial school. His parents worked in the 'Russia' Insurance Company, in the large corner building on Lubianka Square that now houses one of the departments of the KGB. They wanted their son to become a businessman or engineer. Grandmother was an insurance broker.

Suddenly this familiar pattern of existence, which had seemed so stable and unchangeable, was shattered. The insurance company collapsed: nobody now thought of insuring himself. Human life had lost all value, it became hard to distinguish between right and wrong. In the elections to the Constituent Assembly* grandmother voted for the Cadets (Constitutional Democrats) and grandfather for the Bolsheviks. There was not a scrap of bread in the house but there were ample supplies of cocoa and black caviar – the Eynem and Chernyshev stores had hastily sold off all their stock. After a winter in Moscow the family decided to travel south, towards the advancing White Army. In the small town of Oboyan near Kharkov my grandfather, who only a year before had voted for the Bolsheviks, burst into tears at the sight of the tricolor flag and an armoured car with the words 'For Holy Russia' scrawled on it. However, the armoured cars with their tricolor flags soon turned south again. Panic-stricken, grandfather and grandmother thought of emigrating to France, to the 'old country', but, unfortunately, they decided to stay in Russia.

By the time the Civil War was over my father was already fifteen and had to think of finding something to do in life. He volunteered for a Red Cavalry battalion – he was evidently attracted by its romantic name – that had been formed to put down banditry. This unit was used to liquidate the remnants of the many irregular detachments still fighting on in the Ukraine. However, a year later grandmother returned to Moscow with her son and nephew. Shortly after they got there they received a telegram informing them of grandfather's death.

In Moscow, grandmother got a job in the newly created State Insurance Company and went to live with my father in the same room on Nikitsky Boulevard (subsequently renamed Suvorov Boulevard) where I was to spend my childhood and youth, and where Bushmakin and Kiselev were to make their search. After a great deal of trouble my father managed to get work as a lighting effects man with a film outfit and later travelled round the whole country with a

* Elections for a Constituent Assembly were called by Kerensky's Provisional Government, but by the time they took place in 1918, the Bolsheviks had seized power and Lenin ordered the forcible dispersal of the deputies of the various parties that had competed in the elections.

newsreel team. In 1928 he married my mother, who was working as a producer's assistant. She was six years older than my father, but she was remarkably young in appearance for her age and kept her good looks right up to the war. I was born in 1938, a long-awaited, much desired child.

My father, who had been in the third year of his commercial school at the time of the Revolution, was always hoping that he might somehow complete his education. He was particularly encouraged in this by my mother's older brother, Evgeni Grigoryevich Shableyev. I have already mentioned my mother's family and my uncle. My uncle was a very versatile man who, after finishing at the Institute of Commerce, had also graduated in history, literature and law from the university. He was a great lover of poetry and was a friend of the remarkable poet, Velimir Khlebnikov. He had a very chequered career: at one time he was Art Director of a cartoon film studio, then he became director of the museum at the Donskoi Monastery and finally a Prosecuting Attorney for Special Cases. In 1937 he was arrested and was about to be sentenced to five years (in those days this was the minimum sentence given simply to be 'on the safe side'), but my uncle was evidently an idealist and he was by now so disgusted, on closer acquaintance, with what he had long thought was right, or at least necessary for Russia that he lost his temper with his judges and shouted: 'This is not a Soviet Court, but a fascist torture chamber!' This outburst cost him his life.

With my uncle's encouragement my father took a higher degree at the Film Institute and in 1935 enrolled in the History Faculty at Moscow University. But no sooner had he done so than he was asked to leave in order to make room for another candidate who had been recommended by the Party. Only with great difficulty, after an appeal to the Ministry of Higher Education, did my father manage to get this decision reversed.

In 1939, when the Soviet Union invaded Poland, my father was drafted. By the end of this brief campaign he had been promoted to lieutenant. During 1940 he served in the Northern Fleet. In June 1941 he finished his university studies and took his final examinations just as the war began. He had to report for duty immediately.

At first he again served in the Northern Fleet. When the Germans reached Moscow my father remarked in the presence of some fellow officers that the fault for the debacle in the first months of the war lay with Stalin. The next day he was arrested and shortly afterwards brought before a tribunal which sentenced him to eight years. My father told me that just before the Judge read out the sentence a fat-faced official of the N K V D* who was sitting at his side handed him an envelope, but the Judge waved it aside and said, 'Later'. After his trial my father was put in a block for prisoners condemned to death; every day a few people were taken out to be shot and my father waited his turn, thinking that the envelope which had been proffered to the Judge must have contained an order for his execution. But his fears were not borne out, and after a few days he was transferred to the island of Yagry in the White Sea where there was a concentration camp that had been built by the British during their occupation of Archangel in the Civil War. To judge by my father's account, it would be difficult to imagine a more terrible place. The prisoners got scarcely anything to eat and there were frequent cases of cannibalism. Whenever any bread was brought to the camp some of the prisoners, stampeding the guards, would seize a hunk of it, wolf it down, and die on the spot from burst intestines. Everybody suffered from scurvy, and for the rest of his life my father had black marks on his legs as a result. When the battle of Stalingrad started and the need for officers became particularly acute, my father was given a pardon and told to join a unit at the front. However, owing to the chaos on the railways the train in which he was travelling wound up in the Urals. He spent about a year there in command of an officers' reserve company and was sent to the front only in 1943. He first commanded a company with the rank of captain, then a battalion, and in spring 1944 he was badly wounded by a mine. He lay in a swamp for a whole day until he was picked up and taken to a field hospital. A

---

* Pre-war name for the Soviet secret police (now K G B).

splinter from the mine had gone right through his liver, punctured his diaphragm and damaged a lung. There was no chloroform and he was operated on without an anaesthetic. A nurse gripped him by the hand and by the end of the operation she had bruise marks where his fingers had crushed her hand. Shortly after this he was invalided out of the Army.

When the war ended the whole country lived in hope of change and I well remember how my father spent the evening arguing with grandmother. It was difficult for me to follow, but the main question was: What will happen now? It seemed inconceivable that there could be any return to the previous terrible state of affairs. But that is just what happened. When my father went to the university to take the examination still needed for his diploma, Academician Tikhomirov, who was then Dean of the History Faculty, and knew about my father's anti-Stalinist views, began to create such bureaucratic difficulties, that my father lost patience, banged his invalid's cane on Tikhomirov's desk so hard that the oak top almost split in two, and never went near the university again. For a long time after this he made his living by installing and painting iron grilles along the Moscow boulevards. He also began to drink heavily. He kept having nightmares about the war which made him jump out of bed and shriek in a way that chilled my blood as I lay in my cot. He would try to overturn the table or the sideboard, and it was all my mother and grandmother could do to hold him back and somehow make him calm down.

In 1950 my father managed to get work in connection with the preparation of an historical atlas; a little later he began to write articles on historical topics and, together with an old friend from the university, he was able to publish two popular books on archaeology.* But the fact is that for a long time he was not able to work on the sort of thing that his university studies had qualified him for. His ordeals of previous years also began to take their toll. In

---

* *In Search of Vanished Civilizations* (published by the Soviet Academy of Science) and *What Is Archaeology?* – Both were written in co-authorship with the well-known archaeologist A. L. Mongait.

1957 he had his first slight stroke and his health began to get worse and worse until in the spring of 1960 his right arm and leg were completely paralysed and he lost the power of speech. He was in hospital for a long time and even got a little better, but he could no longer work, and he could scarcely read or speak; he had great difficulty in getting out his words and couldn't pronounce them properly. My mother's death from cancer of the brain in January 1961 was a further severe blow for him. After this he and I lived alone. Difficult as our life was, we were nearly always on the best of terms. After my mother's death he had another stroke, and then a heart attack. With enormous difficulty I managed to get a pension for him. In the Welfare Department they procrastinated for six months, refusing to give an answer one way or the other. The trouble was that after the war my father had never had regular employment. By a strange irony it was the K G B that eventually got a pension for him. When they questioned me about the study on the Kiev Principality that I had tried to send to Denmark I thought they were going to expel me from Moscow, and I therefore asked them to do something about my father, who was simply unable to get a pension. When I next went to the Welfare Department I was received with great solicitude and the following day the pension came through. For this reason I cannot speak only ill of the K G B.

While my father and I lived together he could always feel confident that he would have someone to look after him. Then suddenly he was alone. His condition was by no means hopeless. He would not have died if I had not been sent away or if he had at least had some guarantee that he would be looked after until I returned. In effect he was killed by Judge Chigrinov and the sort of attitude Chigrinov represented – all this at the height of a demagogic campaign concerning the need to help war veterans.

In the country, so I was told, my father kept crying and saying over and over again: 'I'm sorry for Andrei.' One of his friends tried to console him by saying I would soon be back. 'No,' he replied. 'I shall never see him again.' Before he had gone to the country we had had a slight quarrel. As I helped him get into the car with an irritable look on my face, I did not realize this was the last time I should ever see him. I well remember how he looked in his old age: tall, broad-shouldered, his hair completely white and his dark blue eyes unblinking.

CHAPTER 19

Moscow

A FEW days after my arrival I had a meeting with my lawyer. He struck me as a cultivated and friendly man who – even more important for someone in my predicament – had a good understanding of the whole administrative and legal machinery, and might possibly be able to find some way out of the labyrinth which to me seemed so hopeless.

'They killed your father,' he said. But he did not think that we should give up the struggle: 'In the City Prosecutor's office they were sympathetic to my application at first but they have evidently met with some resistance from the Moscow branch of the KGB, so we must try to get the case transferred to the republican level.'*

He suggested that I write out in my own hand an appeal from a draft that he would prepare for me, address it to the RSFSR Prosecutor's office and take it there myself. In the draft that he would give me the main emphasis would be on the fact that I had had no permanent work because of the need to look after my father, and that for this reason I could not be regarded as a 'parasite'.

'Yes,' I replied, 'but they may say: All right, you had to look after your father, but now he's dead he doesn't need your help anymore, so you can stay in Siberia.'

'Very well,' said my lawyer, admitting this possibility, 'then why don't you date your application earlier than your father's death?'

He then told me about his meeting with Judge Chigrinov. 'What do you think of the case?' Chigrinov had asked. 'I find it appalling,' my lawyer had replied, 'the man has been exiled without any good reason.' 'Not at all,' the Judge had said. 'You should just read the sort of thing he writes in those plays of his, then you wouldn't talk like that.'

* i.e. to the Prosecutor's office of the RSFSR.

This once again convinced me that the whole case hinged
on my plays and that no arguments, however weighty, about
my not being a 'parasite' would be of any avail. I thanked
my lawyer for the trouble he had taken but, after thinking it
all over, I decided not to go to the Prosecutor's office. Feeling very depressed, I knew I should find it highly unpleasant
to deal with officials, and what is more, I simply did not believe they would show any objectivity about my case. I
thought my only hope would be to obtain my release on the
spot in Siberia after serving half my sentence. Before I left I
asked my friends to apologize on my behalf to the lawyer for
not taking his advice and for not phoning him.

My next move was to try to get back the things that had
been confiscated during the search of my flat. This I was
entitled to do since my sentence did not provide for the
confiscation of my property. I managed to locate Captain
Bushmakin, who had carried out the search, but he referred
me to Novikov, the officer who had interrogated me. With
some difficulty I managed to find Novikov in the Investigation Department of the Ministry of Public Order. Seeing me,
he looked startled and hustling out an old man he was
questioning, he asked me into his office. He immediately
wanted to see my travel warrant and then began to talk to
me without the official air of aggrieved solemnity that he
had put on while interrogating me. He began by emphasizing
that neither he nor his department had anything to do with
my expulsion from Moscow.

'As you know yourself,' he said, 'it wasn't us who expelled you but the Committee [K G B]. They just wanted to
do it through us, though we did our best to get out of it.'
He seemed a little surprised at the relatively liberal way in
which they had dealt with me : 'The Committee isn't what it
was. In the old days you would have disappeared for twenty
years without anyone ever knowing it.'

He took exclusive credit for the fact that criminal proceedings against me had been stopped, and said that the
experts would have given the opinions demanded of them.
On the second point I agreed with him entirely; as to
whether or not it was he who had stopped the criminal proceedings, I reckoned that his role had been rather more

modest. He went on to say that the Moscow Prosecutor's office had obtained my file from him and had at first intended to ask the court for a reversal of my sentence, but they had run into difficulty with the head of the Moscow branch of the KGB, General Svetlichny, who had said: 'Let him stay where he is.' For this reason Novikov thought my case was pretty hopeless.

'The law on parasites,' he explained, 'is a funny business and they can do what they like.'

As to my pictures and plays, he said that they were all in good order and that the next day I could go and collect them from him in the district office of the city police. At the appointed time I went there with a friend. I had to wait for quite a long time, but at last Novikov appeared, brandishing a bulky briefcase, and took us to the room where my things were being kept.

Here there was a man in civilian clothes and a fat, coarse-looking woman. All the pictures were returned to me, though several of Zverev's water-colours were in extremely bad shape. When I unrolled a bundle of his things, I found an empty vodka bottle inside. 'This,' I said, 'was not among the objects taken from me.'

The police officials in the room looked extremely embarrassed and the fat woman who up to now had been making fun of Zverev's pictures, picked up the bottle with two fingers, as though giving expression to her squeamishness, and threw it into the waste-paper basket.

Next, Novikov showed me the report of the experts. The conclusion of the graphic arts section of the Moscow branch of the Artists' Union was very brief and said that Zverev's drawings were the 'work of an abnormal person containing elements of erotic fantasy'. Tatyana Sytin had given her opinion at much greater length and the tone was very crude. She referred to me for instance as a 'twenty-year-old nincompoop'. This surprised me, since I had begun to write my plays at the age of twenty-five, and at the time of my arrest I was twenty-seven. It is possible, however, that the disdainful tone of her report worked to my advantage.

We started arguing about Zverev's drawings. 'This stuff,'

said Novikov, 'is pornography. I'm going to keep it here and
burn it.'

'But,' I replied, panic-stricken, 'the experts say it is not
pornography, only erotic fantasy.' 'And why should the
Soviet public have to look at erotic fantasy?' Novikov shot
back at me.

'Well,' I replied with the air of one willing to compromise,
'I won't show it to the Soviet public.'

Satisfied by this answer, Novikov returned the drawings to
me. He also gave back the manuscript of my biography of
Zverev, but both typewritten copies with the accompanying
drawings had disappeared. The file with my manuscripts was
short of about half its previous contents. Novikov said that
this was all he had received from Goncharenko in the KGB.
However, all of my plays were there: only the first drafts
and copies were missing. The typewritten collection of my
verse was also missing, but I was so concerned about the
fate of my plays that I did not at first notice this. Later on
I was able to get the verse from Novikov.

But I was really surprised and horrified when Novikov
opened a safe and took out some icons. One of them was
mine, but instead of my two seventeenth-century icons
Novikov handed me two worthless daubs which were not
even nineteenth-century but were from the early twentieth-
century. They were exactly the same size as mine, one of
them was a bad painting of the Virgin and Child, while the
other depicted a saint who could have passed for Theodore
Stratilatus.

'These are fakes,' I said. 'They are not mine.'

Novikov seemed genuinely surprised.

'These are the icons I was given by Goncharenko,' he
said. 'I haven't exchanged them for any others – I have no
need of this kind of thing.'

He gave me Goncharenko's telephone number so I could
ring him for an explanation, but he insisted that I sign a
statement confirming receipt of all the items listed in the
inventory made after the search of my flat; without this,
he refused to let me have anything. After a moment's
thought I decided to sign the list, preferring to lose two
icons to risking the loss of all my pictures and the plays as

well. But I refused to take the two substitute icons and left them with Novikov.

I telephoned Goncharenko at the number Novikov had given me. Someone with an old man's voice that was almost cloying in its affability said he had replaced Goncharenko who no longer worked there. I explained my business and this new official asked me to ring again the next day. The following day he told me in even more dulcet tones that he had spoken with his superiors, who had informed him that the KGB no longer had anything to do with my case and could not therefore deal with any claims I might have on them. As I was to learn later, Goncharenko had been transferred from the KGB to the Ministry of Culture, where he evidently put to good use the practical experience gained during his handling of my case. Shortly after my departure he phoned Novikov and asked him to let him have my things for some exhibition or other, but fortunately I had already collected them; otherwise I should never have seen them again.

I also decided to track down the old school friend who had been in the cell with me on Mogiltsev Street, in order to find out what exactly he was up to. After a lot of trouble I found the house where he lived, but I was told there that he left for work early in the morning and returned only late at night, and that nobody knew where he worked. So I had drawn a blank. But shortly afterwards I unexpectedly met my other friend – Tolya Zverev. We ran into each other by accident near the Moscow headquarters of the KGB. But this was an innocent coincidence, we both had an acquaintance who lived in the building opposite, that had once been the old French almshouse. 'Do you know my flat was searched because of you?' Zverev said, to which I was able to reply that my flat had been searched on account of him. He was upset when I further told him that in the opinion of the experts at the Moscow branch of the Union of Artists his work contained 'elements of erotic fantasy'. To confound the experts he said he would go to the Artists' Union with some totally unattractive, flat-chested woman who would provide living proof that he had no erotic inclinations whatsoever. However he decided against this plan since it occurred to him that even flat breasts might have their erotic side.

Shortly after our meeting Markevich came to Moscow again.

'Have you heard the sad news, Tolya?' were his first words to Zverev. 'Your friend Andrei is dead.' 'What do you mean, dead?' said Zverev, taken aback, 'I saw him quite recently and I've heard that he's in Siberia.'

'No, he's dead,' Markevich insisted. 'I wrote a letter to him from Paris and it came back with a note from the Moscow post office saying he was dead.'

My lawyer and interrogator had pointed out to me a new and grave difficulty that now faced me. Since I'd been expelled from Moscow, my father's death meant that I had lost all right to the room we shared, and it would now be given to new tenants; all our things would be inventoried in the presence of a notary, valued and put in storage somewhere. They might later be returned to me, or, if they were lost, I would be paid a sum equivalent to the value at which they had been assessed. I would forfeit not only the room but with it the right to live in Moscow. Though 'parasites' are entitled to renew their permit to reside in Moscow on termination of their sentences, this would not apply to me because I had no close relatives left in the city. I talked with the police superintendent of my district, but he just shrugged his shoulders and repeated what my interrogator had told me – that it was a hopeless case under existing regulations. In other words, I would be obliged to live beyond the regulation distance of 'a hundred and one kilometres from Moscow'.

The only solution, proposed by my friends, was that I should enter into a marriage of convenience with some girl merely for the purpose of using her address to register for a residence permit on my return to Moscow, after which I should be free to rent a room of my own somewhere. Such marriages of convenience concluded in order to get a residence permit, or a room, are a regular feature of Moscow life. I do not know whether my friends would have been able to find a suitable 'bride' for me, but in the end everything turned out differently.

Not long before my arrest I had met a girl whom I liked very much. Her name was Gyusel, and she was an artist. We happened to meet the day before my trial. Unfortunately, I didn't know her address and had not therefore been able to write to her from Siberia. On my way back to Moscow, wondering what to do about my father, I had hoped she might agree to move into our apartment and keep an eye on him. Soon after I got back to Moscow I found out where she lived and we saw each other almost every day. Shortly before my return to Siberia I asked her to marry me and she agreed. Her parents, who were bigoted, narrow-minded Tartars, were horrified on learning that their daughter wanted to marry a Russian – and a 'convict' at that! Her mother begged her to come to her senses, and tried to hide her identity papers and possessions; her father solemnly laid his curse on her, and she left home accompanied by her mother's tears and her father's malediction.

We had to put off the registration of our marriage until my arrival in Siberia since I had no other documents than my travel warrant. My chances of obtaining a residence permit through marriage with Gyusel were in any case nil, since the parents of my wife would never agree to allow me to use their address for this purpose. I therefore decided at least to save my books and pictures from being valued and stored by the authorities, knowing full well what this meant. Apart from anything else I hated the idea of anybody rummaging around my possessions. But I no longer had the time to take them to the friends who had agreed to keep them for me. My travel warrant expired on the 12th of October and on the 13th I was supposed to present it to the Commandant in Krivosheino. For this I should have to leave Moscow on the 9th at the very latest, but I was so depressed by my father's death that I had done practically nothing and on the 9th all my things were still in our flat on Suvorov Boulevard. I then decided, on the strength of a slight cold, to go to my old clinic and try to get a medical certificate of unfitness to travel. The doctor who had always attended us there, a large elderly woman, was sympathetic to my request but said she could not give me a certificate since I was no longer registered as a resident in that district. She called in the head of her section who decided to risk it and make out a certificate for me. The woman clerk whose duty it was to put the official stamp on such certificates was rather startled when instead of an identity card with a Moscow residence permit I handed her my travel warrant. Nevertheless, she stamped the certificate for me, and I now had the right to stay in Moscow for three more days. I next phoned the head of the Housing Department and asked them not to take possession of my apartment until after I left on October 12th.

On the evening of the 9th, helped by a woman acquaintance, I began to sort out my papers. Many of them I tore up, shouting: 'To hell with it!' and threw them all over the room, so that the floor was soon white with scraps of paper. Later Gyusel and the husband of my friend arrived and all four of us drank to our melancholy marriage and the end of my life in Suvorov Boulevard. We put on some records and I remember how my wife, slightly tipsy, danced Spanish dances in her red boots, kicking up the scraps of white paper and making them swirl around the devastated room.

I had bought tickets in advance for the Moscow-Tomsk train, which departed from the Kazan Station at eleven o'clock at night. I was so tired of Moscow that I was even eager to get away as soon as possible. About three hours before we were due to leave I suddenly realized that my troubles were not over. I had kept a little money in Moscow, but it had just about been enough to live on for two weeks; after paying for the moving of my things to a friend's house and two tickets to Tomsk, I hadn't a kopeck to bless myself with. There was nothing left for food on the way, not to mention the journey from Tomsk to Guryevka. An hour before the train left we were already waiting impatiently for my friend who had promised to get us twenty roubles. At last he appeared, and after drinking a bottle of wine for the road, we went off to the station. Thus we set off on our wedding journey with its sombre overtones of death, deportation and complete uncertainty about our future.

That day it began to snow in Moscow, but the farther east we went the warmer it became. We arrived in Tomsk late on the 15th of October. We found that the next steamer would leave only at twelve o'clock the following day. We

put our things in the luggage room at the pier (besides clothing we had taken a drawing board and a roll of paper for
Gyusel, and my typewriter) and went on foot right across
the town to the station – the waiting room at the pier closed
at night. At the station all the benches were occupied, and
we passed the night on the floor next to some gypsies in
brightly-coloured clothes.

The next day we might have chosen between an express
hydrofoil boat and a steamship. But we hadn't enough money
for the hydrofoil, so we took the steamship and spent a
whole day going down the river in its stuffy hold. By the
time we got to Krivosheino it was night and only dim lights
on the landing could be seen glowing in the pitch blackness.
We were the only passengers to get out here. In complete
silence we walked down the wooden gangway, barely able to
carry our things with us. We went first to the police to hand
our travel warrants and medical certificates to the duty officer. We had nowhere to go, and I asked the officer whether
we could spend the night at the police station. He looked
quizzically at Gyusel's papers and observed that our marriage
had not yet been registered, but he nevertheless allowed us
to stay there one night and even gave us some fruit juice to
drink.

We spent the night in a corridor and early the next morning went off to the edge of the village in the hope of getting
a lift. The Siberian frost had already set in and the trees were
covered with hoarfrost. A peasant from a neighbouring village took us as far as Novokrivosheino in his cart, and there
we got a lift in a truck going to Malinovka. By a strange
coincidence it was driven by Zharkov, the deputy chairman
of the kolkhoz who had taken me to Guryevka the first time.
We went past fields from which the oats had been harvested
and where cows were now grazing, and then at a turn in the
road we looked down and saw the houses of Guryevka
scattered over the hillside.

CHAPTER 20

Guryevka

BEFORE they left, the students had nailed old shoes, trousers and caps to the outer wall of my house, so that from a distance it looked to Gyusel and me like some product of American Pop art. Inside, everything was bare and cold. The moment we put down our things Aksinya appeared. Aksinya – the woman Leva had lived with – was a kind of village newspaper, always the first to learn and pass on the latest gossip. She said that Leva had left her and urged us to go and stay with her, asking how we could possibly spend the winter in this tumble-down shack, and without any firewood at that. Gyusel, who was bewildered by everything and upset by the cold hut, thought we should accept the invitation. But I had firmly decided not to lodge with anybody and to live on my own. After Aksinya, our neighbour Sonya came in and invited us to have a bite to eat. I had seen very little of my neighbours before this.

I got my things back from the woman who looked after the kolkhoz store – she had taken them there after my departure – and we began to make ourselves at home. I dismantled the bunks the students had set up and lit the stove, while Gyusel swept the floor and spread a checked blanket on the bed. The place even began to look quite comfortable. I mixed some clay with water and used it to repair the cracks in the stove and then to plaster over some of the cracks in the walls and the window frames, but this did not help very much. Later on, when it began to get really very cold, we had to stuff straw and rags into these cracks and put more clay on top, even reinforcing it with boiled macaroni. We made a mattress out of sacking and stuffed it with straw so that we didn't have to sleep on bare boards. Gyusel washed the windows. Though it was October, the weather was still bright and sunny. Through the window we could see horses trudging over the ground that was brownish with dead grass.

I went to see the foreman the first day. As if he were reporting to his superiors in the district office, he told me that all work in the fields had been completed. I was much more interested in the question of what Gyusel and I would do about food. The Tomsk students had taken with them all the meat and eggs from the kolkhoz store. There was still some sugar, sunflower oil, millet and macaroni. I asked the foreman whether – since there were no eggs or meat – we could be given two litres of milk instead of one. He said he could not decide on this himself and we should have to ask the kolkhoz. But he thought they were unlikely to grant our request since I was already very much in debt to them. I didn't pursue the matter. He did say, however, that I could take some potatoes that had not yet been stored away for the winter. A couple of days later Gyusel and I filled ten sacks full of them, took them home on a cart and put them in our cellar. Those potatoes saved us from starvation during the winter. There was no bread left in the store, but I got some flour which the old woman who lived next door, Sonya's mother-in-law, agreed to bake for us. When we later quarrelled with our neighbours, Gyusel began to do her own baking with soda. We didn't have a proper oven and could only bake small rolls in the stove.

At first we had frequent visitors: people came to have a look at Gyusel and were in general curious about how 'these Muscovites' were getting on. They would come in silently without knocking, sit down in the doorway and spend a long time scratching the backs of their heads while they laboriously thought of something to say. We looked back at them just as silently from our bench at the table. One of the first to come and see us was Leva, who instead of me was now taking the heifers out to graze with Sanka. Leva had also recently married. When he came to Guryevka he had constantly criticized Sanka for setting up house with a woman ten years older, and he kept saying what a disgrace it was. But as the hungry winter approached, Leva had begun to get worried. While I was still away he had taken up with the hunch-backed Polya who was twenty years his senior, and moved in with her. (The trouble with Aksinya, who was even a little older than Polya, was that she had neither a pig nor a cow.) Leva now felt very well off: instead of the meagre summer rations from the kolkhoz store he ate his fill of bacon fat washed down with home-made beer and, being very straight-forward by nature, he swaggered around the village, boasting about how he was living off the fat of the land ('I never had it so good in Moscow'). To enhance the conjugal pleasures of life with his elderly bedmate he drunkenly invited all the men in the village to come and stand outside his window at a specified time in the evening, lit a light inside the house and together with his Polya performed various unsophisticated tricks for the benefit of the onlookers.

Sanka also used to come and see us. He was almost always drunk and sometimes he was followed by his girl-friend Nadya, a brawny woman with a drooping lower lip and an unusually loud and raucous voice. She explained the loudness of her voice by the fact that her mother had been deaf and all the children had had to shout. She was a firm-minded woman and not bad-natured; she treated Sanka like a child who had been committed to her care.

Then we were visited by two elderly brothers: Grisha who had had concussion during the war, so that one of his hands shook all the time, and Petya, who stammered. Later on I often used to go and wash in their bathhouse. During the winter Grisha looked in almost every day to have a game of cards, of which he was tremendously fond. But because of his concussion he couldn't hold the cards properly and kept dropping them all over the floor.

At the beginning we saw a lot of our neighbours: the small red-cheeked Sonya and her husband Mitya, who was a tractor driver and looked very much like Charlie Chaplin. They had three daughters, of whom the eldest was five, and they lived with Mitya's younger brother and mother, who baked bread for them. Mitya's brother was also a tractor driver, but having done his military service, he rather looked down on the other village people, refused to hand his papers in at the kolkhoz office, and said he would soon be leaving. In November Mitya and Sonya were going to celebrate the birthday of one of their daughters and, having brewed some beer for the occasion, asked us whether they could hide it for the time being with us. That summer Sonya had quarrelled with her eldest sister, Katya – the one who lived with the 'parasite' Fedya – and denounced her to the police. The police had arrived just at the moment when Katya was making vodka in their still. She had been fined a hundred roubles and had sworn to get even with Sonya. This was why Sonya and Mitya were now afraid to keep the beer they had brewed at home. We kept two large containers full of it behind our our stove until November, and as a reward for keeping it Sonya invited us to the birthday party. The guests, about twenty altogether, sat at two tables placed end to end. At first we sat in almost complete silence drinking home-distilled vodka and then the beer, with which we ate cold mutton, jellied pigs' trotters and meat pies, though not in any great quantity. The monotony was broken only by the drunken Leva who had been invited along with his Polya. He made a great din trying to propose toasts and all the time made fun of the other guests, saying they were ignorant clodhoppers who didn't know how to speak properly, 'unlike us Muscovites!' Then the women began to sing in chorus and not at all badly, but tired after my day's work and not used to drinking strong home-brewed beer, I soon fell asleep at the table. The party continued into the next day.

We had arrived in Guryevka on the 17th and I had begun work on the 19th. The foreman sent me to work in the linseed-drying shed. Flax, as in many other collective farms in Siberia, was the primary source of income. However, this year the seed had not been properly dried and the linen works in Krivosheino had refused to accept it. It had been dried a second time, but still insufficiently, and now it was being dried once more. The work was being done by the blacksmith, Ivan; my job was to bring him the sacks of seed, empty them and shovel the contents up to the drying flue. The seed was at last accepted, but we were much less fortunate with the flax itself. Flax has to be carded, and there was nobody to do it. Later, the foreman managed to get five or six women to work at it every day in the stables; even so the greater part of the flax was just left to rot away in the

fields. The obvious solution would have been for the factory
to accept the flax in its raw state at a lower price and do the
processing itself by machine; the poor-quality processing
done by hand in the kolkhoz resulted in very great wastage.

After I had worked several days in the drying shed the
foreman put me to work carting fodder out to the cows.
Both herds were still at pasture, but the milch-cows were
being given silage because their yield fell steeply if they ate
only autumn grass. For this job I was given an old piebald
gelding, Sokol, who had once been the strongest horse in the
village but was now so ancient he could scarcely move.

We had to get the corn silage from the pit behind the cowsheds where I had myself helped to put it earlier in the year.
The hard frosts had not yet begun and the silage was not
frozen, so it was quite easy for me to get it out with a pitch-
fork and load it into an iron trough on the cart. Taking only
a little at a time, I made four trips a day. When, three days
later, it began to snow, the milch-cows and some of the
heifers were brought back to the cowsheds, and the rest were
put for a while in a large paddock where, covered with white
hoarfrost, they stood huddled together. It was no longer possible to use a cart and I had to work with a sledge. I was
given two men to help me and every day I had to cart ten
centners of silage and two cartloads of straw to the cowsheds, as well as a certain amount of silage to the heifers in
the paddock. I had now started backing the slow-moving
Sokol right into the silo; the silage was already frozen and
difficult to handle, and as we got deeper into the pit it
became progressively harder to throw it up on to the sledge.
I was not very good at the job, and Sokol was in any case
scarcely able to move the load. Pulling the sledge out of the
silo he fell down several times, and lay helplessly on his
side. I had no end of trouble getting him up again. Then we
had to cover the five hundred metres to the sheds where the
women looking after the cows met me with curses and
obscenities because the cattle were still not fed and they
wanted to get home to attend to their own business there.
I had to unload the silage from the sledge onto a platform
scale; then I dumped it on the ground and the women began
to feed it in pails to the cows while I went off for the next

load. Whenever I carted straw the load often collapsed on the way because of my clumsiness, and I always brought less than the others. From long practice the village men managed this work very much better. I got nothing but curses from the women and eventually the foreman put me on to carting fodder for the heifers only.

But this was even more difficult. The milch-cows were at least stationary, but the heifers roamed freely about their paddock. As soon as I arrived with my load they surrounded me on all sides and started pulling the silage straight from the sledge. The pandemonium was unbelievable as I hit out at their flanks with my pitchfork, trying to get through to the two large wooden troughs and dump the silage there. In their excitement some of them even tried to mount poor old Sokol.

I was again struck by the extremely inefficient way in which this work was done. The two silage pits were right behind the cowsheds. What would be simpler, I kept saying to the kolkhozniks, than to put a row of posts in the ground, lay a steel rail along them and convey the silage straight to the cowsheds in a large bucket driven by an electric motor? It would have taken much less in the way of resources and energy to install something like that than was spent on setting up the preposterous supports for the power cable poles. There were other silo pits three or four kilometres (and some even as far as ten kilometres) away from the village. Every day during the winter a work team went out with large tractor-driven sledges to load the silage and bring it to the farm where it was transferred to horse-drawn sledges and taken to the women in the cowsheds. It was very difficult to go out so far, particularly in snowstorms or during a hard frost. Again, I asked, wouldn't it be simpler to dig all the silage pits near the cowsheds? And how much cheaper and simpler it would be to bring the silage in during the summer, when there were plenty of trucks available in the kolkhoz, rather than transport it with such difficulty in the winter. The kolkhozniks just dismissed me with a wave of the hand: things had always been this way and they didn't need to be told their business by a stranger like me! Their reluctance to make things easier for themselves is due, I believe, to the way they have been taught to think that their job is simply to obey orders, while anything that might make their work easier or harder is a matter for those in authority above them. Their feeling is that even if they do think of some improvement, they will get no reward, and may even get into trouble for doing something out of turn. I don't want to put all the blame on the authorities for this; it is partly a result of traditional peasant inertia.

I found the work very exhausting and there was practically nothing to eat into the bargain. At nights I kept dreaming I was carting silage. I was very pleased, therefore, when on the 30th of October the foreman transferred me to a new job: cleaning the shed where the calves were kept. This was alongside the cowshed; it was slightly over fifty metres long and had doors at both ends; there was a passage in the middle with stalls for the calves running down both sides. One half of the shed was for the baby calves, and in the other half, on both sides of the passage, they kept the heifers. In October and November the finishing touches were still hectically being put to the building by the tractor drivers who, with the onset of winter, would otherwise now be idle. They put slate on the roof, made the floor, the stalls, the feedracks and the doors; a stovemaker came and installed a stove with a cauldron to boil drinking water for the calves. But there were still gaps in the walls and the roof which had to be filled in somehow with straw. In hard frost white wisps of straw hung down from the roof like stalactites and the cows' backs were covered with hoarfrost.

The heifers were looked after by the loud-mouthed Aksinya who always shouted at me angrily for cleaning her section last. The calves were cared for by two women who took things more easily. At first I worked with Sokol and then with another horse called Spiridon who was even older than Sokol but much more spirited. Whenever I harnessed him, he tried to bite me – not so much to hurt as to show me what he felt about the work I was making him do. There was something cat-like in the way he walked, and with his grey mane and clever old eyes he reminded me of Einstein.

Between the stalls and the passage there were gutters into which the women shovelled all the manure; I was supposed to get it out of there, load it on to a sledge and take it out to a field where there were already great piles of it. It was never used as fertilizer, and just went to waste. I took out about six cartloads a day as well as all the wet straw from an outhouse built onto the shed where they kept the newborn calves. For this I was paid at the rate of one and a half 'labour-days' per day. It was very difficult to dig the frozen manure out of the gutters and load it onto the sledge. Steshka, the woman in charge of the cattlesheds, gave me a small shovel which soon broke and then replaced it with one that was even worse. Meanwhile she wandered around the shed saying: 'A fine workman they've sent us, shovelling shit all day, but no idea how to do it.' When the second shovel broke I went to the foreman who told me that Steshka had taken the only good shovel home with her. I went to her house and took it back, and then the work went much better. I also laid wooden boards along the gutters to make a smooth surface from which it was easier to scrape the manure.

Another thing that made life difficult for me was that the kolkhoz had not issued me any boots and I had to work in summer shoes in November frosts when the thermometer went well below zero. The suède gloves I had brought from Moscow were soon in tatters and I had to work with my bare hands. During the whole winter my fingers got so stiff at night-time that in the mornings I could scarcely bend them enough to move the latch on the door. They were giving me no cash in the kolkhoz, so I couldn't buy anything and though I asked the kolkhoz chairman, the Party representative and the foreman to have the kolkhoz issue me gloves and boots by way of an advance, I could get nothing out of them. One day, when the kolkhoz vet saw me cleaning the shed in my light shoes, he took pity on me and gave me a pair of old and worn leather boots. I wore them nearly the whole winter, wrapping sackcloth round my feet. In forty or fifty degrees of frost the sackcloth froze to the sides of the boots and it wasn't easy to get it off. In February the boots almost came apart on my feet, but by then we had a little money and Gyusel bought me some new ones for twelve roubles.

By the middle of November the shop had run out of flour so we were left without bread which, with potatoes, was our staple food. When at this point Steshka again started nagging me and complaining that I was not doing the job properly, I couldn't take it any more and threw my shovel at her, saying I was through and didn't care if the calves drowned in their own shit. I unharnessed the horse and went home. This was the only time I lost my temper. There were many times before and after this that I wanted to send them all to the devil, but I kept myself under control so as not to spoil my chances of getting out of here when half my sentence was up.

Two hours later the foreman came to see me. He spoke to me very pleasantly and gave me a pair of his old patched gloves, adding that he was going to Ivanovka that day and would take a sack of grain with him and have it ground for me there at the mill. I wore these gloves until the spring and every time they got torn Gyusel stitched them up with sacking so that in the end they were as large and heavy as a pair of boxing gloves. Gyusel and I suffered a great deal from lack of proper clothing. Between us we had one pair of old felt boots, which very soon got full of holes. Her sister sent us another pair from Moscow but they were not very suitable for the Siberian weather. Mitya had let us keep the ragged old sheepskin coat that we had used to cover up his home-brewed beer; Gyusel mended it and wore it during the day, and at night we used it as a coverlet. I wore a padded coat and old ski trousers.

From the very beginning firewood was a serious problem for us. A great number of wood blocks had been left over from the building of the day-nursery and at the end of August the foreman had asked one of the drivers to bring a truckload of them to my house. Some of them had been used by the students during September, and Gyusel and I had to get along with what was left. Not far from Guryevka a large quantity of timber had been felled for firewood during the summer by the Krivosheino light-industry co-operative; at the time I could have hired some workers and a truck to go over there, saw some wood for me and bring it back, but I had no money. I had asked my friends to send me twenty-five roubles, but the money came only when I had already left for Moscow. When I got back I was able to collect the money, but there were no longer any workers who could have gone over to saw the wood for me. In any case we needed this money for food and various household needs, such as a kettle, material for curtains, etc. Curtains for the window were absolutely essential because in the villages people are very curious: in the mornings I sometimes found footprints under our windows, and even the woman in charge of the village shop warned me that several people came to eavesdrop under our windows, trying to peer in.

In the taiga, not far from the village, there were some tree trunks with the branches already chopped off (this was left over from timber felled the previous year for the light-industry co-operative). I figured that when our wooden blocks were finished, Gyusel and I might be able to go over and saw some wood for ourselves. One day I managed to get off work earlier than usual and we rode there on the faithful Sokol. There was still not too much snow, and the fallen tree trunks were easy to spot. We began to saw, but either because of our clumsiness or because of the poor quality of the saw, the work went very slowly. With a lot of trouble we sawed off several lengths of about two metres and loaded them onto our sleigh. At home we had to saw them into smaller blocks. The saw they had lent me in the kolkhoz store was too short, it was very blunt and several of its teeth were missing; also we didn't have a trestle. This meant that we just about managed to saw enough for two days, and very soon we had to go out again and fetch more. It was now getting much more difficult to find the tree trunks under the snow. Not far from the place where they were lying, I noticed that there were lots of logs already sawn, split and stacked in neat piles. I thought that they too must belong to the co-operative and couldn't see any reason why we shouldn't take a few of them home with us. Later in the day, when it was already getting dark, I drove back there with Sokol and began to load some of them onto my sleigh. The sleigh got caught on a stump hidden under the snow and I bent down to free it; when I looked up again I suddenly saw that several yards away there was an old man silently pointing a gun at me. I was startled and, seeing who I was, so was the old man. He was someone called Govyazov who lived in our village and this was his firewood. He had been hunting nearby and had heard somebody moving about near his stacks of firewood. Coming up close he had decided with peasant callousness to shoot the thief on the spot, for no trace would ever be found afterwards in the taiga. Fortunately I had raised my head and he had recognized me. I told him I hadn't realized who the wood belonged to and, to try to smooth the matter over, I offered to take the wood I had already loaded to his house. I was very much afraid that it would now get about in the village that I was a thief. However, although Govyazov did indeed tell his story with many embellishments to the whole village, the kolkhozniks were on the whole amused and their attitude to me did not change. Our firewood situation remained difficult.

We had even more trouble with food. The kolkhoz store soon ran out of sugar, and then there was no macaroni or sunflower oil (which we used to fry potatoes). So all we had left was our daily litre of milk for two, millet and potatoes of which, fortunately, we had laid in ample supplies. For days on end we had no bread. It was hard to do without meat, and even harder without sugar. We later sold my shirt for a rouble and my raincoat for three roubles, and bought sugar with the proceeds. A little before this I'd got a small piece of fat from Leva in lieu of a rouble he owed me from the summer. Leva sometimes came in to see us, always drunk and happy to be living so well, and he would say to me: 'Forgive me, Andrei, for living better than you.' But he had an idea that I was pretending to be poor and really had plenty of money. Knowing that I had not been deported for drunkenness like himself, and that I'd spent some time in prison, he took it into his head that I must have been arrested for black market dealings in gold, and he kept telling the kolkhozniks that I had a lot of it hidden away in Moscow. Whenever Gyusel went to the well past his house in her borrowed coat, battered fur boots and my cap, Leva standing on his front steps, would loudly shout: 'I don't believe it, I don't believe it.' He thought it was all a masquerade and all we had to do was take our gold out of its hiding place and buy ourselves proper fur coats.

Several times I told the kolkhoz authorities that they should replenish the supplies in the store, since I could work only if I was fed properly. But they paid no attention. Meanwhile the kolkhozniks, seeing how thin I looked, thought it was a huge joke and said: 'That's what comes of having a young wife – no wonder he's as thin as a rail.' Some of them, however, tried to help me a little: the blacksmith Ivan gave me a few heads of cabbage which we pickled and ate with our potatoes; and old Grisha supplied us with onions throughout the winter. I wrote them letters of gratitude.

When at the beginning of December the District Prosecutor unexpectedly arrived in Guryevka, I decided to complain about the kolkhoz not giving me any food. The Prosecutor, a burly grey-haired man with a puffy face and a thin voice because of all the fat around his throat, replied that the kolkhoz was paying me money and I could buy anything I wanted in the village shop. He went on to express surprise that the kolkhoz had made it its business 'to look after parasites'. I pointed out that the kolkhoz was only paying me small advances and that I could therefore only obtain food through the kolkhoz store on the promise of payment at the end of the year. In the meantime I wanted to eat.

'A kolkhoz isn't a Morozov factory,' the Prosecutor retorted, remembering what he had been told in political instruction classes, at which Morozov factories were always quoted as an example of how the workers were exploited under the Tsars. (The workers drew food in the company store against payday, then when they got their wages they always found they were still in debt to the factory owner.)

'A kolkhoz,' I replied, 'is ten times worse than a Morozov factory. If I work I should be able to eat.'

The Prosecutor's reply to this was: 'The only way of dealing with people like you is to give you a heavy spade and make you dig the frozen earth with the highest possible work norm and then, if you make your norm, give you some black bread.' My complaint, to the great satisfaction of the woman in charge of the kolkhoz store, was thus to no avail.

The Prosecutor, needless to say, had not come to Guryevka to listen to my complaint. The business that had brought him there is a good example of what I was saying earlier about the hazards of being a herdsman.

After I had been switched to other work, the heifers had been taken out to graze by Sanka. In a drunken state he had run into the branch of a tree, injured his head and had to stay at home. The foreman had then ordered Mitya, my neighbour, to take Sanka's place until he got better. Mitya was a tractor driver but at the time his tractor was being repaired. Mitya went out to graze the herd for a day, but the second day he refused and instead, on the instruction of the foreman of the tractor team, began to repair a threshing machine. The hungry heifers, fretful in their paddock, began to try to force their way between the iron pipes with which the gate was barred. Unluckily for him, Kritsky, the herdsman who looked after the milch-cows, happened to pass by at this moment. He too was drunk. Seeing that one of the heifers had got caught between two pipes, he removed all the pipes and the cows made off in different directions. The same day two of them died from no apparent cause. It was said they had eaten too much rye, but nobody could be sure without a proper examination. The kolkhoz authorities were not themselves capable of a proper investigation, and they started legal proceedings in the hope of making whoever was guilty pay the six hundred roubles at which they esti-mated the value of the dead heifers. The Prosecutor had come to look into the matter on behalf of the kolkhoz. After questioning Mitya, Sanka, Kritsky, the foreman, Steshka and others, he went away again. That was all until the trial. I was surprised at the way in which everybody tried to blacken the others in the eyes of the Prosecutor, even though it didn't help them to clear themselves. This was particularly true of Steshka, who did everything she could to damn Kritsky, even though she herself was completely in the clear. I thanked my lucky stars that I hadn't been in charge at the time it happened.

Gyusel and I generally spent our day as follows: In the morning Gyusel lit the stove and made breakfast which usually consisted of fried potatoes. I then left for work, Gyusel went to fetch water, and after that she generally managed to get on with her drawings. Then she lit the stove again and prepared another meal, now of mashed potatoes, for around five o'clock when I came back home. After that we sawed wood. Until suppertime we sometimes studied French, but I must say that we made little progress. On several of those winter evenings I started writing a letter to the head of the Moscow K G B, General Svetlichny, request-ing him not to put difficulties in the way of my release, but I never sent it because I could not write in the required tone of repentance – and to write in any other way would have been useless. Late in the evening we again lit the stove, ate more potatoes and went to sleep on our rickety wooden bed. We lit the stove only to cook our meals and it was very cold in the hut during the night – snow got in through the door and into one corner; later I managed to keep it out by cover-ing the door with sackcloth stuffed with straw, and I got some extra panes of glass from the cowshed to put over our windows.

At night there were always loud squeaking and rustling noises from the mice running around the room; there were so many of them that they seemed to be doing a dance about the table. Besides getting on our nerves they gnawed a hole in the sack of flour which we had incautiously left on the floor. Gyusel had brought two pairs of socks with her, a light and a dark pair, and the mice made off with one of each and gnawed holes in them so that all winter she had to walk around in socks of different colours. At last we could stand it no longer and decided to get a cat.

From the woman who looked after the store I got a small black kitten which we christened Dima in honour of Dima Plavinsky. It was a thin, puny creature and had something wrong with its eyes; it lay curled up on the bed all the time and showed no interest whatsoever in the mice. It also made messes all over the place. I tried to house-train it by shoving its nose into the piles it made and throwing it outside. It then begged to be let in again and immediately climbed right up to the rafters and started crying up there. However much I called it, it would not come down and just ran around meowing piteously. I then went around to the back of the house where there was a gap under the roof and, hanging onto the icy beams, managed with great difficulty to climb up into the attic. But by this time the cat had climbed onto the roof, so I had to scramble up there after it. Since it would have been very difficult to climb down with the kitten in my arms, I just threw it down in the snow. When I came down it was lying in the snow without moving and crying loudly. I brought it in and put it near the stove where it gradually came round. After this it continued to make messes in the room. The struggle between us went on, with increasing cruelty on my part and hopeless despair on the part of the kitten. It all reminded me somehow of the struggle waged by the authorities with runaway prisoners. Finally I compromised by removing a board that covered the trapdoor to the cellar, so that the kitten could go down there to do its business. It accepted this compromise but sometimes continued to misbehave abominably from its hiding place in the cellar, crying in a manner that was either threatening or pathetically imploring. It gradually got used to this way of life, but there was a constant danger that one of us might fall into the cellar, and indeed this happened once to Gyusel who bruised her leg very badly as a result.

The kitten perked up a little after it had eaten some of the fat given us by Leva. Soon it began to play, and then once it caught a mouse that had the insolence to come out in broad daylight. It soon caught a few more, and the mice disappeared from our hut. It began to grow up into a very devil-may-care creature who in the summer even went for dogs, not to mention other cats. Although I treated it very badly, it unaccountably became much more attached to me than to Gyusel, and it particularly liked to sit on my shoulder. Gyusel even began to paint my portrait with it sitting there.

Gyusel had begun to work in the middle of November when we managed to get a large board to which we could fasten her drawing paper. Since we had no canvas she worked with pastels on large sheets of rough paper. On sunny days the hut was quite bright from the reflected light of the snow, although one window was covered over with plywood and the other two were coated with a thick layer of frost. During our whole time in Guryevka Gyusel was able to finish only three things: my portrait, her own portrait and a double one in which she drew herself in the nude – a remarkable feat of endurance considering how terribly cold it was inside the hut. At first some of the kolkhozniks wanted her to do their portraits, but they did not much like the pastel technique – they preferred their pictures to be bright and glossy, and furthermore they were not willing to pay more than five roubles, so that nothing came of all this.

The village women then began to gossip about Gyusel, saying that here she was living in the village, but not doing any work in the kolkhoz – and come to that, who knew whether she was really my 'legal' wife? To register our marriage we had to go to Krivosheino and get my papers which were being kept by the police there. A couple of weeks after our arrival I had finished work early, harnessed the rust-coloured mare Koshka instead of Sokol, and driven over to Krivosheino with Gyusel. But we were too long on the way and by the time we arrived the Commandant had left and we had to drive back empty-handed through the dark Siberian night. The tired Koshka went along very slowly and we took turns running alongside her to try to get warm. After this we kept putting off going there again, because we never had the time, and went on living 'in sin'.

At the beginning of December, when I got my first day off, and Gyusel had just begun to paint my portrait with the kitten on my shoulder, Mitya suddenly appeared in the doorway and solemnly announced with a stupid expression on his face: 'The police want to see you.' He took us to a hut near the cowshed where we found the local policeman and somebody else in civilian clothes who I assumed must be the district representative of the KGB. On the benches along the wall village women were sitting all agog with anticipation of what was to come. The policeman asked for Gyusel's papers and immediately passed them to the man in civilian clothes who copied out all the particulars. The policeman then said that if she wanted to live here she must register as a resident and work in the kolkhoz. This would have meant losing her permit to reside in Moscow, and with it any hope of ever returning there. I therefore replied that Gyusel had come here for a short time only, with no other purpose than to formalize our marriage, and that after this she would leave. The policeman said that in that case we must go to the Commandant and get my papers. I replied that we had already tried to do so and would go there again as soon as possible. The man in civilian clothes said he doubted whether they would register our marriage, in view of the fact that Gyusel was not a resident here. To this I answered that it would really be the limit if marriages were allowed only between people who resided in the same district. After this they let us go, but it was clear that we mustn't lose any more time.

We again set off for Krivosheino on the 16th of December as soon as I had finished work. In the winter there was a daily bus in the afternoon which stopped at Guryevka on the way to Krivosheino, and we had thought we would go on it, spend the night at the bus shelter in Krivosheino and present ourselves to the Commandant the following morning. For some reason the bus failed to appear that afternoon, but we managed to get a lift in a truck going the same way. When we got to Krivosheino we discovered that the bus shelter there closed at eight in the evening. We had supper in the restaurant and then started walking around the streets. It was now night and getting colder all the time. We went to the post office and sat on a bench in the corner, hoping we might be allowed to spend the night there. But we were thrown out. I did not want to go and ask permission to stay in the police station because Gyusel had been here two months without a residence permit. I thought we would have to walk the streets all night but then I suddenly remembered that there was a boarding house. By the light of a street lamp we counted up our money and found we had about a rouble. The boarding house was a large wooden building in a lane just off the main street. The woman in charge of it was very friendly and told us that a bed cost seventy-eight kopecks. Since we had money only for one, she put Gyusel in a room and let me sleep in the lobby on a bench, even giving me a blanket. In the morning we went to the police station.

Here we had an unpleasant surprise: the Commandant had gone off on a trip somewhere. Leaving Gyusel to wait in the corridor, I went to the Chief of the station, Lieutenant Colonel Korotkikh who remembered me, received me very courteously, asked how I was getting on in the kolkhoz, and expressed sympathy when I told him about the shortage of food. When I inquired about my papers, he said they had been locked up in the safe by the Commandant who had taken the key away with him. But he was evidently moved by our plight and went on to say: 'I tell you what. Go to your village soviet and ask the secretary to telephone me, and I will tell them to register the marriage without your papers – they can have them stamped later.'

By midday, having begged a lift in a police car driven by a sergeant who knew us, Gyusel and I managed to get to the village soviet in Novokrivosheino. The secretary, who incidentally was the wife of the chairman of our kolkhoz, expressed her astonishment.

'How can I register you without papers?' she protested. But she agreed to phone Korotkikh, who fortunately was still in his office. 'But suppose he's married already,' I heard her say. 'I'm supposed to look and see in his papers.' He succeeded, however, in persuading her that it would be all right to go ahead, and she began to make out the marriage certificate. We now learned that it would cost us one and a half roubles, and since we had only a few kopecks left I went to the kolkhoz office to ask for another advance.

'How much does he owe us already?' the chairman asked the accountant. But then he decided to be generous and said: 'I suppose we can give you an advance on an occasion like this.' And they solemnly paid out two roubles.

All we needed now was witnesses. The local school mistress, who just happened to come into the village soviet at that moment, agreed to sign as witness for my wife, and the chairman of the soviet, a talkative old man of about sixty, agreed to sign for me. After this he went out into the next room, changed the expression on his face and returned in his capacity as a representative of Authority. Congratulating us in pompous language, he handed me the marriage certificate. This was the last official act in which he was to take part: a few days later he was fired for embezzlement.

That evening we returned home to be greeted by the

squalling of our famished cat. With the fifty kopecks left over from our advance, we had bought some sugar in Novo-krivosheino and for the first time in many days drank our tea sweet. This was how we celebrated our wedding.

CHAPTER 21

Slave Labour

I HAD scarcely got the knack of cleaning out the calves' stalls when the foreman took me off the job. It was regarded in the kolkhoz as a soft job and one of the kolkhozniks who had hitherto worked as a stableman now asked to take over from me. But it was simpler to take me off my present job than to find new work for me. The foreman could hardly send me to help bring in the silage from the outlying silos because he realized perfectly well that I would not survive for several hours in an open sledge without a proper coat and boots, and on my starvation diet. He gave me a day off and then on the 1st of December sent me to help Fedya and Katya clean out the cowshed.

In the winter there were twenty-two people working with the cattle: six milkmaids, three women to look after the calves, three men to bring fodder, four people to clean out the stalls, a water-carrier, a woman to separate the milk, a man to take the milk to the butter factory, a mechanic in charge of the electric milking machine, a watchman and a woman supervisor who was also supposed to weigh the fodder. If one adds that the kolkhozniks who usually worked in the fields were now employed solely to bring in fodder from the silos, it will be seen that in winter the whole village was employed to look after the livestock.

The cowshed was longer and wider than the other shed for the calves. It held over a hundred and fifty milch-cows and heifers. After some of the heifers had calved the number of milkmaids was increased from four to six, each of them being responsible for about twenty-five cows. The milking was done electrically, except in the final stages when the job was finished off by hand. But in winter the pipes kept getting frozen and several times a week the milking had to be done entirely by hand; apart from this, the machinery was always breaking down. The cowshed was not properly insulated against the cold, and in very low temperatures – that winter there were sometimes frosts of fifty degrees centigrade below zero – the calves froze in their mothers' wombs, and the loss of new stock was very high. In winter the milk-maids had to work very hard indeed. The first milking was at six in the morning. Then they had to clean out the stalls and feed hay to the cows. After a short break they had to milk them again, and then once more at one o'clock, after which they cleaned the stalls and waited until the fodder was brought. They had to load the silage and bran by hand into the feed racks; they also had to bring water to the calves by hand. At seven o'clock they again milked them. In addi-tion to all this, several times a month they had to take the cows out for exercise and herd them all back in again.

Those milkmaids who lived at the far end of the village came to work at six in the morning and only got back home late in the evening; the luckier ones who lived nearby had time to run home for a while between milkings. So it went on day after day, without a break – they never got time off. For this reason, even though their wages in winter were about three times as much as anybody else's, nobody liked to work with the livestock. Because of their back-breaking work the milkmaids were always bad-tempered, and there were constant scenes and outbursts of obscene language, as they accused each other of stealing hay or diluting the milk with water. When they ran out of bad language, they hitched up their skirts and showed each other their bare behinds. I don't think they actually stole hay from each other, but I do know that it was impossible to leave a shovel or pitch-fork lying around without it immediately disappearing.

There was also constant verbal warfare between the milk-maids and the supervisor, Steshka. She was a small, sly woman of about forty with a sing-song voice. Since she could barely read or write she was quite unsuitable for the job, constantly making mistakes in the work-sheets. People had several times written to complain about her, but to no effect. It must be said in all fairness, however, that she was the best supervisor one could have hoped for: the situation would have been even worse if she had been replaced by one of the milkmaids. A great scourge of Soviet agriculture is semi-illiteracy combined with an unwillingness to learn and a belief that experience is much more important than training.

My new job was exceedingly unpleasant. As in the shed where the calves were kept, there was a long passage with gutters on either side down the whole length of the building; the cows stood on both sides, on one of which there was a double row with another narrow passage and gutter between the stalls and the wall of the cowshed. Since it was impossible to bring the horse into this second narrow passageway, a large bucket had been installed on an overhead rail and the manure had to be loaded into this sliding receptacle. This was where they put me to work; I had to pull down the bucket, load manure into it and gradually push it along the rail. When it got full I had to slide it along the whole length of the shed, slipping in the liquid excrement underfoot, and tip out the contents into the sledge on which Fedya loaded the manure from the central passageway. He then took it out to the field next to the shed and dumped it there. The gutter was very narrow, and in hard frosts it was terribly difficult to scrape out the frozen muck. When the weather got warmer, on the other hand, I had to shovel out a sloppy mixture of liquid dung and urine, always watching out lest one of the cows should do its business on me in this confined space. Sometimes the bucket fell over and I had to reload it all over again. I kept thinking of a drawing in my history book when I was a child at school: a Roman slave chained to a wheelbarrow.

The cowshed was completely unsuitable for its purpose, yet year after year nobody did anything about it. This winter several beams had become warped and the whole place was in danger of collapsing.

Far from thinking about repairing it, nobody even bothered to nail down a loose board in the floor on which the horses stumbled every time they were backed down the central passageway. 'Why should I bother?' everybody asked. 'It's not my shed and they'd only pay me five kopecks for doing it.' You might well ask why I didn't nail it down myself, since I seemed to be so fond of giving advice. I can only say that, if somebody had come up and advised me to change a rotten floor board while I was clearing out the manure, swearing in the foulest language as I slipped on the icy floor, I should have said: 'The shed can go to hell as far as I'm concerned and all the cows can die. I'm not doing this of my own free will and I couldn't care less!' This is more or less how the kolkhozniks felt as well. 'The work of the slave is uncaring', runs a line from a poem by Ovid that I once studied in the university.

In general, the kolkhozniks do not work as hard as all that. It only looks as though they do because of the constant strain of their bad working conditions, which turn the simplest job into an ordeal. But they boast unceasingly about what terrific workers they are and ask how townsfolk would make out if they had to work in such conditions. I always told them they were very bad workers for not trying to make things a little easier and simpler for themselves.

Because Fedya was always getting drunk, I often took on the additional job of carting the manure into the fields, as well as loading it into my bucket. This had the great advantage that I could occasionally leave work a little early and use the horse for my own purposes. The fact is that Gyusel and I very much needed a horse to go and fetch firewood. Our situation in this respect was now very precarious. As I've already said, we had been able, before there was too much snow, to go out and saw tree trunks previously felled for the co-operative, and I'd also been able to get some more of the large blocks left over from the building of the day-nursery. But it was now impossible to find the tree trunks under the deep snow, and our wood blocks were rapidly coming to an end (some of them got so deeply covered in the snow outside the house that I did not find them again until the spring).

The previous summer, a few miles from the village, I had seen something that struck me at the time: several large clumps of bare birch trunks, without leaves and almost without branches, standing in the middle of a swamp and holding their naked tops to the sky. There was something poetic and awesome about these enormous dead trees still rearing skyward. Now, however, I took a more practical view of them:

it would be good to chop them down for firewood. They stood about a hundred yards from the road which was cleared every day by a bulldozer. Gyusel and I went out with the rust-coloured Koshka with whom I'd been working in the cowshed from the end of December. She was a tough but rather stubborn mare and didn't like going into the snow; I had to clear a path for her every time, from the road to the trees.

Nearly up to our waists in snow, Gyusel and I would saw one of the birch trees until it began to lean over, then we would jump back as it fell into the snow with a loud swoosh, disappearing completely and leaving only a brownish trace of lose snow on the surface where it had fallen through. Then, floundering like swimmers in deep water, we went alongside the fallen trunk and sawed it under the snow into two or three metre lengths; each trunk yielded between five and seven of them. We also felled some of the smaller birches, which we cut into two or three pieces. In the meantime Koshka would stand meekly on the path that we had made from the road and munch the hay that I stole each time from the hayloft next to the cowshed. Then I manhandled the sawn logs over to the sleigh and loaded about six of them at a time, leaving the rest behind in a pile, and we set off home. We went out to fell trees like this for three days running; then for another five days I went out alone to bring back the sawn lengths we had left behind. I tried to pick days that were not so cold, but in Siberia the weather changes very quickly, and by the time we started back home it had sometimes become viciously cold. I remember that my hands were once so frozen that I couldn't pick up the reins, and if I touched them it was like getting an electric shock. My gloves and trousers got wet while I worked in the snow, and then they became crusted with ice. Whenever I moved I felt as though someone were slapping me on the backside. The going was hardest of all for Gyusel.

Towards the end of December our life became not only warmer, but less hungry too. The reason was that on the 25th of the month Gyusel suddenly got a money order from home with a letter saying that her mother was very sick in hospital, and asking her to return to Moscow as quickly as possible.

Gyusel was on the point of going, but she suspected that it was all a ruse, and that her parents were simply trying to get her away from me. So she did not leave and we began to spend the money that had been sent to pay her fare. As we learned later, her guess had been right.

Thanks to this money we were able to buy a few kilograms of bacon fat on the cheap. Leva had quarrelled with his Polya; he had torn her dress with his teeth, threatened to burn the house down and then run off taking several pieces of bacon fat with him. This he sold us for half its value in order to get money for vodka.

Shortly afterwards I was also able to bring home the head, feet and insides of a sick cow that had been slaughtered by the kolkhoz. They had sent the carcass to the restaurant in Krivosheino, and I had bought the rest from them. We got all the fat out of the intestines and melted it down, throwing everything else away. A little later, in February, the kolkhoz slaughtered a small lame calf and sent the carcass to Krivosheino to be fed to the hens at the poultry farm there. Since this meat was not being sold, nobody bothered to weigh it, and the foreman let me have one of the legs. Gyusel and I ate veal for almost a month.

During the winter we got to know several other 'parasites' living in the district who always came to see us when they were in Guryevka. At the beginning of December we were visited by an exile from Ivanovka who had previously lived in our house and was greatly surprised to find that it was no longer empty. He was a tall strong man of over forty, a metalworker from Krasnodar who had been deported here about five years ago and had worked in the kolkhoz under its previous chairman, Inglevsky; he had later gone to work in Krivosheino as a driver for the district co-operative. His name was Shaposhnikov, and in Ivanovka he had moved in with a local Latvian woman (he always referred to her as a 'bitch') from whom he had a small daughter. He drank very heavily and once almost froze to death when he fell drunk from his sledge during a visit to us in Guryevka.

As an old-timer here he told us a great deal about his early experiences in exile and about Inglevsky, under whom the present kolkhoz chairman had served as the Party representative. Inglevsky had particularly disliked 'parasites' and was always urging the locals to beat them up. He himself often used his fists both on exiles and kolkhozniks, and everybody had been too terrified to complain. Once he almost beat to death a sixteen-year-old youth right in his office, but on that occasion some students who were then working in the kolkhoz intervened, and Inglevsky was brought to trial and expelled from the Party. He was also sentenced to a year's forced labour, but in practice this only meant that he was appointed manager of a butter factory in Shegarka, a large village on the Ob, at a considerably reduced salary! Three years later he was caught with his hand in the till, tried again and this time sent to prison. Inglevsky had a special hatred of Latvians – up to 1957 there had been about twenty families of them living in exile in Guryevka – and he had put some of them in prison for 'sabotage', though most people in the village had a very good opinion of the Latvians as hard-working and skilled people. When Gerasimov, the former Party representative, took over as chairman from Inglevsky, he had once asked Shaposhnikov: 'Why are you always drunk?' 'And why are you always hunch-backed?' Shaposhnikov had answered back. Offended, Gerasimov had complained to the police and Shaposhnikov got fifteen days for 'petty hooliganism', after which, with the agreement of the police, he had gone to work with the district co-operative. The police jealously guarded the authority of the kolkhoz chairman and the other local bosses: for insulting them you could get at least two weeks in jail, while they could yell at you in the foulest language with impunity.

One evening we had a visit from a very swarthy thick-set man with an enormous hooked nose and horrible-looking ears. He proved to be Vartan, an Armenian who had spent two years in a camp near Tomsk for stabbing someone to death and had now come back to serve the remaining period of his exile in Krivosheino where he worked for the light-industry co-operative as a lumberman. He was very much surprised to see me wearing ordinary boots, and gave me a pair of felt boots (*valenki*) which, though they had holes in them, I later used when I went to fetch firewood. He told us how he had first gone to prison at the age of sixteen,

recounting his experiences with all the eloquence of a professional criminal. He was a card-sharper of genius, and
when we played 'vingt-et-un' with him, he always told us
far in advance how the game would end. However closely
I watched him, I could never catch him cheating. He was
addicted to *chifir* and had a very low tolerance for alcohol.
Once he drank a little vodka, became very aggressive and
started to fight with me. I managed to get a grip on his head,
but he was twice as strong as I and I would have come off
very badly if he hadn't all at once gone completely limp.
When I let go his head, he slumped back and went to sleep
straightaway. Later he said he couldn't remember a thing.

Sanka Glazov, the herdsman from Novokrivosheino whom
I have mentioned already, came to see us several times. I
have never met a gentler and more harmless person. He was
from Lipetsk and had been sent here for five years, but he had
already served two additional years at forced labour for
absenteeism. Several times we drank with him in our hut,
together with the other Sanka from Guryevka, and he sang
songs in a hoarse but pleasant voice. We particularly liked
a song he had made up to the tune of an old underworld
song. Sanka's words went something like this:

> The river flows quickly by,
> Washing the sand and pebbles,
> And a young 'parasite'
> Begs the hunch-backed boss:
> Let me go home.

This because he has a young wife crying her heart out.
But the hunch-backed kolkhoz chairman is unmoved and
replies:

> Let her weep,
> Let her mourn,
> The young 'parasite'
> Must serve his five-year term.

Several times he told me when he was drunk that 'life had
treated him very hard': at the age of just over twenty he
had been in an automobile accident after which he had
become impotent as a result of an operation on his hip; he

had then begun to drink heavily and had been sent to Siberia. Here he drank even more, and it was obvious that he would never leave, except to go to prison. In March he again missed work and cursed the chairman in foul language, so he was tried once more and given another eighteen months at forced labour. He came to spend the night with us before the trial; the previous day he had been paid off in the kolkhoz and immediately spent all the money on drink. He swore he would never work in the kolkhoz again, but after the trial he was sent to Novokrivosheino to work with the livestock there.

Because of these people who came to see me, there was a note in one of Vera's propaganda sheets denouncing me as a drunkard and a bad influence on the other kolkhozniks, but there was no follow-up to this, and later, in April, I was even praised as a good worker who set an excellent example to the others!

Just before the New Year there were rumours that there was going to be a general amnesty, but they proved to be false. There was more truth in another rumour to the effect that, except in Moscow and Leningrad, people would no longer be deported for 'parasitism', but made to do forced labour on the spot. Someone in the police station told me that this rumour was true. At the end of January Fedya had reached the half-way mark of his sentence, and he applied to the kolkhoz office asking them to remit the rest of it. I was eager to know whether our kolkhoz had been affected by the changes now in the air, and whether Fedya would duly be released. But the weeks went by without his getting so much as an answer, and he was afraid to ask the chairman directly. At last he could stand it no longer, got very drunk and missed work for three days. Fortunately, Steshka, the supervisor of the cowshed, took pity on him and didn't report him.

With the New Year (1966) the blizzards started and our small house was soon buried in snow almost up to the roof; we kept the stove blazing with birchwood, and our black kitten lay in front of it. At the end of January the kolkhoz accounts for the previous year were made up, and before long the final settlement was made with us. This year the value of the 'labour-day' came out, as planned, at sixty kopecks and one kilogram of grain. Half the cash had already been paid in advances, and the kolkhozniks were now about to get the balance in a lump sum; for the grain, however, they would have to wait until after the harvest in the autumn.

In half a year I had earned two hundred and seventy-eight 'labour-days', in other words one hundred and sixty-six roubles eighty kopecks, of which eighty-three roubles forty kopecks were still due to me. I had hoped this money would be enough to pay off my debt to the kolkhoz, and that there might even be some to spare. But when the accountant showed me the wage sheet, there was nothing but a dash against my name. The situation was this: after the loan of thirty roubles for my fare to Moscow, two roubles for the marriage certificate, a fine of six roubles for some hay I had spoiled, sixteen roubles for potatoes, five for the cow's head, six each month for milk, and various other debts to the kolkhoz stores, I still owed twenty-six roubles. However, I was later to get nearly three centners of grain worth twelve roubles a centner at the State purchasing price. After subtracting the centner which I had taken in flour I had about twenty-four roubles' worth of grain coming to me, and I would then be more or less quits with the kolkhoz, provided I took no more on credit from the stores.

The kolkhozniks now all got a hundred and fifty, and some as much as two hundred roubles each – even though the kolkhoz had deducted heavy payment for the use of tractors to plough their private plots for potatoes, and for the haulage of hay up to their houses in the winter. For people who were used to getting only fifteen or twenty roubles in cash a month, this was a great deal of money indeed, and they all immediately started drinking. For three days the village shop was opened from early in the morning till late at night; the woman in charge of it was run off her feet, but she exceeded her sales plan for January four times over. The kolkhozniks bought not only vodka, but lengths of cloth to make dresses and curtains, good trousers to wear on weekends, jars of preserved fruit, gingerbread by the kilogram, and in general all the stuff that had been lying around unwanted in the shop all year. There were also one or two accidents: the drunken Kritsky, for instance, set out to visit us, but on the way he fell into the snow and went to sleep. When he woke up both his hands were frozen and he was in hospital for more than a month; they amputated two fingers on one hand and three on the other. From all over the village we could hear drunken shouting and the shrieking of women.

At the beginning of February there was supposed to be a general meeting of the kolkhoz, and according to gossip the district Party committee would use the occasion to dismiss the chairman for repeated failure to fulfill the plan. The kolkhozniks with whom the chairman was not at all popular, were looking forward to this with some glee. However, the Party committee had no intention of firing him and the meeting was the usual futile waste of time. The plan had indeed again not been fulfilled this year, but the kolkhozniks had nevertheless been paid in accordance with the original estimated production figure. The chief source of ready cash for the kolkhoz had been the sale of flax, but they had made only a very small profit on their dairy products, while on grain there had been a net loss: the State paid twelve roubles for a centner of grain that had cost the kolkhoz fifteen roubles to produce.

The kolkhozniks were now drinking away the last cash that would ever be paid in Guryevka under the 'labour-day' system. In December there had already been rumours that in the new year the kolkhoz would switch to a system of monthly wages entirely in cash, as in the State farms (sovkhozes). The kolkhozniks were very apprehensive about this change, wondering how they would feed their private livestock if they received only money and no grain. They were all very upset and kept saying that without their livestock they would starve. But they all meekly awaited whatever fate might bring them.

From January, in accordance with the new economic directives, the kolkhoz did, in fact, go over to cash payment, but it was done in the interests of the kolkhozniks, to give them somewhat better incentives, and their fears proved groundless. Under the new rates of pay, work that had previously been estimated as being worth one 'labour-day', that is, seventy-two kopecks (sixty plus twelve per kilogram of grain) was now paid for at a rate of approximately eighty kopecks or even a rouble and, moreover, a quarter of this payment was made not in cash but in grain at the end of the year, so that the kolkhozniks now received rather more grain than before. They gradually got used to the new system and nearly all of them were satisfied with it.

This is not to say, of course, that the kolkhozniks' wages went up so much. During the winter a milkmaid would now make on the average eighty roubles (2·2 roubles per centner of milk and five roubles for each newborn calf); in the summer it would be less because of the reduced rates for the job. The women looking after the calves would get about the same, while the men employed to bring silage in from the fields during the winter would make twenty to twenty-five roubles, and a little more in the summer for pre- paring it. During the winter the tractor drivers got less than a rouble for each job, so that they hardly made more than thirty roubles a month, unless some of the jobs involved long journeys. Even less was earned by the mechanic in charge of the milking machinery, who after the introduction of the new system even went on strike for three days. The wages for January were paid at the end of February, but later they began to pay people for each month in the middle of the following month.

The kolkhoz was able to switch to this new system thanks to a broader and more flexible policy of giving credits to the farms, and also because of direct pressure from the State – if it had depended on the people in charge of the kolkhozes nothing would have come of it. I heard that there was going to be large-scale capital investment by the State in agricul- ture in order to make it more effective and somehow reduce the catastrophic gap between it and other branches of the economy.

It seems to me that over-hasty collectivization and the forced pace of industrial development at the expense of agriculture were great mistakes for which the country has paid dearly in both political and economic terms. The only possible way to put this right is to give agriculture large transfusions of capital.

I am not a specialist in agriculture and have read virtually nothing on economics, but during the time I worked on the kolkhoz I made a number of observations that I should like to summarize here. The prime condition for a sensible use of any new capital investment, and for the efficient running of agriculture in particular, seems to me to be the granting of much greater independence to the kolkhozes. It is essential to give up not only the detailed supervision of their work but the whole system of planning it from above. Each kolkhoz should be allowed to make its own plan which it would submit to the State, not for approval but simply for information, to enable the authorities to form an overall picture. The State could continue to regulate agricultural production through its fixing of wholesale prices (a sensible policy in regard to these is also, incidentally, a matter of urgent importance). In my view the State should put pressure on the kolkhozes not to step up production in quantitative terms, but to raise the quality of their output. I further believe that the independence of the kolkhozes can be achieved only through the independence of its individual members. If the kolkhoz chairman is to be made independent of the district authorities (to whom at the moment he is completely subordinated), then he should be appointed by the kolkhozniks themselves in real elections, and should be truly accountable to them. The need is not to 'further develop kolkhoz democracy', to use the empty newspaper phrase, but to create, virtually from scratch, genuinely democratic attitudes in the kolkhozes. Without this it will be impossible to make the kolkhozes feel that the development of agriculture depends primarily on their own individual efforts. They will achieve more only if they have a feeling of self-respect and personal responsibility for their jobs. I think this is partly a matter of education. Capital investment in education may perhaps be the slowest to show results, but in the long run it might be the most effective. It is vital to raise teaching standards in village schools and also to introduce subjects of direct relevance to agriculture. There should also be training courses for adult kolkhozniks, particularly for those in positions of responsibility: foremen, people in charge of the livestock, etc. Milkmaids, for example, should have an elementary knowledge of veterinary medicine, and everybody should be given courses in simple accounting. This is something that the students sent to work on the farms could do. It is also necessary to guarantee minimum wages in the kolkhozes and to raise pension rates at least up to the lowest level of the cities, thus giving the kolkhozniks a greater sense of security. Credit on the most favourable terms should be given for building and for purchasing labour-saving devices; there is also a need for mobile building teams that could go from kolkhoz to kolkhoz doing specialized construction jobs under contract. The present small villages should gradually be replaced by larger residential centres properly equipped with modern utilities, shops, recreation rooms, etc. This would go hand in hand with the abandonment of small private plots which take up so much of the kolkhozniks' time and effort. From the economic point of view, this very small-scale farming is a quite irrational anachronism. On no account, however, should the private plots be done away with by administrative pressure, since this would again lead to hunger and neglect of work on the land. The kolkhozniks should be allowed to buy farm products at cost to make it cheaper for them to buy milk and pork from the kolkhoz than to keep a cow or a pig in their own backyards. Once the kolkhozniks saw the advantage of this, they would voluntarily give up their private plots which are, in fact, a burden to them. But anybody who wanted to carry on with his private plot, especially old-age pensioners, should be allowed to do so.

People should not be forced by administrative pressure to stay in the kolkhozes and prevented from going to the towns. The constant flight of labour from the villages to the towns is a natural process common to all countries, and for us it is absolutely necessary in view of the fact that the proportion between the urban and rural population is still not what it should be for an economically advanced country. Agriculture should be improved not by increased numbers, but by raising the level of skills. Least of all does it need the forced labour of 'parasites'. Even in the days of Peter the Great it was found unprofitable to round up vagrants, drunkards, and other such dregs of society in order to put them to work in the 'manufactories'. And finally, agriculture must be developed intensively, rather than extensively, as at present. To increase the production of milk and meat we need to raise the productivity rather than the numbers of livestock; to improve the output of grain, we need a better yield per acre rather than an extension of the amount of land under cultivation.

But the main thing, as I have already said, is to create democratic forms of management and to instill in the kolkhozniks a sense of really being in charge of their own affairs. It is possible that there is a kind of vicious circle here: economic democratization is impossible without political democratization – which, in its turn, is impeded by poverty and ignorance.

CHAPTER 22

My Wife's Departure

ONCE we had laid in firewood for the winter, I decided I would use some pretext to get out of my work in the cow-shed, which I found intolerable, not least because of constant rows with Fedya and Katya. In February I asked Shapovalov to let me help bring in the silage, pointing out that it was now not so cold. But he was against this, saying it would mean certain death for me, since I would freeze on the open sledge in my flimsy padded jacket. But a little after this they needed someone to cart water for the livestock – the man who had been doing it until now had left because the work took up the whole of his day. I started this new work on the 17th of February. People were always glad to give up work in the cattlesheds, and it was difficult to get anyone to work there, even though the earnings, as I have said, were about four times as much as for other jobs. Apart from some-one to carry water, they needed an extra hand to look after the calves. A great many were born during the winter and the milkmaids had no one to pass them on to once they had grown a little. There was also need for an extra woman to help with the milking so that the milkmaids could take it in turn to have a day off once a week, though nobody seri-ously imagined that they would really be permitted such a luxury. To fill the job of looking after the calves they at first tried to bring in a woman with two young children whose husband had drowned that summer. Despite all their arguments and threats she categorically refused because it meant working from morning to night and she had no one who could look after her children. 'After the death of my husband the kolkhoz promised to help,' she said, 'but they have done nothing for me, and now look at the terrible state my house is in – I shall get out of here as soon as I can.' 'Good riddance to you,' the chairman shouted. 'Did you expect us all to make a great fuss over you just because your husband died?' The next day they tried to give the job to the bookkeeper's wife, but she, too, refused because of her two young children; they threatened to make her pay for two calves that had died, but she still wouldn't take the job. Neither would the wife of the man who supervised the tractor drivers: she also had a young child. The women who were already working in the cowsheds cursed and swore at these others who were shirking it: 'Bitches! We've got children too, but we have to work – we've got even more kids than you!' The other women answered back: 'Shouldn't get laid so often, then you'd have fewer!' The chairman and the foreman could only stand by helplessly while they swore at each other.

The village women had been grumbling for some time about the way my wife had been living in the kolkhoz all these months without a residence permit and refusing to do any work. The most vicious among them, such as Sonya, who had taken a great dislike to us, had been threatening to phone the police and denounce her. They now began to insist that Gyusel should either leave or go to work in the cowsheds. The situation was indeed paradoxical: here I was, exiled for not working, yet my wife had spent four months in the same place without regular work or a residence permit. At the beginning of January the local policeman had come to ask whether Gyusel was working in the kolkhoz. I had replied that she would shortly be leaving. This was now a month ago. Since I had managed to keep in with the foreman, the chairman and the police, Gyusel had so far been left in peace, but she might at any moment be served notice to leave within twenty-four hours. After two such warnings, as I knew only too well, she could make herself liable to prosecution under Article 198 of the Criminal Code for infringing the regulations on residence permits.

Of course, if Gyusel had taken one of the jobs in the cowshed she could have expected to be left alone for some time, since the regulations were enforced less strictly in under-populated Siberia than in the large cities. But I was firmly opposed to this and said that, though I was doing forced labour here, my wife was a free agent and would not work in the kolkhoz for nothing. There was another possibility: in December Gyusel had been offered the job of managing the recreation room in Novokrivosheino, which would have enabled her to live here with me till the end of my term. But this, too, would have meant that she would have to register as a local resident, thus forfeiting her right to live in Moscow and losing all hope of ever returning there. For this reason we refused the offer. Also, regardless of the local situation, if Gyusel were absent from Moscow for more than six months she would risk losing her right to live there. If this were to happen, we would find it impossible to take up residence not only in Moscow but in any other large city.

Gyusel herself was very reluctant to leave and, moreover, we did not have the money for her fare. In February I received only seven roubles for the previous month's work, and that was all we had. Not to be taken unawares by a notice from the police, I wrote about our desperate situation to an old friend of my father's and we decided that in the meantime she would immediately go and work in the cowshed at the first sign of trouble. For a long time there was no reply to my letter and we became very nervous. Next I was told that the police had phoned the village soviet and instructed them to tell me that my wife must either leave immediately or take out a residence permit here and get a job in the kolkhoz. The situation was desperate, and I wrote to another friend with a request for money. I kept putting off the foreman with promises that Gyusel would either leave the next day or go and work in the cowshed as a relief milkmaid (the calves had by now been transferred, for want of someone to look after them, to the farm in Ivanovka). We were quite overjoyed when, on the point of despair, we suddenly got a money order by cable for fifty roubles, and then a friendly letter from my father's old comrade. We could now breathe more freely, but Gyusel still put off her departure, using the blizzard that now began to rage as an excuse. In this way she gained a whole week. However, there was at last nothing to do but for her to leave, and on the 8th of March we said goodbye, not knowing when we should see each other again. Though I no longer had to worry on Gyusel's account. it was hard for me to go back into the empty shack where there was now only the black cat, Dima.

After Gyusel left, I took to drinking occasionally by myself – under the new system I received a little cash and was thus able to afford it. I also began to worry a great deal about how and where I should live on my return from exile. I even played with the idea of trying to settle in one of the towns in the Baltic States and enrolling in the university there: I had almost lost hope of returning to Moscow.

My new work – hauling water to the cattlesheds – was not terribly hard, but it took up almost the whole day. I began at eleven in the morning by harnessing a horse to a sledge on which there were two barrels, each holding about twelve bucketfuls. I got water from the pumphouse and took it to the six milkmaids in the cowshed and to the two women in the shed for the heifers, most of which had by now calved. Altogether, I had to provide water for about two hundred head of cattle. I drove the sledge right into the cowshed so that each milkmaid in turn could draw water in a bucket from the barrels and give each of the cows some to drink; each needed about three or four bucketfuls, and the work went very slowly. At one time the job had been mechanized. The cowshed still had pipes leading from the pumphouse, but the system had long since broken down, the pipes were frozen and covered with rust, and nobody thought of trying to repair them. I suggested placing several barrels in the cowshed and connecting them to the nearby pump with a long hose; as long as the hose was emptied of water and stowed away after use it would not freeze. The whole job would then have taken an hour instead of the best part of the day. There was a suitable hose in the kolkhoz, but as usual it was impossible to overcome the general inertia. I did not myself persist, since I was paid ten kopecks for every barrel, whereas I would have received no reward for my suggested improvement and would simply have been sent to clean out manure again. As each milkmaid finished giving water to the cows in her charge – each girl took about two barrels – I drove the sledge out of the cowshed, filled the barrels again and took them to the next girl. Since they all had to wait their turn, there were constant scenes and shouting matches. One of them was always demanding that I serve her first, or they would try to seize the reins of the horse from me; sometimes they would all refuse to water the cattle until the fodder had been brought, and I would then have to wait around doing nothing. Occasionally I would leave and simply go home, cursing them all and telling them to get their own water. There was also trouble when some of them borrowed my horse to get water from the pump to take to their homes; carrying water over any distance was difficult in winter, and they needed a great deal of it. I didn't mind this as long as they didn't take the horse without my knowledge, but if I found they had taken it at a time when I needed it, I just went off home without saying a word; in this way I did manage with great difficulty to make them see reason. My greatest struggle was with my neighbour, Sonya, who always shouted: 'You're a parasite, but I'm a kolkhoznik! Do you think I couldn't get water myself?' And, for emphasis, she pulled up her skirt and held up her bare bottom for me to admire. I was tempted to kick it, but didn't because I knew I would have no end of trouble with talk about 'that parasite molesting a kolkhoz girl'.

By the time I had finished my work, unharnessed the horse and gone home it was usually eight or nine o'clock. I worked with a completely white mare who looked like a circus horse. She was very intelligent, hardy and placid; it was very tough on an unshod horse to pull two full barrels of water along the slippery wooden floor of the cowshed. I had to watch out in case the runners should get into the gutter; this could cause terrible trouble. We sometimes had to struggle hard for half an hour to move the sledge a couple of yards.

Hay was also the cause of constant scenes. By spring fodder was very short and there was a daily ration of one kilogram a day per cow. But the fence around the place where the hay was kept was broken down and cows let out for exercise often got in there, as did the horses. Steshka had constant rows with the stableman over this and even reported him for it. She also accused me of feeding hay to the horses. This did nothing to prevent the loss of hay, and it never occurred to her or anyone else to mend the fence.

Carting twenty barrels a day at a rate of ten kopecks per barrel, I was due to get more than sixty roubles in March, if I took no days off. 'See how much Andrei is getting,' the kolkhozniks grumbled. 'We shan't get that much. And there's nothing to the work: he just holds a hose in his hands and the water flows into the barrel by itself.' In fact, I didn't even hold the hose, as I had made a hook out of wire to attach it to the rim of the barrel, while I just walked around. This only made the kolkhozniks madder still. Even Leva was very upset at earning only twenty roubles, and he no longer asked my forgiveness for living better than me but hinted that it was uncomradely for one 'parasite' to earn three times as much as another. I never ceased to marvel at the psychology of the village people. Even those who seemed well disposed towards me spoke reproachfully about my sixty roubles. The one who kicked up the greatest fuss was Sonya, who shouted that her Mitya, though a kolkhoznik, had not earned as much as this. Mitya, incidentally, was in trouble.

At the end of March a judge with two assessors and a prosecutor arrived in Guryevka and turned the school building into a courtroom. They were trying Shapovalov, Gorbachov (the foreman of the tractor-drivers' team) and two herdsmen, Kritsky and Mitya, who were accused of causing the death of two heifers in the autumn. The Judge, a large, bald man who looked a little like Chigrinov, sat down with his two assessors at the teacher's desk; the Prosecutor sat at a small table on his left and the Clerk of the Court on his right; the accused sat on a bench before him, and behind them practically everybody in the village had crowded in to watch – all but the milkmaids who could not leave the cowsheds.

In his speech the Prosecutor called for a fine of six hundred roubles (one hundred and fifty each), to be paid by the defendants to the kolkhoz. Mitya was accused of having refused to graze the cows, Kritsky of having let them out of the paddock, Gorbachov of having sent Mitya away to repair the threshing machine, and Shapovalov of bearing overall responsibility as the man in charge of them all. Next the Judge began to question the accused and the witnesses. None of the accused pleaded guilty, though Kritsky declared at first that it was a tricky business in which he was both guilty and not guilty. The Judge then asked him how he would estimate the extent of his guilt in roubles. When it was put like this, Kritsky firmly pleaded not guilty. I think this was a mistake, since the Judge had been pleased by his partial admission of guilt, and if he had named a small sum he would have fined him by that amount, whereas now it would be very much more.

It was quite beyond Shapovalov to understand how it was that he, a foreman, who was there to protect the interests of the kolkhoz, could find himself in court, and he kept insisting that he should be tried 'in accordance with the law'. The foreman of the tractor drivers, Gorbachov, really had no connection with the case and the Prosecutor was charging him only because, as he put it: 'There are too many cases in which foremen cover up for tractor drivers who have committed offences, and we must put a stop to it.'

The witnesses were Sanka, the deputy chairman, Steshka, and the veterinarian, Suslikov. Both the Prosecutor and the Judge handled them all very roughly, but they were especially unpleasant to Suslikov. He was about to take up another job in the Tyumen region where his parents lived and was due to leave any day. 'You've done well for yourself here and now you're clearing out,' the Prosecutor told him. And the Judge was no better: 'We've heard all about you – you'd better watch out or you'll come to a bad end!' This is perhaps how a teacher might tell off a schoolboy, but it was hardly the way for a judge to address a witness.

After the interrogation of the witnesses – who were very much afraid that they themselves might be charged and therefore incriminated each other as well as the defendants – the court retired to consider its decision. In the meantime the Prosecutor announced that while we were waiting he would give a talk on 'Soviet law'. The talk was all about how a woman would denounce her husband for beating her, and he would get three years, but then a month later she would come and beg for him to be released. The moral was, as the Prosecutor impressed on his listeners, that wives should think twice before denouncing their husbands, because once they had been jailed they would have to serve their sentences to the end. The Prosecutor also spoke a little about the legal status of kolkhozniks. 'You're always complaining,' he said, 'that you're not allowed to leave the kolkhoz. The kolkhoz is right not to let you go – it's like a big family, and it knows best whether to let you go or not. You live very well – the workers in the towns don't have half as much to eat as you, so instead of complaining you should get on with your work. In America one farmer produces more by himself than the whole of this village here.' At this point I interrupted to say, in defence of our kolkhozniks, that there was much more mechanization in America, but they were so frightened at the idea of anyone arguing with a prosecutor that they all hissed at me. The Prosecutor next went on to emphasize, much to their pleasure, that the chairman and foreman were not entitled to beat them. In another kolkhoz, he said, the foreman had beaten up some of the kolkhozniks and locked one woman in his office without food for a couple of days, but he would shortly be brought to trial for this.

The Judge now came in from the next room, everybody stood up and he read out his decision. Kritsky and Mitya were both to be fined two hundred and twenty-five roubles each, and Shapovalov and Gorbachov seventy-five roubles each, and they were all to share court costs in the same proportion. Kritsky and Mitya heard the sentence with a look of bewilderment, while Sonya (Mitya's girl-friend) broke into shouts and curses. The Judge said they could appeal within five days, but nobody wanted to do this lest they be fined even more. Two hundred and twenty-five roubles is half a year's earnings for a kolkhoznik.

The kolkhozniks wandered off to their houses, scratching the backs of their heads, while the Judge and his two assistants left with the feeling of work well done, convinced that discipline would now improve.

I witnessed one other public event in the school – whether before or after the trial I don't remember – when a voting booth was set up there for 'elections' to some local soviet or other. In Moscow I had never voted, since I did not take 'elections' seriously, but here I was afraid not to in case I should jeopardize the possibility of a remission of my sentence. The schoolmaster handed me a ballot with the name of a single candidate and I put it in the ballot box. On the other side of the room there was a booth covered with red cloth where one could vote 'in secret'. I don't think anybody went into it. I was a little surprised by the ambivalent attitude of the kolkhozniks: on the one hand they looked on the election as an empty formality, but at the same time it was a 'holiday', just like the First of May or the Seventh of November, on which the thing to do was to get drunk and 'have a good time'.

At the beginning of April the ground was still covered with snow, the wind was cold and there were no signs of the thaw. It was also pretty cold in my shack, since my firewood was coming to an end; but at least my food situation had improved. I now bought supplies in the village shop and from other kolkhozniks; Gyusel often sent me packages of soup mixes, and I was able to make soup and *kasha* for myself. Nadya Kabanov baked bread for me, though again I had to do without during the first half of March until I managed to have fifty pounds of flour ground for me in Novokrivosheino.

I had brought several popular books on mathematics with me from Moscow, and whenever I had a few hours to myself I studied the theory of probability; but I didn't get very far with it, since I had very little time and, what was worse, it was so cold that my hands got stiff and I couldn't take notes. Progress on the notes for this book, which I also began to write then, was likewise very slow. I worked on them only in fits and starts, and by July I had got no further than the story of my visit to the diplomat after the raid on my apartment by the KGB. These solitary activities of mine were suddenly interrupted, anyway, in rather comic fashion.

The other exiles often quarrelled with their girl-friends, threatening to leave them and move in with me. Whenever they mentioned this I would only laugh, knowing they would never leave the women who fed them on cabbage soup and bacon fat. But then, at the end of April, Fedya had a terrible row with Katya – they even came to blows – and said he was coming to live with me. Katya told him to go to the devil, but when he came early next morning to tell me he would be moving in with me that same day, I still thought he would very soon make it up with her. I was astonished and dismayed when he later drove up to my house on a sledge with an old wooden bedstead, a suitcase and a sack of potatoes. 'All right,' I thought to myself, 'I'll put up with him for a couple of days and then I'll smoke him out of here.' I meant this literally: my stove was now in very bad shape, the flue was partially blocked, and whenever I lit it the room filled with black smoke, so that I had to lie on the floor in order not to suffocate. Fedya let out a yell and tried to poke around in the stove, but this made things even worse. He set up his bed in the corner opposite me and spent most of his time on it, sighing sadly. He and Katya continued to scream at each other in foul language for all to hear, and swore they would never make it up: 'If ever I let that parasite come back, you can all spit in my face!' Katya shouted to all the other girls in the cowshed. But on the third night there was suddenly a loud knock at our door. 'Open up, don't be afraid,' came a loud voice from outside. Then in came Katya, blind drunk, with her twelve-year-old daughter, and begged Fedya to get up and go back home with her. Overjoyed, Fedya made a show of resistance for five minutes and then began to pack his suitcase. The happiness of reconciliation was slightly clouded when Katya in her drunkenness fell down into the cellar through the opening in the floor that I had made for the cat. The next day I put Fedya's bed on the porch and it was soon taken away by Katya.

Three weeks later Fedya's example was followed by Leva. He had got a package from home, sold all the things and immediately spent the money on drink. At the time his girl-friend Polya was distilling some liquor to give to the men who were sawing wood for her. Leva insisted that she give him a little first, but Polya refused, saying she had made it to exchange for firewood. 'Very well, then,' Leva bawled. 'If you won't give me a drink, I'll phone the police and tell them you're making vodka,' and he left the house. Polya was so terrified that she poured it all away, hid the still and made off somewhere. When Leva returned he found a pad-lock on the door. He was very upset and went to his previous girl-friend, Aksinya, but after a fist fight with her he finally

came to me: 'Polya's kicked me out and I'm going to live
here now.' But I wouldn't let him in and said he could
come here only if the chairman or foreman ordered it, in
which case I would leave myself. He swore and threatened
for a while, but then went away. Soon he sobered up a little,
made peace with Polya, and asked Aksinya to forgive him,
so she wouldn't complain to the police.

From the first of January a new system was supposed to
have started in the cowsheds: for each two milkmaids there
was to be a man to clear the manure from their stalls and
bring up supplies of fodder. There was at first great scepticism
about the idea; everybody said nothing would come of it
because nobody would be able to force someone like me to
do both these jobs. The milkmaids with whom I had once
worked were particularly eloquent on this point. Our six
milkmaids were given three helpers: Fedya, Mitya and the
sixteen-year-old Tolya Kabanov. Since nearly everybody in
the village was related, this meant that Mitya was now working for his wife and aunt, while Tolya found himself teamed
up with his aunt and his uncle's wife; as a result, the usual
bickering and complaints about favouritism only intensified,
and after a while Tolya Kabanov could stand it no longer and
refused to go on with the job. For a few days the two
women he had been working for had to bring in the fodder
themselves, and the manure just piled up; they wept and
swore while Steshka the supervisor, stood by shrugging her
shoulders and cooing in her sing-song voice. The foreman
then made me take Tolya Kabanov's job (he always made
me do the work that nobody else wanted to do), while Tolya
took over my job of carting the water.

I started my new duties in the middle of April. The work
was now much easier than when I had done it before, because
the weather was warmer and the cows were driven out every
day, I could even get into the narrow passageway at the side
with my sledge and didn't have to use that ghastly bucket
on the rail. Apart from fetching silage, I was expected to
bring bran from the drying shed. With my weak heart it
was difficult for me to shift sacks of bran weighing fifty-five
kilograms each, but during the whole time I had been in the
kolkhoz I had never called attention to the fact that I was

specifically exempted from doing very heavy work, in case this should adversely affect my hope of a remission.

I soon got the hang of the work and even managed to do it more quickly than the others, so that my two milkmaids, who had once feared I would not be able to cope, were now very pleased with me, particularly as I never missed work, like Mitya and Fedya, because of drunkenness. It was at this point that I was praised for my efficiency in the kolkhoz bulletin.

CHAPTER 23

'The Drinks are on You'

JUST before the First of May the kolkhozniks were given a lecture on the international and domestic situation by a lecturer sent out by the district Party committee. Up to then most of the propaganda work in the village had been conducted by Vera, the manageress of the recreation room, who from time to time somewhat incoherently read out newspaper articles which she barely understood herself and then explained to us – an article on Sinyavsky and Daniel, for example, she reduced to the simple proposition that they were American spies. She also read out to us day after day the infinitely long-winded statement issued at the end of the 23rd Congress of the CPSU.* Hardly anybody listened, however, since they were too busy with their work, or if they did listen it made no sense because they didn't even know what CPSU meant. One schoolboy asked her what it meant, but she wasn't able to tell him. Only Filimon, the mechanic in charge of the milking machinery, who had once attended a course in the town, was able to say what it was.

The lecture was given in the school. The lecturer, who had a round, good-humoured face and looked like a well-read peasant, began by saying he had been at a meeting in Tomsk at which he and other lecturers had been briefed by Obrikov, a representative of the Central Committee of the CPSU, and that he would be giving us the gist of what he had been told there. The main point of his talk was that not only abroad, but even inside the country, there were people who did not believe that the domestic situation was good, and thought some things were wrong. Since it was impossible to make such people change their minds, Party lecturers had now been instructed to admit that there were indeed shortcomings in the country. 'In particular, comrades,' he

* Communist Party of the Soviet Union.

said, 'as you well know yourselves, our agriculture is in a very poor way.' He explained this, with an air of great shrewdness, by saying that our country was a very large one with too much variety in climatic conditions. By this he evidently meant to imply that, though conditions vary all over the country, the authorities expected everybody to obey the same instructions. He also said that Soviet tractors were too heavy and cumbersome. After this he spoke only about our strong points, of which the chief was the military might of our country. He said that on this score – unlike in agriculture – we had no reason for anxiety at all. He condemned the Americans for the war in Vietnam, attacked West Germany and praised France. About China he said: 'They live even worse than we do.' Since many people in the village had heard Chinese broadcasts, they asked him a few questions: Who is helping Vietnam most, we or the Chinese, and is it possible that we might become friends with China again? He said the Chinese were helping Vietnam only in words, and that it was quite possible we would be friendly with them again after the death of Mao Tse Tung. He ended his lecture on a quite unexpected note by saying we should not worry about the fate of Khrushchev, who was living at liberty in Moscow and not complaining about life.

A month later we got another lecture, this time in the recreation room, and after it there was a concert. On this occasion the lecturer was a rather pretty girl who in a hushed voice, constantly wringing her thin hands, spoke mostly about the war in Vietnam. When she invited questions, Leva, who had fought in the Korean War, drunkenly got to his feet and said he was very interested to hear about events in Vietnam, because he had once been in Korea. 'When were you there?' asked the girl sweetly. Delighted to be taken notice of, Leva replied: 'I was there in the days when we used to sing that song "Stalin and Mao Are Listening to Us".' He then tried to start singing it, but he was quickly made to sit down. The concert was given by a group from one of the Tomsk factories. First a small chorus sang a song about comradeship among soldiers and then one about rockets standing at the ready. Next somebody sang a song about how we should not forget the last war and be prepared for the next. Finally someone recited a poem on the same general theme.

After the first lecture in the school, we had a meeting to decide the question of who would graze the cattle during the coming summer months. There was no difficulty about the village herd, which Fedya and Katya again agreed to take on. What was more difficult was the question of the kolkhoz herd as a whole, which consisted of a hundred and fifty head of cattle for which three herdsmen would be needed. But nobody wanted to do the job, particularly after the recent trial. Kritsky had the excuse that he had lost some of his fingers and couldn't even hold a whip; Pashka Kabanov said that he had a hernia which prevented him from riding a horse; and Sanka pointed out that his three-years' sentence would terminate at the end of May. I also was determined to get out of it at any price. If I agreed to do this job, I would never get out of Guryevka, so I said I was nearsighted and without my glasses, which I had accidentally broken in November, couldn't tell a cow from a bush. Luckily I was backed up in this argument by the chairman, whose wife and son were also nearsighted. Finally the choice fell on Leva, Sanka and Pashka Kabanov, who took the herd out on the 17th of May.

The spring sowing began on the 2nd of May: first wheat, then oats, corn, and finally clover and potatoes. Flax was sown at the same time as wheat. This year, almost for the first time, the wheat was sown on land where rye and corn had grown the previous year and the oats were sown in the place of corn and wheat. For many years previously the same crops had always been sown in the same fields. No fertilizer was put in the soil, even though there were heaps of manure near the cattlesheds which during the summer had even caught fire. The ploughing was done with two tractors, and a third followed them along the furrows with two mechanical seeders. I was put to work carting the seed from the barn, where it was loaded on to carts by women. The work was done in two shifts of twelve hours each. After three days we had to work eighteen hours a shift: the whole day and half the night (or vice versa). Loading the sacks on to the cart and then transferring them to the seeders was very hard work and I got pains in my chest. I was choked with dust, my eyes watered all the time and, as the weather became a little warmer, we were plagued by gnats. On top of it all I caught a bad cold and had a constant temperature. The night shift was the hardest, particularly because I could not see in the dark and did not know my way around the fields.

The area of land sown for crops had not increased since collectivization in the early thirties; some land had even grown over with scrub. As a legacy from the days when there had been small individual farmsteads here, the fields were still small and divided by rows of trees. On these small plots of land the tractors burned up much more fuel in manoeuvring back and forth than they would have done in larger fields. With modern equipment it would have been the easiest thing in the world to remove the trees between the fields, but nothing was done about it year after year, ten times more money was wasted on fuel than it would have cost to make larger fields. I pointed this out to the foreman and he readily agreed with me, but it made not the slightest difference.

When all the sowing was over, I thought I might be able to rest for a couple of days, but I was in for new trouble. During the winter, as I have mentioned, many calves were born, and some of them were already old enough to be taken out to pasture. The foreman now ordered me to do this, despite my pleas that without glasses it was even more difficult for me to see a calf than a cow. So I decided to play a trick. I took seventy calves out and after a few hours came back with only five, saying that the rest had got lost because I was too nearsighted to keep track of them. They had great trouble finding them – one had even strayed as far as Ivanovka. The next day I went to see the oculist in Krivosheino to ask for a certificate declaring me unfit for work in which good eyesight was essential. I also wanted to have my heart examined by the specialist in the clinic there, but it turned out that he had gone off on a trip to another village. Unluckily, the head of the clinic was also away and the oculist was afraid to let me have a certificate in his absence, but I had the presence of mind to get a paper from him giving me an appointment in the clinic next day. I showed this to the foreman and the matter ended there. I didn't go back to the clinic and the grown calves were shortly afterwards taken away to Novokrivosheino.

The 28th of May was the first anniversary of my trial and in three months' time, by August, I was due to reach the half-way mark of my sentence. I was very concerned about whether I should be released then. During my visit to the clinic I called at the police station and spoke to the Commandant. He said the police would have no objection, if the kolkhoz were prepared to release me. The foreman and the Party representative told me they would let me go – though not in August, only sometime in October after the harvesting was over. Their answers, however, were somewhat lacking in conviction and to make matters worse the Party representative, with whom I got on very well, was at daggers' drawn with the chairman and soon after this left the kolkhoz. I had made up my mind that if I wasn't released when half my sentence was up, I would not stay in the kolkhoz, but ask the police to let me transfer to work in Krivosheino. I would give as my reasons the fact that the kolkhoz did not provide me with food and also that I had no proper place in which to live. In the third place, I would say the kolkhoz was constantly underpaying me, not giving me the money I had earned. Nobody's wages were in fact correctly calculated, partly through illiteracy and partly because the kolkhoz hoped to improve its situation by 'economizing' on wages. A special offender in this respect was Steshka, who was always putting people down for five or even ten roubles less than they had earned. I sometimes refused to sign work-sheets, and twice made her re-do them, but on three other occasions she took them to the accountant's office without bothering about my signature and I was not paid in full for my work. At the beginning of May I wrote a long complaint detailing all Steshka's little frauds, and also quoting cases in which the earnings of other kolkhozniks had been wrongly calculated. I solemnly handed this document to the deputy chairman in the presence of the Party representative and Steshka herself. I did not expect it to have any practical effect in terms of getting back any of the money owed to me, but I thought it might help me to show a copy of it to the police when I asked them to transfer me to other work. I must say that the kolkhoz officials in general were not very finicky in money matters. The deputy chairman, for instance, to whom I had so solemnly handed my denunciation, once spent on drink all the money for bonuses due to be given to the women who looked after the cows, and when the time came he merely handed them a rouble each with an embarrassed smile. They whispered a little among themselves but were too frightened to make any real protest. Needless to say, I received no reply to my complaint, and Steshka continued to falsify the amount of my earnings.

After the business with the calves, I did nothing at all for three days. Following the spring sowing there is generally a small break in the work of the kolkhozniks which they use to plant potatoes on their private plots; then, from the middle of June, they have to start preparing silage, and after that the hay-making begins. I thought I should probably have to do the same job as the previous summer, but on the 10th of June the foreman came to see me and said he would like me to drive the milk cart. In the summer the cows were not kept in the shed but were milked in a paddock at the far end of the village from where the milk was brought three times a day to the farm to be separated.

At first I was glad of this proposal because I did not want to work on the silage, but the work turned out to be much more difficult than I had expected. I had to get up at half past five in the morning and go to look for the horse. It was all right if the stableman had brought the horses back to the village the previous day, but if he had been drinking and let them run wild I would have to go out in the fields hunting for them. By seven I had to have the horse already harnessed and ride a couple of miles to the place where the cows were milked by automatic milking machines. The machinery, as mentioned before, often broke down, and the milkmaids had to finish the job by hand. Sometimes I would help them, to speed things up, and I discovered for the first time what hard work it was. After taking the milk cans to the farm I had to bring eight sacks of bran from the barn, take them to the cows, then go back for the empty cans and return them to the milking place to be washed. After all this I was able to go home for a bite to eat and a short rest. Three hours later, at lunchtime, the whole process had to be repeated, and again in the evening; the milkmaids finished their job only at ten, and I still had to deliver the milk to the farm and wash the cans myself, so they would be ready for use early the following morning. I never got to bed before twelve and had no days off. One of the worst things now in the summer were the gnats and gadflies which almost ate one alive, particularly in the morning and evening – though this year they were not as bad as the previous year.

I soon had more trouble with Steshka. She calculated the amount of milk in the cans one way, while the woman who worked the separator weighed it and got a different result, sometimes amounting to twenty litres. She and Steshka accused me of drinking it on the way from the milking place to the farm; this seemed all the more likely to them since I had stopped claiming the daily litre to which I was entitled. It was clear to everybody, however, that it would be a Gargantuan feat to drink that amount of milk a day. I went to the foreman and suggested he replace me by somebody more trusted than I. 'Nonsense,' he said. 'Who has ever heard of a sailor who didn't drink water? You don't have to sign for the milk, so why should you care how much is missing?'

I was paid twenty kopecks for every hundred litres I carried, while the herdsmen got forty kopecks and the milkmaids, if I am not mistaken, around one rouble twenty kopecks per hundred litres. The yield was very low: each cow gave four litres a day in the winter, and this rose only to six in the summer. This meant that the average daily yield, with a herd of a hundred and fifty, was never more than nine hundred litres a day (and sometimes as low as six hundred) so that my average wage was a little more than one rouble fifty kopecks a day. The herdsmen earned three roubles a day each (if there were two of them) and two roubles a day if there were three of them. The average daily wage of a milkmaid was anything between one and a half and two roubles.

After the middle of June the yield did not go up and in

July it even began to fall. Matters were not helped by two placards with slogans, one of them calling on the milkmaids to redouble their efforts to raise the yield, and the other to increase their efforts to double the yield. The milkmaids, however, were not responsible for the low yields. If anybody, it was the herdsmen. At first all three of them grazed the cows, each of them taking a day off every two days. But then Pashka Kabanov refused to go on with the job because of his hernia and managed instead to get himself the job of taking the cream to the butter factory. This left only Leva and Sanka, who did not know where the best grazing places were and disliked the job anyway. Sanka had come to the end of his sentence, but he had stayed in the village because there was nowhere else for him to go, and he just went on living with Nadya Kabanov. On the day his release came through he got drunk and lay down to sleep it off on the main street in Krivosheino. The police took his papers away, so that he had to borrow money from me to pay the fine and get them back. Both he and Leva were drunk all the time when they were out grazing and they ended up by having a fight and abandoning the herd, as a result of which the cows got among the oats and trampled down several acres of them. Before they were summoned to the police and replaced by another herdsman, about whom I shall have something to say later, there was a further incident involving Sonya. For the umpteenth time she had shown her bare behind to the other milkmaids, but for once one of them complained, and Sonya was had up before the Judge and fined twenty-five roubles. She had been afraid they might jail her for several days, and before going to court in Krivosheino, she had come to see me to borrow money for bread so that she would have something to eat beside the prison food. I gave her the money, smiling to myself as I remembered how often she had upbraided Gyusel and me because her mother-in-law baked our bread for us. After she was fined, Sonya wouldn't have anything more to do with the other milkmaids and refused to continue, so that Steshka herself had to take her place. This wasn't the end of the matter. When they were interrogated by the police, Leva and Sanka behaved very badly and testified that the reason they had quarrelled and left the herd was that on the night before they had drunk home-brewed beer at the house of Marusya Kabanov, the wife of a previous herdsman. Because of their evidence, the police started criminal proceedings against her for the illegal brewing of beer.

In the midst of all these unsavoury happenings it was suddenly announced that there was going to be a public meeting in the recreation room at which a representative of the police would make an important announcement. A few days before this, rumours had started going round to the effect that the police were going to get tougher, and in particular that they were going to be equipped with truncheons. On the platform at the meeting were two of the local policemen, a man in civilian clothes, the kolkhoz chairman and the Party representative. The meeting was opened by the man in civilian clothes, who said that meetings such as this were being held all over the country, in factories, offices, kolkhozes and State farms, in order to 'explain to the working people' two new measures: the decree on increased penalties for hooliganism and the equipment of the police with truncheons. The second point was an especially delicate one, since up to now truncheons had always featured prominently in anti-American propaganda, and ever since I was a child I could remember how in our newspapers, books, films, posters and other propaganda material the truncheon was writ large as a symbol of the 'American way of life'. The man went on to read from a mimeographed circular, adding his own remarks. He started by saying what a sad comment on the times it was that the 'Central Committee and our Government' had found it necessary to introduce truncheons just before the fiftieth anniversary of the October Revolution. Reading from his bit of paper, he went on to explain that the crime rate was continually going up, notably among the youth. Hooliganism accounted for the highest percentage of the crimes committed and must be regarded, therefore, as particularly dangerous; there had been an extraordinary increase in the use of various kinds of homemade weapons – flick-knives, knuckle-dusters, etc., which were often made by people at their place of work, while others looked on and pretended not to notice. He ended by emphasizing that the life of the Soviet people was nevertheless getting better and better as the years went by. 'For instance,' he said, 'I was here in your village five years ago and I'd never seen such a miserable lot as you, but now you look more or less like everybody else.'

As one of the policemen made a short speech to say that only lawbreakers need fear truncheons, the look on his and his colleagues' faces suggested that they could hardly wait to get their truncheons and start a new fight against crime. He then made a point of saying that the kolkhozniks should not, however, put all the blame for crime in their district on the 'parasites', since they themselves were not much better. 'Look at this parasite in your village here, Amalrik, who has done nothing wrong so far – though he did once try to steal some wood, but that's something quite excusable.' The last to speak was the kolkhoz chairman who complained that the people in Guryevka, even sixteen-year-old girls, were so foul-mouthed that he hated coming here. The meeting ended with the election of a *druzhina* to be headed by Shapovalov.

Curiously, almost all the kolkhozniks took what they had heard to mean that truncheons would be used to punish people when they had been sentenced by a court, i.e., that they would be used instead of fines or imprisonment, or in addition to them. Some of them grumbled that it was funny to beat people with clubs in these days, but others calmly pointed out that we were just going back to the old days – we used to have a landlord and now we have a kolkhoz chairman; they used to beat the peasants with switches and now they would use truncheons. All in all, I think the decision to introduce truncheons was taken rather badly, and considering the vague idea our police have of the limits of their authority I think it is going to cause a great deal of trouble – as, for example, in Tula in the summer of 1967 when there was a pitched battle between police and workers after somebody had been struck with a truncheon.

In July the kolkhoz expected that students would come from Tomsk again, and I began to hear rumours that the secretary of the Party committee had decided to throw me out of my shack to make room for them. I said they could put anybody they liked in with me, but that I wouldn't leave

myself. The upshot was that they didn't put the students
there, but I did have to leave the house much earlier than I
had expected. This came about through the arrival of a new
herdsman who appeared out of the blue in Novokrivosheino
with his wife and two children at the beginning of the
summer and expressed a desire to work in the kolkhoz.
At first he worked for a short time grazing the cattle in
Novokrivosheino, but when a new herdsman was needed in
Guryevka (because of the incident I have described) he was
sent here. The kolkhozniks made fun of him, saying that he
must be the lowest of the low to go and work in a kolkhoz
of his free will and that somebody like that was a thousand
times worse than a 'parasite', who at least had been forced
to do so. The chairman, on the other hand, was so pleased
at the idea of someone coming to work for him voluntarily
that he wanted to make a special fuss over the man, thereby
encouraging him to serve as a shining example to everybody
else.

It was decided to put him in my house. The place was
whitewashed on the inside, and a day later the herdsman's
belongings were brought over on the tractor. Nobody paid
any attention to me or asked me to leave.

The first night was utter hell. I had been used to keeping
down the mosquitoes by spraying the room with an insecti-
cide, but now the herdsman's wife, a languid and sleek young
woman, said this would be harmful to the children, so during
the night I was bitten all over. She also lit the stove and I
nearly died of the heat. All night long the herdsman and
his wife quarrelled and the two children bawled their heads
off. There was a stench of urine and dirty underwear. It was
the same again the next day. Only my cat, Dima, was happy
because he suddenly got a lot of fish: the herdsman had
spent all his money on drink and was feeding his family on
fish that he had caught in the pond; they had no oil to fry it
in so they boiled it in water and ate it with black bread. I
gave the children some sugar and a packet of cocoa that
Gyusel had sent me. But I cannot say that the children
aroused any warmth of feeling in me. Both of them were
boys, one a year old, who was somehow undersized and
wrinkled, and howled nearly all the time; the other was

already three but had not yet learned to talk and went around naked all the time, stubbornly refusing to let himself be dressed.

Things were no better on the third day. Previously, I had looked forward to my short nap at home when I took a break from work during the morning, but now I had to sit out in the yard because of these squalling children. There was no question of my being able to do any writing. I hid away all my papers and put my typewriter under the bed. The herdsman's wife offered me two books of hers to read, saying how wonderful they were. One was Maxim Gorky's novel, *Mother*. After a couple of pages I gave it up – this fore-runner of 'Socialist realism' seemed to me utterly stilted and pretentious, in the worst style of *fin de siècle* decadence. The second book, from which pages were missing at the beginning and the end, seemed to be a collection of Bulgarian tales and was more unpretentious. But the book was so impregnated with the combined smell of children's porridge and urine, the pages were so sticky and dirty, that it was disgusting to hold in one's hands, let alone read. I decided I must get out of the house; the only place where I could go was the shack next to the stables, which was used by the stableman and where in winter harnesses and oats were kept. It had once had a porch, but this had been torn down and sawn up for firewood during the winter. It had an iron stove, two small windows facing each other and benches by the door. There was no electricity and no proper roof, only boards covered with earth. In dry weather earth was always coming through the cracks, and when it rained mud oozed down in great quantities. But there was no alternative and, after speaking with the foreman, I loaded all my possessions on a cart – my large table, the bed, a saucepan, kettle, frying pan, basin, mattress and other things – and with Sonya's little daughter sitting on top with my black cat in her arms, I drove the whole lot past the school and the farm to the stables. Village women standing at the roadside shook their heads in astonishment at the amount of property I had accu-mulated. There was indeed so much that it would not all go on the cart and we had to make a second trip. When we reached the stable, the frightened cat jumped out of the girl's arms and started to run back the way we had come. I decided that, as is usual with cats, he didn't want to leave his old home. But late that night I heard him scratching at the door and meowing to be let in.

I cleaned the walls, moved my furniture in and old Razuvanov, my neighbour, put panes of glass in the windows for me; one of the milkmaids washed the floor and I put sacking over the door to keep the mosquitoes out. The only thing wrong with this luxurious dwelling was the state of the roof, but I hoped that before it rained again I would have time to rig up something like a canopy over my bed. It was also very hot, but at least I now had privacy and could be sure that nobody would ever want to take the place away from me.

I had no sooner moved to the stable than there was more trouble on the kolkhoz. One morning all the herdsmen failed to come to work, and the worried milkmaids, seeing the cows still in the paddock, went to look for them. When they went to the house which I had just left, they found complete pandemonium. The new herdsman was beating his wife, Sanka was making love to Katya, Fedya was lying blind drunk under the table, and on the table there was a vodka-making still and a huge bottle full of the stuff. The milkmaids raced off to call the newly-organized *druzhina* headed by Shapovalov and telephoned the kolkhoz office. By the time the *druzhinniki* came, the still and the bottle had been hidden away in the cellar, where they were found by Shapovalov's men and confiscated. I thanked my lucky stars I had got out of the place at the right time. The upshot was that all ended happily as far as the three herdsmen were concerned: the members of the *druzhina* succumbed to temptation, drank all the liquor they had confiscated, and then quietly forgot the whole matter. It occurred to me, as I sat thinking about it all in my new quarters, that the new herdsman would probably not last very long here and that I might yet be able to return to my old home. But shortly after this my life was changed by an event of much greater importance than the chance of moving back again.

On the 8th of July I had just unharnessed my horse after the morning milking and gone to the village to buy myself some onions when I was stopped near the shop by the post-woman. 'Looks like a telegram for you,' she said, handing me a yellow envelope. It was exactly the same sort of envelope in which I had received news of my father's illness ten months earlier. I was very alarmed, thinking that some-thing had happened to Gyusel, and it took me some time to take in what was written in the telegram. It read: 'Sentence reversed. Official notice follows by letter. Drinks on you. Ginzburg.'

CHAPTER 24

Flight; The Prosecutor's Decision

I WAS so dazed that I took a very long time to walk back along the dusty road to the stable, trying to grasp what had happened. I could not think why the sentence had been reversed and assumed that it was the result of continued efforts by my lawyer who had not been discouraged by the rejection of the first appeal and my lack of faith in a successful outcome.

I went on with my job of carting the milk, but I was now eagerly awaiting the official notice from the court so that I could take it to the police. After a week I got a letter from my lawyer which made me feel much less confident: 'Andrei Alexeyevich,' it read. 'You have probably already received a telegram sent to you at my request by A. I. Ginzburg. The hearing of your appeal has taken an exceptionally long time and it was only on the 20th of June that the Supreme Court of the RSFSR reversed the unjustified decision of the People's Court to expel you from Moscow. The Prosecutor's office of the Frunze district has been instructed to re-examine the evidence submitted to them in connection with your case. Phone me as soon as you get back to Moscow. Congratulations and best wishes.'

What bothered me was that the evidence was to be re-examined by the Prosecutor's office. Did the court order mean that I could expect to be released immediately without waiting for the results of this examination, or would the police here insist on waiting until these were known? It was also uncertain whether the Prosecutor's office would now drop its case against me and also how long it would take for them to make a decision – perhaps a whole year, as the court had done?

Next day I took this letter to the police. The Commandant studied it for a long time, arching his brows with a puzzled

look, and at last said they had so far received no instructions.
'You'll have to wait a while, but,' he suddenly remembered,
'there was a package today from Moscow and when the secretary comes we'll have a look at it.' In fact it did contain
a notification of the Supreme Soviet's decision, which had
been reached on the 20th of June but had taken a month to
get here.

'We don't quite know what to do,' the Chief of the station,
Lieutenant Colonel Korotkikh, said to me. 'We've never had
a case like this before. We'll have to wait for a decision
from the Prosecutor's office, and until then you'll have to go
on working here as before. In any case we'll let you go when
you've served half your term, whatever the Prosecutor
decides.'

As usual with the police, they wouldn't let me read the
court's decision itself. The Commandant invited me into his
office to give me back my identity papers and work-book.
This was not done because of the Supreme Court's decision,
but simply in accordance with new instructions that all
exiles must have their papers returned to them. While I was
sitting there my old friend Shaposhnikov was brought in
under guard. His five-year sentence had been about to end
in July, but just before he was due for release he got in trouble
again: after leaving the kolkhoz in the spring to work in the
district co-operative he had been caught in a minor theft.
Only thirty-six roubles were missing and he had immediately
paid them back, but even so they still wanted to take him to
court. Shaposhnikov now told me, as we met here for the
last time in the police station, that the outlook was very
poor. I got a lift back to Guryevka, and on the way the rain
began to pour down again. After getting the telegram, I had
decided I wouldn't worry about the roof of my shack, thinking I should now be returning to Moscow any day. But when
I got home I found the bed and table and a bench with my
food supplies all covered with mud. The next day I took some
squares of slate intended for the roof of a new barn and built
a little shelter over my bed and table. I could now sit in
comfort and read *The Brothers Karamazov* which I had
borrowed from the library in Novokrivosheino.

After getting my lawyer's letter I had written at once to

Ginzburg, asking him to find out exactly what I should do now, what the implications of the re-examination of my case by the Prosecutor's office were, and how long I might have to wait for the results. The people in the village also waited with interest to see whether I would be released. When I got the telegram, I had been so overjoyed that I could not refrain from telling them I would soon be leaving, but now, as they could all see, the days kept going by and I was still stuck in Guryevka. Hearing I had received a letter from my lawyer, some of them said he was just trying to string me along – I'd paid him good money no doubt, and now he just wanted to keep me happy.

On the 24th of July the postwoman came to the stable and handed me a new telegram which read. 'Return immediately. Your presence essential. Papers already in your possession quite sufficient. Ginzburg.'

'Well, what do they say?' the postwoman asked.

'I'm leaving tomorrow,' I replied.

That evening I agreed with the foreman that Vera's eldest son should take my place at work, and in the morning I again went to see the police to talk about my departure. I intended to say that, since the court had reversed the sentence by virtue of which I was here, they had no good grounds for keeping me any longer; if, on the other hand, the Prosecutor's office decided to start a new case against me or demanded that the previous sentence be left in force, then it was up to them to send me back here. In any case, I was going to say, I should be given a travel warrant to enable me to go to Moscow, since I had been informed that my presence there was essential.

'Is the Commandant here?' I asked the duty officer.

'No.'

'And the Chief of the station?'

'There's nobody here,' said the officer. 'They've all gone to work on the building site.* Come again tomorrow.'

What was I to do? I could stay overnight here in the boarding-house and go back to the police in the morning, not knowing whether they would allow me to leave or not;

---

* i.e. to do a stint of 'voluntary' labour, as is traditionally expected of Party members and other 'activists' in the Soviet Union.

alternatively, since I had been requested to go back to Moscow 'immediately', I could simply leave in the morning without asking permission of the police. Brooding over this as I walked around the streets of Krivosheino with their rotting fences, I made up my mind to risk it and just leave.

All I had to do was to go to the kolkhoz office and get the money they still owed me: my wages for July and the quarter of my six months' earnings that was due to be paid in grain.

I would have to get them to convert this into cash, but I knew that without a note from the police releasing me the kolkhoz would not settle accounts with me. Perhaps the money I had in my pocket would be enough for the trip, but I had to have something to live on in Moscow. So I decided on a subterfuge.

'Is the chairman here?' I asked, going into the kolkhoz office.

'He's not here. He's gone away on holiday and won't be back for a couple of weeks,' the accountant, a miserly-looking old man, told me to my surprise.

'I'm here in exile and working on your kolkhoz,' I said to him though he knew this as well as I did. 'The court has reversed my sentence and I have to leave urgently for Moscow tomorrow, so I would like to get my money.'

'Give me your notification of release and a list of the supplies you have had from the store this month.'

'I don't have either of those,' I said, and the accountant just shrugged his shoulders: 'Well, how do you expect us to settle with you?'

'I've just come from the police,' I said, 'and they're all out working on a building site, so I couldn't get my notification. But I'll pick it up in the morning and leave for Moscow without coming back here – I had an urgent telegram telling me to come at once. Can't we do it this way: you just give me an advance on my earnings now and send the rest to me later in Moscow when you get confirmation of my release from the police?'

He hesitated for a long time, saying that this was a matter for the deputy chairman, who was also not there. We sat and waited for him a long time, but in vain. At last the accountant plucked up his courage and said he could give me fifty roubles, but no more, because he didn't know how much I had taken from the store in July. In fact I had taken nothing, and the kolkhoz thus owed me eighty roubles.

That evening I went back to Guryevka. There was one more thing I had to do : to find a home for my cat. I took it to Pashka Kabanov, who was a decent and kind person. I also arranged to go to Krivosheino with him the next morning when he drove there with the cream. I went to say goodbye to the milkmaids and also to many other kolkhozniks, and I handed back to the kolkhoz store all the things I had borrowed from them. I was going to take my typewriter and suitcase home with me, but all my other things I gave away. I shaved off my beard so as not to attract attention on the journey.

Early in the morning we drove off to Krivosheino where I intended to get the boat to Tomsk. The cart lumbered slowly along the muddy road past the birch trees, which were beginning to turn yellow. We drove through Dolorez, a ghost village where there was nothing except the rotting frames of a few half-ruined houses. Would I ever see all this again?

At the pier I had an unpleasant surprise. None of the boats were stopping in Krivosheino that day because they had already taken on too many passengers. So I went to the bus station at the other end of the village, fearful of being seen with my suitcase by somebody from the police. There was no direct bus to Tomsk and I had to change twice. When I got there at about eight in the evening, I learned at the station that there were no tickets left for the Moscow train. I was told things were very busy now and one had to buy tickets a week ahead. At first I thought I would try somehow to get to Taiga, from which there were more frequent trains to Moscow, but I found there was no local train from Tomsk to Taiga for the next twenty-four hours or so. As soon as the Tomsk-Moscow train drew in at eleven o'clock, it was immediately besieged by crowds of passengers. When they had all got in and the train was about to leave, I asked an elderly woman conductor if she would let me on just to go as far as Taiga. She shrugged her shoulders, indicating that there were constant ticket inspections. But I pleaded with her and promised to pay her well, and at the last moment she gave in. After an hour, sure enough, there was a ticket inspection.

'You'll have to get off,' said the stern-looking inspector, an elderly man with a moustache. But evidently the conductress had whispered a word in his ear and he didn't insist, though at a tiny station between Tomsk and Taiga, where the trains stop only once every twenty-four hours, ten other passengers without tickets were thrown off. In Taiga I deposited my luggage and went to buy a ticket, but the moment I reached the ticket window I felt a hand on my shoulder.

'Come over here,' said a police sergeant, pointing to the door of the ticket office. 'Where are you travelling to? Where is your luggage? Do you have your papers?'

My first thought was that the Commandant in Krivosheino, learning of my departure, had requested the railway police to detain me.

'I'm going to Moscow and I've put my things in the luggage room,' I said, handing him my identity papers. Instead of the usual stamped residence permit, they contained a note from the Moscow police saying that my permission to reside there had been withdrawn, and that from the 29th of May, 1965, I was under the jurisdiction of the police in Tomsk. I explained that I had been exiled to the Krivosheino district, but that the Supreme Court of the RSFSR had reversed my sentence and I was now returning to Moscow.

'Do you have the court order with you?' the sergeant asked.

'No, it's with the police in Krivosheino.'

'And your notification of release?'

'I didn't have time to pick it up,' I replied. 'I had a telegram from my lawyer telling me to return at once.'

'Well, show me the telegram.'

'It's in my suitcase in the luggage room. I can go and get it.'

The sergeant hesitated. I realized that the Krivosheino police had not sent out an alarm and that the sergeant's suspicions had simply been aroused by my rumpled appearance and lack of luggage. They were not allayed by my failure to produce a notification of release, but he was visibly impressed by my mention of the Supreme Court.

'Do you think they will register someone like you to live in Moscow?' he asked, continuing to examine my papers.

'Of course they will,' I said, 'now the Supreme Court has reversed my sentence.'

'Very well. You can go,' the sergeant said.

The Krasnoyarsk-Moscow express was due ten minutes later. I bought my ticket, and collected my luggage, and while I was waiting for the train the sergeant walked past me several times. It was clear that he still had his doubts. Luckily, the train drew in, and I got on quickly. I couldn't help feeling, however, that the police in Taiga were bound to phone Krivosheino to check on me; the police there would say I had bolted without permission, and I was sure I would be arrested somewhere along the way, or on my arrival in Moscow. I spent three days in this state of anxiety, which robbed me of any pleasure I might have felt at the thought of being on the way home.

But I wasn't arrested on the way, and at seven in the morning on the 29th of July I arrived in Moscow. I immediately went to Ginzburg, who told me that despite my scepticism as to the outcome, my lawyer had filed an appeal with the Prosecutor's office of the RSFSR. The appeal had been accepted and the Prosecutor's office had challenged the decision of the People's Court in the Moscow City Court. The Moscow City Court, however, had upheld the verdict of the People's Court. The lawyer had thereupon filed a new appeal with the Prosecutor's office which this time had taken its objection to the decision of the lower courts to the Supreme Court of the RSFSR. On the 20th of June the Supreme Court had duly reversed the decision of the People's Court to expel me from Moscow, quashed the supporting decision of the Moscow City Court, and referred my case to the Prosecutor's office of the Frunze district for re-examination. I later saw the text of the Supreme Court's order. The court gave three reasons for its decision: in the first place, as was evident from my work-book and the testimony given by myself and witnesses, I had never tried to evade socially useful work, and could not therefore be regarded as a 'parasite'; in the second place, the medical evidence had not clearly established that I was fit to do manual labour; and finally, the People's Court had not established what was meant by my 'incorrect way of life' or the nature of my relations with the foreigners who visited me. There was nothing about my father's illness.

Ginzburg told me that he and his friends had agreed that I should live in their apartment till they returned from their holiday in the middle of August. In the meantime, as soon as the Prosecutor's office closed my case, I would be able to start proceedings for the return of my room; this was why he had been so insistent that I return to Moscow at once. He also told me I would be able to see Gyusel that same day. She was living in a small village near Moscow.

A couple of days later I had a meeting with my lawyer and told him of my worries about my hasty departure from Krivosheino. He said that inasmuch as the Supreme Court had reversed my sentence, I automatically reverted to the legal status I had had before it was passed. Until the final decision from the Prosecutor's office, however, my situation was somewhat complicated and it could be that the Prosecutor's office, on writing to Krivosheino to demand my return to Moscow, might be informed that I had left without waiting for their final decision. It was even possible, he thought, that I might have to go back there to get the notification of release. He added that the Frunze district Prosecutor's office had the reputation of being extremely conservative, and that this might lead to further delay. But in the meantime we decided that I should simply wait to hear from them. So for the time being I lived with Gyusel in the apartment that had been so generously lent to us, and waited impatiently.

On the 19th of August the lawyer informed me that the Prosecutor's office had formally decided to drop the case, and that four days later – that is, after an interval equivalent to the time it would take to travel from Siberia – I should go to the 5th Police District and pick up the official notification. With this it would then be possible for me to start applying for the return of my room. The lawyer also said he had heard from the police that my plays had supposedly been published in Denmark, and that this had been one of the reasons for my prosecution. I was sceptical about this story: in the first place, I didn't know any Danes to whom I could have given my plays, and in the second place the affair of my article on the Normans had made me distrustful of anything involving Denmark.

Lieutenant Gorokhov, from whom I had been instructed to pick up the notification, was a slightly built, tired-looking man who received me fairly pleasantly. He even told me that the next day he was going on holiday in the Caucasus and asked me whether I knew of any good places there. He handed me my copy of the notification and said: 'Well, will you get a job now?' In reply I just shrugged my shoulders. I also met Novikov here and asked him whether it was true that my plays had been published in Denmark. Both of them just looked blank and said they didn't know for sure, it had only been a rumour. Novikov raised the question of the icons that had been stolen from me. To set his mind at rest I said I suspected the people in the KGB and not the police, since the police were less educated and wouldn't know much about icons. Novikov was terribly offended: 'You're quite wrong about that,' he said. 'We have people who know just as much about icons as the KGB, and at Petrovka there are people who have degrees in history from the university.'

The document they gave me was such a curious one that I reproduce it here almost in full:

I, Police Lieutenant Gorokhov, attached to the 5th Police District of the City of Moscow, having examined evidence in the criminal proceedings (Case No. 3381) against A. A. Amalrik, hereby certify, as follows: Amalrik, Andrei Alexeyevich (born in 1938, a native of Moscow, Russian, not a Party member, secondary education, unmarried, of no fixed occupation, with no previous convictions, formerly resident in the City of Moscow at 12 Suvorov Boulevard, Flat 10), as has been established by interrogation, began his working life in 1957, from which year he was employed in a number of positions which he generally left of his own free will ...

[Here followed a long list of all the places in which I had worked.]

On the 5th of March 1965, Amalrik was summoned to the 5th Police District in the City of Moscow where he was warned that he must find work by the 20th of that month, and it was explained to him that he must do so under the terms of the decree of the Supreme Soviet of the RSFSR of the 4th of May 1961, 'On the strengthening of measures against persons evading socially useful labour and leading an anti-social, parasitic way of life.' He was informed of his liability for failure to observe the terms of the decree. After the warning Amalrik did not take up employment and for this the People's Court of the Frunze District of the City of Moscow ordered him to be expelled from the city for two years and six months, with effect from the 28th of May 1965, and to be sent to one of the places designated by law as areas of enforced residence for persons guilty of parasitism.

On the 31st of March 1966 the Deputy Prosecutor of the RSFSR protested this decision in the Moscow City Court and requested its annulment. On the 7th of April 1966 the Moscow City Court examined this request and rejected it. On the 8th of June 1966 the Deputy Prosecutor of the RSFSR entered a second protest in the Supreme Court of the RSFSR which reversed the decisions taken by the People's Court of the Frunze District on the 28th of May 1965 and by the Moscow City Court on the 7th of April 1966, in respect of Amalrik, Andrei Alexeyevich, and ordered that the case be referred to the Prosecutor's office of the Frunze District for further investigation.

In the course of further examination it was established that when he was resident in Moscow at his address in Suvorov Boulevard, Amalrik was often visited by young people, including foreigners, who took away with them pictures of an abstract nature. All the tenants in the building have been questioned, but were unable to say what the citizens who came to Amalrik's room were doing there, nor were they able to give their names.

When a second medical report was called for, its conclusion was that the medical examination undergone by Amalrik on the 30th of April 1965 showed that the condition of his heart (combined mitral weakness of rheumatic origin) has resulted in a reduced capacity for work, and that Amalrik is unable to do work which involves the lifting of heavy objects.

The results of the further investigation have been reported to the Prosecutor of the Frunze District of the City of Moscow, Comrade Orlov, who has given instructions that further proceedings in the case should be discontinued, and that an order should be issued to this effect.

In view of the above facts, the case against A. A. Amalrik is hereby discontinued.

> Signed: Officer in Charge of Interrogation at the 5th Police District, Lieutenant Gorokhov.

This document was witnessed and countersigned by the head of the district station, Lieutenant Colonel Akulov, and by the head of the Police Department in the Frunze district soviet, Lieutenant Colonel Rykalin. It thus appeared, strange as it may seem, that the reasons given for dropping the case against me were all points that had been mentioned in the text of the original court decision to expel me from Moscow.

With this paper I went to the housing department of the district soviet which referred me to its legal officer, an elderly and quite friendly woman. But it was very difficult to explain my situation to her, and she was astonished that I had no notification of release from Krivosheino. I explained how I had not managed to pick it up because of my hasty departure. She then suggested that I write to the chairman of the district soviet enclosing notarized copies of the Supreme Court's decision and the statement from the Prosecutor's office, as well as a note from my former place of residence certifying that I had previously had a room there. In the office of the Supreme Court I obtained a copy of their decision, and when I went to get a note from the office of the building I had lived in before, the girl there told me that my old friend Kiselev had been looking for me in order to hand me an important document. Half an hour later he appeared again, asked whether my exile had 'done me good' and then solemnly handed me the official notification of my release. I learned that the police in Krivosheino had simply mailed it to the 5th Police District in Moscow three days after I left. It was signed by Lieutenant Colonel Korotkikh and said simply that I had been released on the 29th of July 1966 'on the basis of a decision of the Supreme Court of the RSFSR'.

At the beginning of September the district soviet agreed to let me have a room in Moscow, but this was only the start of a long battle with the housing department. They kept putting me off, always asking me to phone the 'next day', and when they did begin to offer me rooms they were invariably tiny and without the most basic conveniences. I refused them all outright, and when they then told me there was nothing else, I decided to try to get my old room back through legal action. I went to the legal consultant at the People's Court where I had been tried. One of the lawyers there told me he was sorry to disappoint me, but that under existing housing regulations I was simply not entitled to be given a place to live in Moscow: 'Once you have been subject to an administrative expulsion order, you automatically, after six months, lose the right to your place of residence, irrespective of whether your expulsion was justified or not, or whether the sentence has been reversed or not. The district soviet has just been trying to do you a favour, or perhaps they don't know the law.'

At the end of August I had to leave the flat in which I had stayed up to then. Till the middle of September I lived with a friend and then, with great difficulty, Gyusel and I managed to rent a room for thirty roubles a month in an old house belonging to an elderly married couple. The man was ordinarily quiet and inoffensive, but when he got drunk he made scenes and told us to leave. That wouldn't have mattered so much, but I became very frightened when his wife once called the police because he had got violent and the policeman demanded to see our papers. Not having a residence permit I would have found it very difficult to explain my situation; we would certainly not have been permitted to go on renting a room like this. I therefore showed him only Gyusel's papers, saying that I was her husband and pointing to the entry recording our marriage. Luckily, the policeman was satisfied with this. This room swallowed up all our money, and we found it even more difficult to manage than in Siberia. We lived mostly by selling off my books.

On the advice of the legal officer in the district soviet, I tried a new approach. On the 16th of September I wrote an application asking for a room twice the size of the one I had had before my exile. I based this request on the fact that I needed more space because of my wife, whose situation was especially difficult. The deputy chairman of the soviet granted this request and at last I was given a room of eighteen square metres. Though a little dark, it was in a flat with a bath and telephone and, what is more, it was in the section of the Arbat where I had lived as a child. I had no more grounds for complaint, and on the 7th of October I received the paper authorizing me to move in. All I had to do now was to get my permit to live in Moscow.

First I had to go to the police station to present my housing authorization. After the presentation of this document, the permit was usually a formality, and I was a little surprised that it took ten days. With the note of authorization from the police I went to the housing department again, paid a small fee and gave them my papers which were now sent once more to the police for the actual permit to be entered in them. At the beginning of November my much-travelled papers were at last returned to me with a new notation duly sealed and signed: 'City of Moscow, 5th Police District. Registered for permanent residence at 5 Vakhtangov Street, Flat 5. November 2nd, 1966.'

With this the story of my exile comes to an end.

1966-1967, Guryevka—Moscow

Note About The Author

Note About The Author

In 1969 Andrei Amalrik's short book *Will the U.S.S.R. Survive until 1984?* reached the West and was first published in Russian by the Alexander Herzen Foundation in Holland. In England it was published in *Survey* and by Allen Lane, The Penguin Press; in the United States by Harper and Row. It received an enormous amount of publicity, both on account of its analysis of political feeling in the Soviet Union and because of its prediction of a future war between China and Russia.

Later he wrote an open letter to Anatoli Kuznetsov (which appeared in the English press) in which he discussed the pressures exerted on Soviet intellectuals by the Secret Police.

On the 21st of May 1970 Andrei Amalrik was arrested at his *dacha* outside Moscow. At the time of going to press he has been transferred to Sverdlovsk.